Our Price
£35.00

98

CW01457158

BEETHOVEN 1806

AMS Studies in Music

BEETHOVEN 1806

Mark Ferraguto

OXFORD

UNIVERSITY PRESS

OXFORD
UNIVERSITY PRESS

Oxford University Press is a department of the University of Oxford. It furthers the University's objective of excellence in research, scholarship, and education by publishing worldwide. Oxford is a registered trade mark of Oxford University Press in the UK and certain other countries.

Published in the United States of America by Oxford University Press
198 Madison Avenue, New York, NY 10016, United States of America.

© Oxford University Press 2019

Library of Congress Cataloging-in-Publication Data
Names: Ferraguto, Mark, author.
Title: Beethoven 1806 / Mark Ferraguto.
Description: New York, NY : Oxford University Press, [2019] |
Series: AMS studies in music | Includes bibliographical references and index.
Identifiers: LCCN 2019002769 | ISBN 9780190947187 (hardcover : alk. paper) |
ISBN 9780190947200 (epub)
Subjects: LCSH: Beethoven, Ludwig van, 1770-1827—Criticism and
interpretation. | Music—19th century—History and criticism.
Classification: LCC ML410.B42 F4 2019 | DDC 780.92 [B] —dc23
LC record available at https://lccn.loc.gov/2019002769

1 3 5 7 9 8 6 4 2

Printed by Integrated Books International, United States of America

For Lisa

CONTENTS

FIGURES

MUSIC EXAMPLES

TABLES

APPENDICES

ACKNOWLEDGMENTS

Beethoven 1806 is a book about Beethoven's relationships, and it's gratifying to begin it by acknowledging some of the relationships in my life that have helped it come into being. I first thank James Webster, Annette Richards, and Neal Zaslaw, the members of my dissertation committee at Cornell University (where many of the ideas for this book germinated). They, along with the rest of the music faculty, have been inspiring mentors and supportive colleagues.

Many other generous colleagues have provided feedback on this manuscript in its various forms, including Stuart Paul Duncan, Emily H. Green, David Hyun-su Kim, Martin Küster, Ellen Lockhart, Lewis Lockwood, Damien Mahiet, Nicholas Mathew, Eric McKee, Sezi Seskir, and Jessica Waldoff. I am especially thankful to Damien Mahiet, who has read and critiqued a decade's worth of drafts with wisdom and wit. I also owe a special word of thanks to Jessica Waldoff, both for encouraging me to begin this journey in the first place and for reading and commenting on the entire manuscript, to its great benefit. My gratitude also goes to Shanti Nachtergaele, who kindly and expertly assisted with proofreading, formatting, and tracking down materials.

I could not imagine a more supportive group of scholars than my music history and theory colleagues at the Pennsylvania State University: Marica Tacconi, Charles Youmans, Vincent Benitez, Maureen Carr, Thomas Cody, Taylor Greer, Stephen Hopkins, and Eric McKee. For their support during my time as a junior faculty member, I also want to thank Barbara Korner, Dean of the College of Arts and Architecture; Sue Haug, former Director of the School of Music; and David Frego, Director of the School of Music. Amanda Maple, Music Librarian at Penn State, offered advice and assistance on numerous occasions, for which I am most grateful.

Several institutions provided invaluable support for this project. The Institute for the Arts and Humanities at Penn State bestowed the gift of time at a pivotal moment with a Fall 2015 Resident Scholars and Artists Grant; my thanks go to former director Michael Bérubé for this opportunity. The American Musicological Society supported this project through both a subvention from the AMS 75 PAYS Endowment (funded in part by the National Endowment for the Humanities and the Andrew W. Mellon Foundation) and a Virginia and George Bozarth Travel Fund Grant, which facilitated a research trip to Austria in the summer of 2016. I was able to return to Austria the following summer as the recipient of a Research Associate Grant from IES Abroad; I thank Morten Solvik, Director of the IES Abroad Vienna Center, for his hospitality and support.

For their research assistance in Vienna, I am grateful to Otto Biba, Director of the Gesellschaft der Musikfreunde archives, and the staff members of both the Gesellschaft der Musikfreunde and the Austrian National Library. I also want to thank Stefan Gschwendtner of the Linz Schlossmuseum for allowing me to examine Beethoven's Erard piano. Perhaps the most exciting experience during my time in Vienna was being able to explore the Razumovsky Palace after years of researching and writing about it. My sincere thanks go to Antonis Stachel for this opportunity.

I have been privileged to work with W. Anthony Sheppard, Editor of AMS Studies in Music, on both the original version of chapter 3 and on this book; his editorial guidance and advice have improved this manuscript in numerous respects. I am also grateful to Suzanne Ryan and Victoria Dixon of Oxford University Press for helping this book reach its final form.

All German and French translations are mine unless otherwise indicated. Martin Küster and Markus Chmielus kindly offered their expertise in proofreading the German translations. I am grateful to the University of California Press for granting me permission to reprint my article "Beethoven *à la moujik*: Russianness and Learned Style in the 'Razumovsky' String Quartets" (*Journal of the American Musicological Society* 67, no. 1 [Spring 2014]: 77–123), here in revised form, as chapter 3. I also want to thank Barry Cooper for the permission to reproduce part of his transcription of the revised solo part for Op. 58 (chapter 2).

The musical examples in this book have been set primarily in reference to the editions of Beethoven's works by G. Henle (Op. 59) and Jonathan Del Mar (Opp. 58, 60, 61). In a few cases, I have instead based my examples on the earliest printed editions, noting this in the captions. In these instances, I have tried to retain as much of the irregularity of these early editions as possible, preserving slurs, beaming, orthography, spelling, and placement of dynamic and expressive markings, and making only slight corrections and emendations for the sake of clarity. The following pitch notation system is used throughout the book: CC, C, c, c^1, c^2, c^3, where middle C = c^1.

Finally, I want to thank my family. I am especially grateful to my brother Michael Ferraguto, Principal Librarian of the Baltimore Symphony Orchestra, for sharing both his professional expertise and his excellent sense of humor. I also thank my father Paul, my late mother Maria, and my grandmother Mary for their constant love and support. To Lisa: I can hardly put into words how to thank you for all that you've done over the last decade as this book took shape. Now our trio has become a quartet, and while life isn't any simpler, it's certainly more fun. This book is dedicated to you.

ABBREVIATIONS

Anderson—Beethoven, Ludwig van. *The Letters of Beethoven*. 3 vols. Translated and
   edited by Emily Anderson. New York: St. Martin's Press, 1961.
Briefwechsel—Beethoven, Ludwig van. *Briefwechsel: Gesamtausgabe*. 7 vols. Edited
   by Sieghard Brandenburg. Munich: G. Henle, 1996–2001.
Thayer/Forbes—Thayer, Alexander Wheelock. *Thayer's Life of Beethoven*. Revised
   and edited by Elliot Forbes. 1967. 2 vols. Reprint, Princeton: Princeton
   University Press, 1991.

BEETHOVEN 1806

INTRODUCTION

Between early 1806 and early 1807, Ludwig van Beethoven completed a remarkable series of instrumental works that included his Fourth Piano Concerto (Op. 58), three "Razumovsky" String Quartets (Op. 59), Fourth Symphony (Op. 60), Violin Concerto (Op. 61), Thirty-Two Variations on an Original Theme for Piano (WoO 80), and *Coriolan* Overture (Op. 62). Despite the enduring popularity of these works, critics have long struggled to reconcile the music of this year with Beethoven's "heroic style," the lens through which his middle-period works have typically been viewed. The challenge is both to find a suitable way to understand and appreciate these works on their own terms and to consider how they fit into a larger and more comprehensive picture of Beethoven. Drawing on concepts of mediation derived from relational accounts of art and society, this book explores the works of 1806 and early 1807 in light of the composer's relationships with the people for whom—and instruments for which—they were composed. Not only did Beethoven depend on performers, patrons, publishers, critics, and audiences to earn a living, but he also tailored his compositions to suit particular sensibilities, proclivities, and technologies. Exploring these relationships in the context of early nineteenth-century cultural and political history opens up new ways of engaging with the music of this banner year.

KNOWING BEETHOVEN

"The familiar," wrote Friedrich Nietzsche, "is what we are used to, and what we are used to is often the most difficult to 'know'—that is, to view as a problem, to see as strange, as distant, as 'outside us.'"[1] Just as Nietzsche struggled to know the quotidian—the "not strange" rather than the "strange"—because of its familiarity, so have we struggled to know Beethoven, a composer who

---

1. Friedrich Nietzsche, *The Gay Science*, trans. Josefine Nauckhoff (Cambridge: Cambridge University Press, 2001), 215. Quoted in Michael Wood, "A World without Literature?," *Dædalus* 138, no. 1 (Winter 2009): 58–67.

exemplifies the musically familiar. Beethoven is a mainstay of popular culture the world over; his image greets us on coffee mugs and T-shirts, and his compositions in car commercials, summer blockbusters, and sports arenas. The influence of his music has been both wide and deep; Scott Burnham has gone so far as to argue that the "values of music" are those of Beethoven's most celebrated works.[2] But the nature of Beethoven's familiarity cannot be fully explained either by the commodification of his artworks and image or by the extraordinary influence of his music. As scholars from Theodor W. Adorno to K. M. Knittel (and beyond) have emphasized, it is not Beethoven but "Beethoven"— the deaf, struggling hero—who fueled both the Romantic and the modern imagination, and who remains familiar to us today.

The tendency to view Beethoven's life through the lens of his Romantic legacy has had far-reaching consequences on the ways in which his career and oeuvre have been conceptualized. As Knittel has suggested, the temptation to read Beethoven's life as a narrative of struggle and transcendence has resulted in an incomplete picture of him: the "events, sources and witnesses that support this Romantic plot have been highlighted, while other conflicting views have been suppressed, generating a limited vision of Beethoven's life—the Beethoven myth."[3] At the same time, the myth has itself generated immense interest in the few works that help to sustain it—"*Fidelio* and the music to *Egmont*; the Third, Fifth, and Ninth Symphonies; and the *Pathétique* and *Appassionata* sonatas," according to Carl Dahlhaus—while obscuring or suppressing the ones that do not.[4]

Partly as a reaction to this, a variety of new scholarly approaches to Beethoven have emerged over the past two or three decades, addressing in particular his so-called middle or heroic period. These studies have ranged from reexaminations of canonical works and genres to explorations of long marginalized ones. As scholars such as Elaine Sisman, Lewis Lockwood, Nicholas Cook, Nicholas Mathew, and Nancy November have stressed, the heroic paradigm, particularly in its narrowly construed sense, falls short of reflecting the breadth and heterogeneity of music from this period.[5] The longstanding focus on the heroic has

2. Scott Burnham, *Beethoven Hero* (Princeton: Princeton University Press, 1995), xiii.

3. K. M. Knittel, "The Construction of Beethoven," in Jim Samson, ed., *The Cambridge History of Nineteenth-Century Music* (Cambridge University Press, 2001), 118–50, 121.

4. Carl Dahlhaus, *Nineteenth-Century Music* (Berkeley: University of California Press, 1989), 76.

5. Elaine R. Sisman, "After the Heroic Style: Fantasia and the 'Characteristic' Sonatas of 1809," *Beethoven Forum* 6 (1998): 67–96; Lewis Lockwood, "Beethoven, Florestan, and the Varieties of Heroism," in Scott Burnham and Michael Steinberg, eds., *Beethoven and His World* (Princeton: Princeton University Press, 2000), 27–47; Nicholas Cook, "The Other Beethoven: Heroism, the Canon, and the Works of 1813–14," *19th-Century Music* 27, no. 1 (2003): 3–24; Nicholas Mathew, "Beethoven and His Others: Criticism, Difference, and the Composer's Many Voices," *Beethoven Forum* 13, no. 2 (2006): 148–87, "Beethoven's Political Music and the Idea of the Heroic Style" (PhD diss., Cornell University, 2006), and *Political Beethoven* (Cambridge: Cambridge

made it especially difficult to hear what Mathew has termed Beethoven's "Other voices," ranging from the lyrical and sentimental to the overtly political.[6]

By fixing our gaze on a single year in Beethoven's life, this book seeks to elaborate the specific conditions in which the works of 1806 and early 1807 were conceived, composed, and heard; in this sense, it is a microhistory. In Sigurður Gylfi Magnússon and István Szijártó's oft-quoted formulation, micro-historians hold in their hands a microscope instead of a telescope. Magnússon and Szijártó highlight three characteristics of the genre that resonate with the present study: the analysis of specific cases or circumstances (instead of developments across decades or centuries), the emphasis on using microinvestigation to answer larger historical questions, and the treatment of historical individuals as "conscious actors" as opposed to "puppets on the hands of great underlying forces of history."[7] Drawing on these concepts, this study seeks to understand Beethoven's works less as exemplars of the stylistic phases, periods, and narratives that arose after his death, and more as responses to the people, objects, places, and circumstances in his life. At the same time, this approach invites us to pose larger questions about Beethoven's relationship with his milieu, about the ways in which his reputation was constructed, and about the nature of the creative process itself. Paradoxically, knowing Beethoven implies distancing ourselves from what we already know, making unfamiliar the familiar. My hope is that this approach offers a pathway to reappraising the way we think about Beethoven's music today.

THE FOURTH PIANO CONCERTO AND THE MEANINGS
OF MUSICAL MEANING

Our microinvestigation begins with a single sonority, the G-major chord that opens Beethoven's Fourth Piano Concerto. Without yet hearing the sound of this chord, one can glean a number of details from its graphic representation in the concerto's first printed edition (published in 1808 by the

University Press, 2013); and Nancy November, *Beethoven's Theatrical Quartets: Opp. 59, 74, and 95* (Cambridge: Cambridge University Press, 2013).

6. Mathew, "Beethoven and His Others."

7. Sigurður Gylfi Magnússon and István M. Szijártó, *What Is Microhistory? Theory and Practice* (Abingdon, Oxfordshire: Routledge, 2013), 4–5. See also Giovanni Levi, "On Microhistory," in Peter Burke, ed., *New Perspectives on Historical Writing*, 2nd ed. (University Park: Pennsylvania State University Press, 2001), 97–119; and Thomas Robisheaux, ed., "Microhistory Today: A Roundtable Discussion," *Journal of Medieval and Early Modern Studies* 47, no. 1 (January 2017): 7–52. Recent musicological studies that explicitly draw on microhistory have included Mark Everist, *Music Drama at the Paris Odéon, 1824–1828* (Berkeley and Los Angeles: University of California Press, 2002); Tamara Levitz, *Modernist Mysteries: Perséphone* (Oxford and New York: Oxford University Press, 2012); and Peter J. Schmelz, "'Shostakovich' Fights the Cold War: Reflections from Great to Small," *Journal of Musicological Research* 34, no. 2 (2015): 91–140.

EXAMPLE I.1. Beethoven, Piano Concerto No. 4 in G Major, Op. 58, i, m. 1, first edition (Vienna: Bureau des Arts et d'Industrie, 1808).

Viennese firm Bureau des Arts et d'Industrie) (Example I.1). First, while the pitches are unremarkable in and of themselves, their distribution is unusually thick, involving the full triadic spread from the low G (played by the fifth finger of the pianist's left hand) all the way to b¹ (played by the fifth finger of the right hand). Second, the rhythms are slow and static and the sense of meter ambiguous, perhaps more suggestive of the opening theme of a slow movement (or a slow introduction) than a movement marked Allegro moderato. Third, the dynamic is emphatically hushed, marked both *piano* (quietly) and *dolce* (sweetly). Fourth, and perhaps most crucially, this chord is to be played by the piano. The allocation of the concerto's opening idea to the soloist rather than the orchestra is, if not entirely without precedent (Mozart had tried something similar), certainly among the most radical opening gambits for such a piece. Our eyes tell us, in short, that this is a special chord indeed.

But what do our ears tell us? Here, I refer to a 1999 recording by the fortepianist Robert Levin.[8] In this sonoric representation, one hears reinforced many of the features just described—the full triadic spread, the prominent melodic third, the sense of rhythmic stasis, the hushed dynamic level, and of course, the commanding presence of the soloist (and absence of the orchestra). But one also hears elements not necessarily implied by the chord in its notated form. Levin, playing on a Viennese-style fortepiano, delicately rolls the chord from bottom to top rather than playing all of its pitches simultaneously. He raises the fortepiano's damper mechanism, allowing the strings to resonate and vibrate sympathetically. The overall effect, given the translucent but overtone-rich timbre of the fortepiano, is akin to the strumming of a harp. It recalls a long tradition of associating this concerto (especially the second movement) with the legend of Orpheus, a demigod of music and a figure to whom Beethoven himself had sometimes been compared, most notably in Joseph Mähler's 1804

8. John Eliot Gardiner (director), *Beethoven: The Piano Concertos/Choral Fantasy*, Orchestre Révolutionnaire et Romantique with Robert Levin, fortepiano, 4 compact discs (Archiv Produktion, 1999).

FIGURE I.1. *Ludwig van Beethoven* (1804). Portrait by Joseph Willibrord Mähler (1778–1860). Photo: Rudolf Stepanek. Used by permission of the Beethoven-Haus Bonn.

portrait where he is depicted holding a contemporary instrument known as the lyre-guitar (see Figure I.1). Our ears, then, confirm much of what our eyes have told us, but they also perceive things our eyes could not, allowing us to peer (or hear) down different interpretive pathways.

While neither Levin's performance nor that of any other pianist since Beethoven's day can be considered definitive, it serves to illustrate the fact that the realization of even so ostensibly simple a musical utterance as this G-major chord depends on a performer's creative intervention. If the printed score reveals crucial details about pitches, harmonies, rhythms, tempo, and so on, it tells us little or nothing about other important matters like the kind of instrument to be used, how it should be tuned, what temperament to set, what kind of touch to employ, or whether or not to make use of devices such as the damper pedal, moderator, or *una corda*—all of which might plausibly be used here. Nor does the score in this case indicate that the opening chord should be rolled; however, given the relatively rapid decay of the fortepiano's tone and the chord's function as an exordium, this too seems plausible. Indeed, Beethoven's pupil Carl Czerny advocated precisely this effect in an annotated example of

EXAMPLE I.2. Beethoven, Piano Concerto No. 4 in G Major, Op. 58, i, m. 1, according to Czerny.

the concerto's opening theme in his Op. 500 treatise[9] (Example I.2). Neither interpretation—playing the chord as notated or in the manner suggested by Czerny—supersedes or invalidates the other, but they do produce markedly different results.[10] These varied approaches, in turn, help to widen the horizon of possible musical meanings.

Owen Jander, a scholar who wrote prolifically on this concerto, was one of the first to articulate the importance of hearing it on period instruments. Beginning with his 1985 article in *19th-Century Music*, Jander advanced the theory that the concerto's second movement—a highly dramatic series of exchanges between piano and strings in E minor—represented a dialogue between Orpheus (as represented by the pianist) and the furies (as represented by the strings), followed by Orpheus's failed attempt to rescue his beloved Euridice from the Underworld.[11] His argument built on a tradition of quasi-programmatic interpretations by A. B. Marx, Franz Liszt, and Donald Francis Tovey, among others. The evidence for his case, however, was and remains circumstantial—nowhere did Beethoven suggest that the movement or the concerto was either based on such a program or in any way connected with the Orpheus myth. Both Edward T. Cone and Joseph Kerman took issue with Jander's approach; as Cone put it, whatever the value of Jander's investigation in probing Beethoven's literary and cultural interests, "its effect on our aesthetic enjoyment will always be tainted by the suspicion of illegitimacy."[12] Nonetheless, Jander continued to defend his

9. Carl Czerny, *Vollständige theoretisch-practische Pianoforte-Schule*, Op. 500, 4 vols. (Vienna: Anton Diabelli, 1839), vol. 4 (*Die Kunst des Vortrags der ältern und neuen Clavicompositionen oder Die Fortschritte bis zur neusten Zeit*), 111; English translation of the Beethoven chapters in Paul Badura-Skoda, ed., *On the Proper Performance of All Beethoven's Works for the Piano: Czerny's Reminiscences of Beethoven and Chapters II and III from Volume IV of the Complete Theoretical and Practical Piano Forte School, Op. 500* (Vienna: Universal Edition, 1970), 19–109.

10. The decision to roll or not to roll this chord has provoked a remarkable amount of controversy among critics and pianists. See Neal Peres da Costa, *Off the Record: Performing Practices in Romantic Piano Playing* (Oxford and New York: Oxford University Press, 2012), 42–4.

11. Owen Jander, "Beethoven's 'Orpheus in Hades': The *Andante con moto* of the Fourth Piano Concerto," *19th-Century Music* 8, no. 3 (Spring 1985): 195–212.

12. Edward T. Cone, "Beethoven's Orpheus—or Jander's?" *19th-Century Music* 8, no. 3 (Spring 1985): 283–6, 286.

ideas in print, elaborating them in a 1995 retrospective article in *19th-Century Music* and in a 2009 monograph that provocatively extends his Orphic interpretation to all three movements.[13] While the controversy surrounding Jander's argument is well known among musicologists, few scholars today recall the emphasis his readings placed on period instruments. The reason for this emphasis is clear enough: the tone and timbre of early pianos are perhaps more suggestive of Orpheus's lyre than the modern piano; this is particularly true in the concerto's second movement, with its imploring arpeggiated figurations.[14]

In spite of his interest in historical performance practices, however, Jander was ultimately concerned with advancing his reading of the concerto's "plot," as developed through juxtapositions of specific moments in the score with lines from Ovid, Virgil, and Kanne. Indeed, his desire to unearth a hidden Orphic program in the concerto may be understood as stemming from the same methodological impulse as Joseph Kerman's later narratological account (in spite of the fact that Kerman framed his account as a corrective to Jander's original article); namely, the impulse to reveal a kind of inner coherence that explains the music's unusual qualities. As Carl Dahlhaus observes, this impulse—which underlies the main analytical and hermeneutic traditions of twentieth-century music scholarship—originated in the only seemingly contradictory views of the nineteenth-century "formalists" and "content aestheticians," both of whom took Beethoven as their primary analytical object:

> Unlike most controversies, these views [of formalists and content aestheticians] at least have an underlying premise in common—namely, that Beethoven's music conceals an "idea" which must be grasped in order to do the work aesthetic justice. . . . To unearth a constellation of a few notes from which all the structures in a movement by Beethoven supposedly derive, and to search for a subject or "poetic idea" whose depiction or expression imparts sense and coherence to a piece of instrumental music: both are consequences of the belief that before one can come to grips aesthetically with a work by Beethoven one must penetrate to a "second level" of the music. Analysis and hermeneutics—or rather the "analytic principle" and the "hermeneutic principle"—arose in music history (or at least attained historical significance) simultaneously as opposite ways of unraveling the difficulties posed by the reception of Beethoven.[15]

13. Owen Jander, "Orpheus Revisited: A Ten-Year Retrospect on the Andante con moto of Beethoven's Fourth Piano Concerto," *19th-Century Music* 19, no. 1 (Summer 1995): 31–49, and *Beethoven's "Orpheus" Concerto: The Fourth Piano Concerto in Its Cultural Context* (Hillsdale, NY: Pendragon Press, 2009).

14. Jander originally suggested that the Fourth Piano Concerto was composed for the six-octave Viennese piano, but later amended his argument to propose that Beethoven's five-and-a-half-octave Erard piano, acquired in 1803, was the important stimulus. See chapter 5.

15. Carl Dahlhaus, *Nineteenth-Century Music*, 11.

While Jander locates the underlying idea of the concerto's second move-ment in the legend of Orpheus, Kerman reads it as a "relationship story" whose Orpheus-like protagonist, "the individual who is the piano . . . overcomes a hostile community and then . . . experiences some kind of failure."[16] Using different but equally evocative language, both authors attempt to "penetrate to a 'second level' of the music" and to reveal an underlying narrative, whether literal (in the case of Jander) or metaphorical (in the case of Kerman).

While there is certainly value in these approaches, I want to address some of their limitations and to think a bit more deeply about the relationships among the score, the instruments at Beethoven's disposal, and the various audi-ences for whom he was composing. In particular, I want to ask two related questions: First, in what ways does Beethoven's instrumental music reflect his relationships with the patrons, performers, publishers, critics, and consumers for whom—and the instruments for which—he was composing? Second, and more broadly speaking, in what ways did this music help to establish or articu-late Beethoven's social and professional aims?

In pursuing these questions, I respond in part to the call issued by scholars such as Christopher Small, Georgina Born, and Nicholas Cook for a more "relational" approach to musicology, one that decenters the musical score as a privileged analytical domain and instead locates meaning—to quote Small—in the act of "musicking as human encounter."[17] This methodological reorienta-tion owes much to performance studies, a field that has until quite recently remained awkwardly estranged from music scholarship. As Alejandro L. Madrid observes, performance studies asks a different set of questions from those posed by traditional music scholarship:

> While music scholarship (including performance practice) asks what music is and seeks to understand musical texts and musical performances in their own terms according to a social and cultural context, a performance studies approach to the study of music asks what music does or allows people to do; such an approach under-stands musics as processes within larger social and cultural practices and asks how these musics can help us understand these processes as opposed to how do these processes help us understand music.[18]

16. Joseph Kerman, "Representing a Relationship: Notes on a Beethoven Concerto," *Representations* 39 (Summer 1992): 80–101, 83.

17. Christopher Small, *Musicking: The Meanings of Performing and Listening* (Middletown, CT: Wesleyan University Press, 1998), 10. See also Georgina Born, "For a Relational Musicology: Music and Interdisciplinarity, beyond the Practice Turn," *Journal of the Royal Musical Association* 135, no. 2 (2010): 205–43, and Nicholas Cook, *Beyond the Score: Music as Performance* (Oxford and New York: Oxford University Press, 2013).

18. Alejandro L. Madrid, "Why Music and Performance Studies? Why Now? An Introduction to the Special Issue," *Trans: Revista Transcultural de Música* 13 (2009). On the integration of perfor-mance studies and traditional music scholarship, see also Cook, *Beyond the Score*, and Nicholas Cook and Richard Pettengill, "Introduction," in Cook and Pettengill, eds., *Taking It to the Bridge: Music as Performance* (Ann Arbor: University of Michigan Press, 2013), 1–19.

My aim, from this perspective, is not to ask what Beethoven's instrumental music means (or meant)—the kind of question posed by Jander and Kerman in their readings—but rather what it does (or did). In particular, I am interested in what this music did for Beethoven in the period of its creation (spanning its conception, composition, publication, and earliest performances), and especially how it helped him to negotiate his social position in Vienna while he attempted to make a living through both patronage and the market.

Given my focus in this volume on Beethoven's interactions with people, instruments, markets, and ideas, it seems important to address a potential criticism of this kind of methodology; namely, that in asking what Beethoven's music did for him, one risks glossing over its aesthetic significance at the expense of its social importance. It is true that in some sociologically oriented writing on musical subjects "the music itself"—that is, the kinds of parameters that music critics have typically taken to represent music—has played a minimal role. Charles Rosen criticized Tia DeNora's seminal study *Beethoven and the Construction of Genius* on these grounds, among others.[19] But such critiques not only attempt to impose a universal standard on music scholarship, they also imply that the "aesthetic" and the "social"—or more broadly, text and context—are locked in what Rita Felski has called a "zero-sum game in which one side must be conclusively crushed so that the other can triumph."[20] As she observes, this need not be the case: "[A]rt's autonomy—if by autonomy we mean its distinctiveness and specialness—does not rule out connectedness but is the very reason that connections are forged and sustained. . . . Artworks can only survive and thrive by making friends, creating allies, attracting disciples, inciting attachments, latching on to receptive hosts."[21] The central question of the present study, then, is how Beethoven's compositions not only reflect but also produce the social, how they attempt to "make friends, create allies, attract disciples, incite attachments, latch on to receptive hosts." In other words, my interest lies in tracing some of the many historical pathways linking the aesthetic and the social in Beethoven's music.

The concept of mediation is a valuable tool for investigating these ideas. For Bruno Latour, a mediator is an object, event, being, idea, discourse, practice, or assemblage that does not simply transport meaning but rather transforms,

19. Tia DeNora, *Beethoven and the Construction of Genius: Musical Politics in Vienna, 1792–1803* (Berkeley: University of California Press, 1995); Charles Rosen, "Did Beethoven Have All the Luck?" *New York Review of Books* 43, no. 18 (November 14, 1996), online version (http://www.nybooks.com/articles/archives/1996/nov/14/did-beethoven-have-all-the-luck/), accessed October 17, 2015. See also Tia DeNora (with reply by Charles Rosen), "Beethoven's Genius: An Exchange," *New York Review of Books* 44, no. 6 (April 10, 1997), online version (http://www.nybooks.com/articles/archives/1997/apr/10/beethovens-genius-an-exchange/), accessed October 17, 2015.

20. Rita Felski, "Context Stinks!" *New Literary History* 42, no. 4 (Autumn 2011): 573–91, 584.

21. Ibid.

translates, distorts, and modifies it.[22] To acknowledge the significance of mediation in artistic creation is both to complicate notions of how meaning is produced and to recognize the messiness and irreducibility of the creative process itself. As Antoine Hennion has observed, highlighting the role of mediators forces us to acknowledge that artistic creation is not governed by the artist alone but is rather a form of "collective work." Artistic creation is "far more widely distributed" than traditional models of authorship imply, taking place "in all the interstices between . . . successive mediations."[23] At the same time, embracing mediation as an analytical paradigm does not mean rejecting traditional ideas like authorship, style, or the work concept; on the contrary, these ideas have the potential to gain clarity when viewed as the products and instigators of innumerable mediations. In shifting the emphasis from representation to mediation, the relationships among author, work, and context become more fraught and more complex, but none of these constructs disappears. What results is a greater appreciation for the contingency of these constructs and the possibility of posing new questions that seek to understand musical meaning from a different vantage point.

THE CASE FOR 1806(–7)

The period from early 1806 through early 1807—during which Beethoven focused almost exclusively on instrumental music—is of particular interest for an approach that seeks to reunite the aesthetic and the social. From a historical point of view, it is noteworthy because it marks an expansion of Beethoven's social networks. Both Archduke Rudolph of Austria (brother to Emperor Francis II) and Count Andrey Razumovsky (Russian ambassador to Austria) extended their patronage and support to Beethoven around this time. Like the other major patrons in Beethoven's life, notably Prince Lobkowitz and Prince Lichnowsky, they provided the impetus for new works, arranged for performances, and generally promoted Beethoven's brand. The works of 1806–7 are for this reason representative of Beethoven's reliance on the patronage system while also reflecting the changing and unstable nature of patronage in his life. Beethoven also began or deepened collaborative relationships with other artists at this time, including the violinist Franz Clement (resulting in the Violin Concerto, Op. 61), Razumovsky's house quartet led by Ignaz Schuppanzigh

---

22. Bruno Latour, *Reassembling the Social: An Introduction to Actor-Network Theory* (Oxford and New York: Oxford University Press, 2005), 39.

23. Antoine Hennion, "Music and Mediation: Towards a new Sociology of Music," in Martin Clayton, Trevor Herbert, and Richard Middleton, eds., *The Cultural Study of Music: A Critical Introduction* (London: Routledge, 2003), 80–91 (1–9 in online version, https://hal.archives-ouvertes.fr/halshs-00193130), 7.

(resulting in the Opus 59 quartets), and the poet Heinrich von Collin (resulting in the Overture to *Coriolan*, Op. 62). But this period is characterized by distant as well as close relationships. Only by achieving international recognition, Beethoven believed, could he be considered a "true artist" (*ein wahrer Künstler*), and he spent much of the year aggressively marketing his new compositions (Opuses 58, 59, 60, 61, 61a, and 62, as a set) to firms in France, England, and the German-speaking lands.[24] His ideal audience during this period, then, was much more heterogeneous than is often assumed: it included not only Viennese concertgoers and consumers, but also foreign publics, as well as specific patrons, performers, firms, and even critics.[25] This complex matrix of relationships makes the music of this period both challenging and worthwhile to study from the perspective of mediation.

In terms of historiography, the instrumental works of 1806 have long presented a problem. Despite the now canonic status of these works, critics have struggled to reconcile their character—often described as "lyrical," "spacious," or "serene"—with the other music of Beethoven's so-called heroic decade (roughly 1802 to 1813). Beginning in the mid-nineteenth century, critics championed the heroic ethos of struggle and transcendence that characterizes many of the compositions of this decade. But the works of 1806 do not conform easily to this paradigm, and rather than reject the paradigm, critics have tended to view these works either as temporary regressions or, more optimistically, as evidence of Beethoven's penchant for alternating between phases of radical growth and restraint. The latter idea appears in many biographical studies but is expressed most clearly by James Webster:

> Within and independently of the three large periods, [Beethoven] seems to have alternated between phases of expansion into or exploration of new territory and phases of consolidation or repose. . . . The G-Major Piano Concerto, the Violin Concerto, the Fourth Symphony, and the *Waldstein* and *Appassionata* sonatas, like Op. 59, have neither the strain nor the exaltation of the *Eroica*, nor are they charged with comparable extramusical associations. . . . [T]heir relations to Classical norms of form and procedure are clearer. . . . On a more detailed level, Beethoven's middle period often appears to exhibit pairs of individual works; in these pairs, the first work

24. Beethoven's desire to achieve international recognition is indicated by several letters from this period; see especially those of November 18, 1806 (*Briefwechsel*, vol. 1, no. 260, pp. 292–4; Anderson, vol. 1, no. 137, pp. 156–8) and May 11, 1807 (*Briefwechsel*, vol. 1, no. 281, pp. 312–13; Anderson, vol. 1, no. 143, pp. 168–9). Quotation from letter of May 11, 1807.

25. Birgit Lodes has considered some of the ways in which Beethoven's music responds to the tastes and abilities of his noble patrons in a recent essay on Beethoven's dedications: "Zur musikalischen Passgenauigkeit von Beethovens Kompositionen mit Widmungen an Adelige: *An die ferne Geliebte* op. 98 in neuer Deutung," in Bernhard R. Appel and Armin Raab, eds., *Widmungen bei Haydn und Beethoven. Personen—Strategien—Praktiken. Bericht über den Internationalen musikwissenschaftlichen Kongress Bonn, 29. September bis 1. Oktober 2011* (Bonn: Verlag Beethoven-Haus, 2015), 171–202.

to be completed or published usually seems to be the bolder, larger, or more expressive, the second work the more modest, less pretentious, more Classical. This pattern holds for six of the symphonies: the Third and Fourth, Fifth and Sixth, the Seventh and Eighth . . . .[26]

The notion that Beethoven alternated between phases of expansion and consolidation not only adds nuance to the three-period model, but also offers an attractive solution to the problem apparently posed by the works of 1806 (among others). The Fourth Piano Concerto, Violin Concerto, and Fourth Symphony do not represent a regression in the wake of the heroic works of 1803–5, but rather their essential complement. Divergences from the heroic paradigm are absorbed into a governing logic of aesthetic dualism.

Like the three-period model or the notion of the heroic style, the concept of aesthetic dualism provides a broad-brush generalization that can help to make sense of a complex body of works over a long period. But as Derrida reminds us, in any binary opposition, "we are not dealing with the peaceful coexistence of a vis-à-vis. . . . One of the two terms governs the other (axiologically, logically, etc.), or has the upper hand."[27] In this instance, the "expansive," "bold," or "more expressive" works provide the framework against which the "modest" or "traditional" ones are judged, and the former are implicitly (and often explicitly) valorized at the expense of the latter. The reception of the Fourth Symphony provides an apt illustration. As early as 1830, A. B. Marx maintained that this symphony belongs "in the same sphere with Mozart's, Spohr's, and other symphonies in which the composer has not yet risen to a heightened awareness, to a specific idea," arguing that one must "unconditionally recognize a higher meaning" in Beethoven's mature odd-numbered symphonies and the programmatic *Pastoral*.[28] While Marx was referring to the symphony's apparent lack of a *bestimmte Idee* (by which he meant extramusical content), others have responded in similar terms. For J. W. N. Sullivan in 1927, the Fourth, Sixth, and Eighth Symphonies were "not in the main line of Beethoven's spiritual development."[29] And for Joseph Kerman, writing in the authoritative context of the *New Grove Dictionary of Music and Musicians*, neither the Fourth nor the Eighth Symphony celebrates Beethoven's "symphonic ideal," the unprecedented fusion of technical and expressive mastery that he considers "probably Beethoven's

26. James Webster, "Traditional Elements in Beethoven's Middle-Period String Quartets," in Robert Winter and Bruce Carr, eds., *Beethoven, Performers, and Critics: The International Beethoven Congress, Detroit, 1977* (Detroit: Wayne State University Press, 1980), 94–133, 125–6.

27. Jacques Derrida, *Positions*, trans. Alan Bass (Chicago: University of Chicago Press, 1981), 41.

28. Review of March 20, 1830 (*Berliner allgemeine musikalische Zeitung* 7: 92), reproduced and translated in Wayne Senner and William Meredith, eds., Robin Wallace, trans. and ed., *The Critical Reception of Beethoven's Compositions by His German Contemporaries*, 2 vols. (Lincoln: University of Nebraska Press, 2001), vol. 2, 66–7.

29. J. W. N. Sullivan, *Beethoven: His Spiritual Development* (London: Unwin Books, 1964), 87.

greatest single achievement."Through the curious but clearly intentional omission of these two symphonies from his discussion, Kerman suggests that they lack the "forcefulness," "expanded range," "evident radical intent," and impression of a "psychological journey or growth process" that characterizes the Third, Fifth, Sixth, Seventh, and Ninth.[30] Others have resorted to metaphor in order to account for the apparent discrepancy between the Fourth Symphony and its odd-numbered companions. The Fourth, wrote Sir George Grove in 1877, stands between the *Eroica* and the Fifth "like a graceful Greek maiden between two enormous Norse or Scandinavian heroes; the Parthenon between the Cathedrals of Chartres and Rheims; or an idyl of Theocritus between Hamlet and Lear."[31] It is akin, wrote Max Chop in 1910, to "the nadir between two stormy, foam-crested waves, like the peaceful ground lying in the green of the meadow between two lofty ice- and snow-covered mountain peaks."[32] "Poised between the two staggering *yang* peaks of the Third and the Fifth," writes David Tame in 1994, "the Fourth Symphony is a rich, verdant valley of *yin* expressiveness."[33] For Jan Swafford, the Fourth "is virtually the anti-Third. It would be the same with the Fifth and Sixth."[34]

If not for the iconic status of the heroic Beethoven, Victorian-era critics (and their modern forebears) would hardly have needed to resort to the metaphoric oppositions of peaks and valleys, giants and maidens, *yin* and *yang*, to explain, or explain away, the Fourth. Convenient though such oppositions may be, they threaten to reduce the symphony to a platitude. They also paint a bland picture

30. Joseph Kerman et al., "Beethoven, Ludwig van," in *Grove Music Online (Oxford Music Online)*, http://www.oxfordmusiconline.com/subscriber/article/grove/music/40026pg14 (accessed September 29, 2017).

31. George Grove, "Analytical Review of L. van Beethoven, Op. 60, Symphony in B Flat, No. 4," in *Analytical Reviews of Classical and Modern Compositions, for the Use of Amateurs at Musical Entertainments* (New York: C. F. Tretbar, c. 1877–8), vol. 5, 1–8, 1. The oft-repeated claim that Schumann called the Fourth Symphony a "slender Greek maiden between two Norse giants" appears to be erroneous. Schumann (as Florestan) referred to the symphony as both "the slender, Greek-like one" (*die griechisch-schlanke*) and "the Grecian" (*die griechische*, as opposed to the "Roman" *Eroica*). The formulation "slender Greek maiden between two Norse giants" seems to have been Grove's embellishment, and Joseph Bennett attributed it to him in a 1904 program note (Joseph Bennett, "Second Concert: Thursday, March 24, 1904," *Analytical and Historical Programme* [London: Philharmonic Society, 1904]). Grove himself later attributed the formulation to Schumann, and Thayer-Deiters-Riemann (1911) followed suit. See Mark Ferraguto, "Beethoven's Fourth Symphony: Reception, Aesthetics, Performance History" (PhD diss. Cornell University, 2012), 53–9.

32. "Das Werk berührt in seiner Stellung zwischen 'Eroica' und C-Moll-Symphonie eigenartig, etwa wie das Wellental zwischen zwei stürmischen, schaumgekrönten Wogen, wie der friedlich im Grün der Matten liegende Grund zwischen zwei hochragenden eis- und schneebedeckten Gebirgskämmen." Max Chop, *Erläuterungen zu Ludwig van Beethovens Symphonien: Geschichtlich und musikalisch analysiert mit zahlreichen Notenbeispielen* (Leipzig: Reclam, 1910), Vol. 2 (Symphonies 4–6), 3.

33. David Tame, *Beethoven and the Spiritual Path* (Wheaton, IL: Quest Books, 1994), 125.

34. Jan Swafford, *Beethoven: Anguish and Triumph* (Boston and New York: Houghton Mifflin Harcourt, 2014), 468–9.

of Beethoven's oeuvre, impelling us to hear in black and white instead of in vibrant color. The Fourth Symphony owes much indeed to the symphonic tradition of Haydn and Mozart, but it also stands in a complex relationship both to this tradition and to the so-called heroic style. Likewise, to describe the orchestral works of 1806 in general as antipodes of the heroic is to mischaracterize them. In this book, I proceed from the point of view that each work can be approached individually and historically. It would be neither desirable nor possible to ignore considerations about style and period. But by examining Beethoven's music through his relationships, it becomes possible to shift the focus away from these more or less schematic conceptions of his oeuvre, focusing instead on the particularity of each work and the mediations that helped to give it shape.

HEARING BEETHOVEN HISTORICALLY

As an exercise in historically informed analysis, this project seeks to contribute not only to Beethoven studies but also to a growing interdisciplinary literature on the topic of listening in the eighteenth and early nineteenth centuries. As Schroeder (1990), Tolley (2001), Riley (2004), Sisman (2005), Bonds (2006), Lowe (2007), and others have emphasized, only through the careful reconstruction of past listening practices can we begin to apprehend what this music might have meant for contemporary audiences. Beethoven's music has historically presented specific challenges for such an approach, insofar as the Romantic portrayal of the deaf Beethoven as a kind of high priest of art—one whose works resulted from profound, even divine, inspiration—has reinforced the idea that his music somehow transcended the constraints of materiality. The composer's own words have often been cited as evidence for this claim: "What do I care about your wretched fiddle," he allegedly asked Ignaz Schuppanzigh, "when the spirit seizes me?"[35] To be sure, Beethoven sometimes attempted to distance himself from the practical considerations of music making, as for example when he entertained the idea of a "market for art" in a letter to the publisher Franz Anton Hoffmeister.[36] But there can be no doubt that he carefully considered the factors that contributed to the creation of dynamic and

35. Carl Dahlhaus, citing the "wretched fiddle" anecdote, maintains that Beethoven introduced the idea that "a musical text, like a literary or philosophical text, harbors a meaning which is made manifest but not entirely subsumed in its acoustic presentation—that a musical creation can exist as an 'art work of ideas' transcending its various interpretations." *Nineteenth-Century Music*, 10. The source for the anecdote itself is uncertain; possibly it first appeared in A. B. Marx, *Ludwig van Beethoven: Leben und Schaffen*, 2 vols. (Leipzig, 1859), vol. 2, 45–6.

36. Beethoven describes a "market for art" (*ein Magazin der Kunst*), "where the artist would only have to bring his works and take as much money as needed." *Briefwechsel*, vol. 1, no. 54, pp. 63–5; Anderson, vol. 1, no. 44, pp. 47–9.

profitable artworks. His private remarks, his correspondence with patrons and publishers, and the sheer variety of his published works show that he strove to strike a balance between amateur and connoisseur tastes, popular and learned styles, marketable trends of all kinds and the desire to be original. As the breadth of recent literature on eighteenth- and early nineteenth-century music suggests, coming to terms with the music of this era—even, or perhaps especially, that of Beethoven—requires more than merely investigating the scores; it requires positioning the musical work at the intersection of multiple axes: biographical, artistic, social, political, economic, performative, and historical, among others.

The following six chapters merge musical analyses with studies of context, with the aim of providing a fine-grained account of the music of 1806–7. Chapter 1 establishes the book's thematic and chronological framework. In the spring of 1806, Beethoven finished revising and restaging his opera *Leonore*, which had premiered the previous autumn during the French occupation of Vienna. By year's end, he had completed the bulk of the work on his Fourth Piano Concerto, Fourth Symphony, Violin Concerto, and three "Razumovsky" Quartets. As critics have noted, the three orchestral works in particular represent a marked departure from the "heroic" topics and musical characteristics that have often been viewed as central to Beethoven's music of 1803–5 (his "heroic phase," according to Alan Tyson).[37] This chapter explores the nature of and motivations for this shift, focusing on, among other things, Beethoven's reactions to critics, changes in the political climate, and the popularity of Luigi Cherubini, whose rescue opera *Faniska* premiered in Vienna between the 1805 and 1806 productions of *Leonore*.

Each of the next five chapters investigates a single work or group of works, organized by genre rather than chronology. Chapter 2 focuses on the two concertos of 1806, the Fourth Piano Concerto and Violin Concerto. This chapter examines these works through the lens of contemporary debates about virtuosity, demonstrating how an emerging discourse on interiority—understood as the hallmark of the "true" virtuoso—mediated Beethoven's approach.

Chapter 3 turns to the "Razumovsky" Quartets. Beginning in the mid-nineteenth century, Beethoven's treatments of the Russian folksongs in these quartets (borrowed from the well-known Lvov-Pratsch Collection, published in 1790) elicited sharp criticism. This chapter reappraises these treatments through a close engagement with contemporary aesthetic debates, the surrounding political scene, and the cosmopolitan persona of Razumovsky himself.

Chapter 4 examines the Fourth Symphony, a work that has long been thought "Haydnesque" because of its succinct length and proportions, unpretentious orchestration, and witty finale, among other aspects. While the presence of Haydnesque features seems undeniable, the extent and nature of Haydn's

37. Alan Tyson, "Beethoven's Heroic Phase," *Musical Times* 110, no. 1512 (February 1969): 139–41.

influence on Beethoven at this moment in his career has yet to be carefully explored. This chapter reconsiders the symphony in light of the Haydn mania that was sweeping theaters, concert halls, and the pages of journals like the Leipzig *Allgemeine musikalische Zeitung*.

Beethoven's relationship with the instruments at his disposal forms the basis for chapter 5. In late 1803, Beethoven acquired a new piano from the French firm of Sébastien Erard. Nowhere is the piano's influence more apparent than in his Thirty-Two Variations on an Original Theme (1806), a quasi-systematic exploration of piano techniques, textures, and sonorities. This chapter illustrates how the capacities and limitations of the Erard mediated Beethoven's compositional process, suggesting new avenues of interpretation.

Chapter 6 examines the *Coriolan* overture, composed in early 1807, from the perspective of Beethoven's relationship with the playwright for whom it was written—Heinrich Joseph von Collin. Critics from E. T. A. Hoffmann forward have struggled to reconcile the suspensefulness of Beethoven's overture with the more "reflective" tone of the tragedy that inspired it.[38] In response, many critics have attempted to argue that the overture owes more to Shakespeare's *Coriolanus* than to Collin's play. But Beethoven had compelling reasons—both pragmatic and aesthetic—to engage with Collin's tragedy. Probing the relationship between Beethoven and Collin opens up a host of literary, visual, and political associations surrounding *Coriolan* and suggests a new paradigm for thinking about the overture.

As the reader will observe, this book does not attempt to provide "blow-by-blow" analyses of every piece it considers. Rather, the focus here is on distinctive moments, moments that define this music and articulate its significance in particular ways. Moments of expressive interiority in the Fourth Piano Concerto and Violin Concerto, moments of "Russianness" in the "Razumovsky" Quartets, "Haydnesque" moments in the Fourth Symphony, moments of physical limitation in the C-Minor Variations, programmatically suggestive moments in the Overture to *Coriolan*—all of these play with and even transgress formal, aesthetic, or technological boundaries. These moments illustrate the rich variety of ways in which Beethoven's relationships mediated his instrumental music and how, in turn, we modern-day listeners might hear it with new—or perhaps newly historical—ears.

---

38. E. T. A. Hoffmann, "Review of Beethoven's Overture to *Coriolan*," in David Charlton, ed. and Martyn Clarke, trans., *E. T. A. Hoffmann's Musical Writings* (Cambridge: Cambridge University Press, 1989), 286–93, 287. Originally published in the *Allgemeine musikalische Zeitung* 14, no. 5 (August 1812): cols. 519–26.

CHAPTER I

AFTER *LEONORE*

On December 27, 1805, the Austrian Emperor Francis II signed a peace agreement with Napoleon Bonaparte that drastically weakened the might of the Austrian Empire and brought an end to the French occupation of Vienna.[1] News of the Peace of Pressburg reached Vienna the following morning, and a public commemoration was immediately organized and held in St. Stephen's cathedral, where a *Te Deum* was performed. The English physician Dr. Henry Reeve, who had been living in Vienna since late September, described the scene in his private journal:

> All the bourgeois were under arms, and the church was crowded with the citizens of Vienna and the French soldiers mixed among them; the [Austrian] magistrates and what noblemen are here were on one side, while General Clarke and many French general officers were seated on the other. Friends and foes all met together to celebrate the return of peace. It is somewhat ridiculous that prayers have been daily offered up in St. Stephen's for peace for three months past even before the war was fully declared, and now the people return thanks for being most severely beaten by the Lord's anointed. Never was a country so completely subdued, never was a conqueror who used his victory and triumph with such moderation; never did a numerous and victorious army behave with more forbearance and moderation.[2]

The peace ceremony did little to mask the consequences of the occupation on the Viennese. Resources had become severely strained. Due to the requisition of horses for the transport of cannon and baggage, and the slaughtering of livestock for the nourishment of tens of thousands of troops, food had become scarce. "The butchers shut up their shops," wrote Dr. Reeve, "and only give out

---

1. Austria ceded territories to three of Napoleon's vassal states: Venice, Venetia, Istria, and Dalmatia went to the Kingdom of Italy; Trentino, the Tyrol, and Vorarlberg to Bavaria; and the Breisgau to Baden and Württemberg (Tim Blanning, *The Pursuit of Glory: The Five Revolutions That Made Modern Europe: 1648–1815* [New York: Penguin Books, 2007], 656). With the formation of the Austrian Empire in 1804, Francis II restyled himself Francis I. I retain the more common "Francis II" throughout for consistency.

2. Henry Reeve, *Journal of a Residence at Vienna and Berlin in the Eventful Winter 1805–6* (London: Longmans, Green, and Co., 1877), 94.

small portions of meat to families; many can get none. Famine begins to stare us in the face."[3] The Russian soldiers, despite an alliance with Austria, "burnt, and ate, and destroyed everything they could lay hands on, to prevent, as they said, anything being left for the French, who were following them."[4] Until well into the new year, French, Russian, and Austrian soldiers filled the hospitals and the streets, among them the survivors of the bloody Battle of Austerlitz on December 2.[5]

Faced with famine and tax increases to help pay national indemnities, the war-weary Viennese sought the pleasure of diversion. Dr. Reeve wrote that

> Politics are seldom talked of; the people are indifferent upon every topic but mere idle objects of amusement, and the new ballet or play, the dress of the *bourgeois*, the parade of their emperor's return, &c., is more eagerly talked about than the miserable treaty of peace, the loss of an army, or the overthrow of an empire. The subject is "traurig" they say, and in this world we ought to amuse ourselves.[6]

Indeed, although audiences thinned as the members of high society fled the city in droves, the five major theaters were kept open during the occupation by governmental decree. "From the distance," Beethoven's collaborator Georg Friedrich Treitschke remembered, "the storm of war rolled towards Vienna and robbed the spectators of the calm essential to the enjoyment of an artwork. But just for this reason all possible efforts were made to enliven the sparsely attended spaces of the house."[7] Emanuel Schikaneder's *Swetards Zaubergürtel* (with music by Anton Fischer) and *Vestas Feuer* (with music by Joseph Weigl) were lavishly produced, boasting "very extraordinary splendor of decorations and costumes."[8] Special performances were organized to keep the French troops entertained, including, on Christmas Day, a performance of Haydn's oratorio *The Seasons*.[9] And the winter season saw the premiere of two new operas, Beethoven's *Leonore* and Cherubini's *Faniska*.

The story of *Leonore*'s disastrous premiere on November 20, 1805, is a familiar one. The opera's failure had both external and internal causes. Externally, the French occupation resulted in a parterre filled with foreigners who had little appreciation for German Singspiel (though some of them perhaps knew the French play by Jean-Nicolas Bouilly on which the opera was based). Moreover,

---

3. Ibid., 85.

4. Ibid., 85.

5. This battle, Napoleon's greatest victory, came at an extremely high cost. The casualties for the allied Austro-Russian forces were 15,000 dead or wounded and 12,000 taken prisoner; for Napoleon's *Grande Armée* 8,000 dead or wounded and 573 taken prisoner (Blanning, *Pursuit of Glory*, 655).

6. Reeve, *Journal*, 119.

7. Quoted in Thayer/Forbes, vol. 1, 382–3.

8. Ibid., 382 (quoted without attribution).

9. This is especially remarkable as performances were generally prohibited on Christmas.

many of Beethoven's Viennese supporters had fled the city by the time of the premiere.[10] Internally, the opera's length and three-act design proved to be more cumbersome than Beethoven and his librettist Joseph Sonnleithner anticipated. Early reviews were almost unanimous on this point, citing among other concerns the "very extensive" third act, the overture with its "*very* long Adagio," and the "endlessly repeated" text.[11] Beethoven, despite registering to his friends his strong reluctance to make changes, gradually came to realize that revisions would be necessary if the work were ever to succeed. Condensing the opera into two acts would be the thrust of his revisionary efforts over the winter, in preparation for a second run of performances in early 1806.

The restaging of *Leonore* effectively marked the end of a project that had occupied Beethoven for more than two years. What followed was a period of remarkable productivity, the culmination of which was the landmark *Akademie* of December 22, 1808, at which the Fifth and Sixth Symphonies, Choral Fantasy, and Fourth Piano Concerto had their public premieres. While much has been written about Beethoven's preparations for the *Akademie* and about the concert itself, less attention has been paid to the period immediately following the revival of *Leonore*. And yet, the year 1806 has long stood out as exceptional within the context of the middle period. Not only was it one of the most prolific years of Beethoven's career but also, as critics have noted, the works of 1806 seem to represent a departure from the heroic idiom that characterizes Beethoven's music of previous (and later) years. This chapter explores the idea of Beethoven's "stylistic turn" of 1806 from two perspectives. First, it focuses on the commercial, political, and social pressures that mediated Beethoven's compositional approach in 1806. As I argue, Beethoven's pivot toward instrumental music and cultivation of new expressive paradigms in the wake of *Leonore* may be viewed as a response not only to his diminished prospects as an opera composer but also to his political disenchantment after the French occupation. Second, it examines some of the most unusual musical aspects of the works of 1806. Taken together, these seem to suggest a unified aesthetic outlook for the year; however, there are also continuities (some on the surface, others more subterranean) that link these works with the music of the "heroic phase" in interesting and often overlooked ways. This chapter hence provides the historical

10. As Thayer writes, "The nobility, the great bankers and the merchants—all those whose wealth enabled and whose vocations permitted it—precisely those classes of society in which Beethoven moved, which knew how to appreciate his music, and of whose suffrages his opera was assured, fled from the capital." Thayer/Forbes, vol. 1, 386.

11. Reviews of January 4, 1806 (*Zeitung für die elegante Welt* 6: 12–13), and January 8, 1806 (*Allgemeine musikalische Zeitung* 8: 237–8), reproduced and translated in Wayne Senner and William Meredith, eds., Robin Wallace, trans. and ed., *The Critical Reception of Beethoven's Compositions by His German Contemporaries*, 2 vols. (Lincoln: University of Nebraska Press, 2001), vol. 2, 172–3.

and critical framework for the studies of individual works that follow in subsequent chapters.

REVISION, REVIVAL, RECEPTION

Leonore's second run in the spring of 1806 met with a somewhat warmer critical response than its earliest performances, but the financial returns were disappointing. Inexperienced with the business of opera, Beethoven believed that the theater's management had swindled him. The tenor Joseph August Röckel (who played Florestan in the 1806 version) witnessed a scene between the theater's manager Baron von Braun and Beethoven, in which Braun indicated that the low returns were due to the fact that only the boxes and front-row seats had been filled. The issue quickly turned from money to music, and Beethoven's high-flown style came on the line. According to Röckel,

> [Braun] hoped that the receipts would increase with each representation; until now, only the first ranks, stalls and pit were occupied; by and by the upper ranks would likewise contribute their shares. "I don't write for the galleries!" exclaimed Beethoven. "No?" replied the Baron, "My dear Sir, even Mozart did not disdain to write for the galleries." Now it was at an end. "I will not give the opera any more," said Beethoven, "I want my score back."[12]

Röckel may have embellished his account, but it is clear that the revision process caused Beethoven personal strain. Stephan von Breuning, the librettist who helped condense the opera into two acts, confided to his sister Eleonore and her husband, Franz Wegeler, that "probably nothing has caused Beethoven so much grief as this work, whose value will be fully appreciated only in the future."[13] The revision in some sense brought to a head the frustrations that had surrounded the project from the beginning. For Beethoven, mounting an

12. Thayer/Forbes, vol. 1, 398. A more vivid version of this story is related in Sonneck: "[Braun] emphasized that hitherto Beethoven's music had been accepted only by the more cultured classes, while Mozart with his operas invariably had roused enthusiasm in the multitude, the people as a whole. Beethoven hurried up and down the room in agitation, shouting loudly: 'I do not write for the multitude—I write for the cultured!' 'But the cultured alone do not fill our theatre', replied the Baron with the greatest calmness, 'we need the multitude to bring in money, and since in your music you have refused to make any concessions to it, you yourself are to blame for your diminished percentage of return. If we had given Mozart the same interest in the receipts of his operas he would have grown rich'. This disadvantageous comparison with his famous predecessor seemed to wound Beethoven's tenderest susceptibilities. Without replying to it with a single word, he leaped up and shouted in the greatest rage: 'Give me back my score!'" Quoted in O. G. Sonneck, ed., *Beethoven: Impressions by His Contemporaries* (New York: Dover Publications Inc., 1967), 66–7.

13. Stephan von Breuning to Franz Gerhard Wegeler and his wife Eleonore (née von Breuning), June 2, 1806, in Theodore Albrecht, ed., *Letters to Beethoven and Other Correspondence* (Lincoln: University of Nebraska Press, 1996), vol. 1, no. 116, 179. German text in Franz Gerhard Wegeler and Ferdinand Ries, *Biographische Notizen über Ludwig von Beethoven* (Coblenz, 1838), 62–6.

opera had meant navigating an unfamiliar world of impresarios, stage managers, librettists, divas, and censors. As Lewis Lockwood has noted, this plunge into what Beethoven called the "whirlpool of society" (*der Strudel der Gesellschaft*) may have presented special challenges for a composer who was coming to grips with the onset of deafness.[14] In any case, while Beethoven had proven that he could compose and stage an opera to some public acclaim, he had also demonstrated that launching a career as an opera composer would be no light task. Although he would tinker with libretti throughout his lifetime, draft ideas for new operas, and even petition for a position as a court opera composer in December 1807, the only other opera project to take root would be the third and final revision of *Leonore* in 1814 (better known as *Fidelio*).

Leonore's lackluster reception may also have had another cause: Luigi Cherubini. With the Viennese premieres of *Lodoïska* and *Les deux journées* (the latter variously titled *Graf Armand* and *Die Tage der Gefahr*) in 1802, Cherubini had effectively established the demand for French operas in the city. By the end of that year, his *Médée* (*Medea*) and *Eliza* (*Der Bernhardsberg*), with its terrifying avalanche scene, had also had their Viennese premieres. The one-act *L'hôtellerie portugaise* (*Der portugiesische Gasthof*) followed in 1803, along with (between 1803 and 1804) a spate of operas by other French composers including at least six operas by Méhul and works by Le Sueur, Dalayrac, Della Maria, Devienne, Berton, Boieldieu, and Isouard.[15] Cherubini's arrival in Vienna in July 1805 inevitably caused a sensation, and it placed added pressure on Beethoven to compete in a genre in which he was a novice. To further compound matters, Cherubini's latest opera, *Faniska*, composed expressly for the Viennese stage, had its debut at the Kärntnerthor Theater on February 25, 1806, between the premiere and revival of *Leonore*.

Like *Leonore* in its 1805 version, *Faniska* is a three-act rescue opera based on a French play (*Les mines de Pologne* by René-Charles Guilbert de Pixérécourt). Like *Leonore*, its German libretto was adapted by the secretary of Vienna's court theaters, Joseph Sonnleithner.[16] And like *Leonore*, it focuses on a husband and

---

14. The remark appears in a sketchbook entry of 1806: "Even as you plunge here into the whirlpool of society, so it is possible for you to write operas despite all social handicaps—let your deafness no longer be a secret—even in art." Lewis Lockwood, "Beethoven, Florestan, and the Varieties of Heroism," in Scott Burnham and Michael Steinberg, eds., *Beethoven and His World* (Princeton: Princeton University Press, 2000), 27–47, 27.

15. See the entry on Cherubini in Peter Clive, *Beethoven and His World: A Biographical Dictionary* (Oxford and New York: Oxford University Press, 2001), 70, and Winton Dean, "German Opera," in Gerald Abraham, ed., *The Age of Beethoven: 1790–1830* (Oxford and New York: Oxford University Press, 1982, rpt. 2007), 452–522, 463.

16. Sonnleithner based his German libretto for *Faniska* not on the French original by Pixérécourt but rather on an Italian translation that Cherubini had set to music. See John A. Rice, *Empress Marie Therese and Music at the Viennese Court, 1792–1807* (Cambridge: Cambridge University Press, 2003, rpt. 2007), 194–7.

wife, Rasinski and Faniska, whose lives are threatened by a tyrant, Zamoski. See Figures 1.1 and 1.2.[17] (The two female leads were played by the same actress, soprano Anna Milder.) The two operas also share numerous dramatic and musical details, among which perhaps the most striking is the presence of an extended *sotteraneo* in which a slow orchestral prelude depicting the darkness and gloom of the underground dungeon precedes a monologue-like recitative and aria sung by the imprisoned protagonist (Florestan's "Gott! welch Dunkel hier" and Faniska's "Welche Wohnung des Schreckens!").[18] Both operas also include, unusually, vocal canons; whether Cherubini's three-part canon "Hoffnung, du trocknest wieder sanft die Augenlider" was at all influenced by Beethoven's four-part canon "Mir ist so wunderbar" remains unknown.[19]

Perhaps unsurprisingly, *Faniska* was criticized in the musical press for some of the same reasons as *Leonore*, among which its weak libretto and highbrow musical style.[20] And yet, the early Viennese reception of these two operas could not have been more different. While *Leonore* essentially disappeared from the public stage for eight years after its short second run ended on April 10, 1806 (after a total of five performances), *Faniska* garnered an impressive sixty-four performances in its first four years.[21] And while *Leonore* remained unpublished until 1810 (with the exception of three numbers printed by Johann Cappi in 1807), *Faniska* was widely available for purchase in numerous forms within mere months of its premiere.[22] By August 1806, Viennese consumers could already purchase not only two different piano-vocal scores of the opera (including a

17. My thanks to Bonna Boettcher for her help in procuring these images.

18. As Golianek notes, Faniska's aria ("Allzu tief sind des Herzens Wunden") has musical similarities with the 1814 version of Florestan's aria, most notably a lively concluding section in F major. Ryszard Daniel Golianek (trans. John Comber), "Towards a New Aesthetics of the Viennese Singspiel in the Early Nineteenth Century: Beethoven's *Fidelio* and Cherubini's *Faniska*," in Mieczysław Tomaszewski, ed., *Beethoven: Studien und Interpretationen 6: Internationale musikwissenschaftliche Symposien, Warszawa 2012, 2013 und 2014 im Rahmen des Ludwig van Beethoven Osterfestivals* (Muzyczna: Kraków Akad., 2015), 403–11, 409–10. On prison scenes and the two-tempo aria structure more generally, see Stephen Meyer, "Terror and Transcendence in the Operatic Prison, 1790–1815," *Journal of the American Musicological Society* 55, no. 3 (Winter 2002): 477–523.

19. For further similarities between these two operas, see Anton Schindler, "Aus Frankfurt am Main," *Niederrheinische Musik-Zeitung* 8, no. 43 (October 20, 1860): 337–40, 338, and Golianek, "Towards a New Aesthetics."

20. See "Nachrichten," *Allgemeine musikalische Zeitung* 8, no. 24 (March 12, 1806): cols. 376–7.

21. Michael Jahn, "Aspekte der Rezeption von Cherubinis Opern im Wien des 19. Jahrhunderts," *Studien zur Musikwissenschaft* 49 (2002): 213–44, 225. A sixth performance of *Leonore* may have been given at the palace of Prince Lobkowitz on May 4, 1806; see Theodore Albrecht, trans. and ed., *Letters to Beethoven and Other Correspondence*, 3 vols. (Lincoln and London: University of Nebraska Press, 1996), vol. 1, 182, note 4.

22. The first year's issues of Cappi's *Musikalisches Wochenblat* included the trio "Ein Mann ist bald genommen" (no. 22; February 22, 1807), the duet "Um in der Ehe froh zu leben" (no. 26; March 28, 1807), and the canon quartet "Mir ist so wunderbar" (no. 52; September 26, 1807). In 1810, Breitkopf und Härtel published the piano-vocal score of *Leonore*'s 1806 version without the overture and finales.

bilingual one issued by Breitkopf & Härtel), but also an arrangement for string quartet, keyboard and orchestral versions of the overture, and four original works based on the opera's themes, among other items. See Table 1.1.

Hence, in the short term, *Faniska* succeeded where *Leonore* did not. As if to rub salt in the wound, Cherubini—who attended the premiere of *Leonore* and was reportedly unimpressed—ordered a copy of the *Méthode du chant* used at the Paris Conservatoire and presented it to Beethoven as suggested reading.[23] If Beethoven felt at all patronized by this gesture, he did not admit it; on the contrary, he professed nothing but admiration for the elder composer. Around 1817 or 1818, he would call Cherubini the greatest living composer apart from himself, and would later tell him that he valued his operas above all other compositions for the stage. According to Anton Schindler, the French treatise remained in Beethoven's library until his death, alongside its German translation published by Breitkopf & Härtel; a partial copy of the latter (with annotations in Beethoven's hand) is preserved in the Beethovenhaus archive.[24]

A POLITICAL TURN

By the spring of 1806, reports began to suggest that life in Vienna was on the mend. An article in the *Journal des Luxus und der Moden* on music and theater during the winter months concluded:

> You can see from all that has been said, that the Viennese have already long recovered from the horrors of the war, and that amusement, joy, and peaceful arts are paid homage once again. The prosperity among the local inhabitants must be very firmly based, because one does not notice the slightest reduction of luxury either in garments, or in equipages [horse-drawn carriages], or at tables; and where it concerns the advancement of charitable purposes—the support of the poor and the encouragement of the deserving—there the Viennese give with full hands and without reservation. This year earlier than usual we have gentle weather and all the harbingers of spring. Here the whole beautiful world flows on foot to the *Bastey*, and by carriage to the *Prater*; the crowding and mixing of so many glad and well-dressed people from every class earns, among all the plays of Vienna, perhaps the first place.[25]

23. See Anton Felix Schindler, *Beethoven as I Knew Him*, ed. Donald W. MacArdle, trans. Constance S. Jolly (Mineola: Dover Publications, Inc., 1996), 133.

24. As MacArdle notes (ibid., 192, note 89), neither the French nor the German edition is listed among the books Beethoven owned at the time of his death. However, the third and final part of Breitkopf & Härtel's edition, with translations of Italian words in Beethoven's hand, is in the archives of the Beethovenhaus in Bonn (BH 97). This volume, published in 1804, treats "Arias in all meters and of all characters" and includes a short preface printed in both French and German followed by arias by Hasse, Leo, Jomelli, Caffaro, Piccini, Sacchini, Sarti, Cimarosa, Maio, Galuppi, Traetta, and J. C. Bach (doubtful attribution).

25. "Sie sehen aus allem bisher Gesagten, daß man sich in Wien von den Schrecknissen des Kriegs schon längst wieder erholt hat, und daß der Unterhaltung, der Freude, und den friedlichen Künsten wieder wie sonst gehuldiget wird. Der Wohlstand unter den hiesigen Bewohnern muß sehr

FIGURE 1.1. *Faniska*, from *Wiener Hof-Theater Taschenbuch auf das Jahr 1807, Vierter Jahrgang* (Vienna: Joh. Bapt. Wallishausser, 1808). Used by permission of the Division of Rare and Manuscript Collections, Cornell University Library.

FIGURE I.2. *Fidelio*, from *Wiener Hof-Theater Taschenbuch auf das Jahr 1815, Zwölfter Jahrgang* (Vienna: J. B. Wallishausser, 1815). Used by permission of the Division of Rare and Manuscript Collections, Cornell University Library.

TABLE 1.1 Arrangements, editions, and original works based on Cherubini's *Faniska*, as advertised in the *Wiener Zeitung* in 1806.

Date first advertised	Publisher/distributor	Title
May 2	Johann Cappi	*Ouverture aus der Faniska, für das Clavier,* 40 kr. *Märsche aus det[t]o,* 30 kr.
May 24	Thadé Weigl	*Das XXIX und XXX. Heft des mit so vielem Beyfalle aufgenommenen Potpourri, für das Forte-Piano, Preis à 36 kr. welches nebst mehreren andern beliebten Stücken verschiedene Neuigkeiten aus den Singspielen: Die Uniform, Faniska, Die Samniterrinnen, Alane, und dem grossen komisch, Ballete: Paul und Rosette, enthalten.*
June 4	Bureau des Arts et d'Industrie	*Ouvert. de l'Opéra Faniska, arrangée p. le P. F. par A. E. Müller,* 48 kr. *Faniska; im Clavierauszuge, von A. E. Müller, Nr.* 1, 1 fl. 20 kr., Nr. 2, 40 kr., Nr. 3, 30 kr., Nr. 4, 50 kr.
June 28	Chemische Druckerei	Franz Clement, *VI Variationen über ein beliebtes Thema aus der Opera Faniska von Cherubini, für eine Violine,* 18 kr. Abbé Gelinek, *VI Variations avec un Polonoise sur le thême de l'Opera Faniska de Chérubini pour le Piano-Forte,* 40 kr. Joseph Lipavsky, *Partie finale de l'introduction de l'opera Faniska de Cherubini en Rondo pour le Clavecin ou Piano-Forte, Oeuv. 30,* 48 kr. F. A Neumann, *VII Variationen über ein beliebtes Thema des Cherubini'schen Singspiels Faniska für das Forte-Piano,* 1 fl. *Aus der Cherubini'schen Oper Faniska: Die Ouverture für das Piano-Forte,* 40 kr., *Der Tanz der Kleinen Hedwig für das Piano-Forte,* 15 kr., *2 Märsche für das Piano-Forte,* 12 kr. each.
July 19	Bureau des Arts et d'Industrie	*Faniska, Ouverture à grand Orchestre,* 3 fl.
	Artaria / k. und k. priv. Kunsthändler in Wien am Kohlmarkte	*Faniska, Grand Opera en Quatuors pour 2 Violons, Viole, & Violoncelle par Cherubini,* 3 fl. 30 kr. *Faniska, im Klavierauszug,* 4 fl. 30 kr.
	Kunst- und Musik-Verlage / Chemische Druckerei	Subscription notice for a bilingual vocal score to be published by the end of August 1806: *Faniska, eine grosse Oper in drey Acten von Cherubini. In vollständigem Clavier-Auszuge mit deutsch- und italiänischem Texte,* 10 fl. (6 fl. 40 kr. for subscribers). [Possibly Breitkopf & Härtel's edition, arranged by Gottlob Bierey.]
August 6	Bureau des Arts et d'Industrie	Subscription notice for a vocal score to be published by the "Bureau de Musique zu Leipzig [A. Kühnel]" by the end of August 1806: *Cherubini's grosse Oper Faniska, in drey Akten; im vollständigen Clavierauszuge, von A. E. Müller,* 6 fl. 30 kr.

If the city's social life had returned to normal, however, its political life remained troubled and chaotic. Count Franz Joseph Saurau, one of the most influential ministers on the imperial council, wrote to the emperor on March 16, 1806, that the country's internal conditions posed a far greater threat than did Napoleon.[26] In addition to having to fund its military operations, the Austrian nation now owed vast sums in indemnities as a result of the Peace of Pressburg. Worse, the government seemed to be in a state of paralysis, unable to agree on even the most superficial decisions. In a diplomatic cable to the Russian court, Count Razumovsky compared the Viennese cabinet to "a debilitated body, escaped from total destruction, hoping to regain its forces in calm and tranquility, and dreading at every instant a new tremor that would be able to overpower and annihilate it."[27]

More broadly, the year 1806 brought momentous changes in the political structure of Europe. The Holy Roman Empire, dating back to the ninth century, fizzled out of existence as Francis II was compelled to abdicate his title of Holy Roman Emperor. Meanwhile, Napoleon organized the German states into the *Rheinbund*, or Confederation of the Rhine, and placed garrisons throughout Germany at the expense of his hosts. By year's end, he had embarked on a new military campaign, with French troops entering Berlin on October 27 and Warsaw on December 19.

Composers on both sides of the Rhine commemorated these events with characteristic symphonies of a nationalist tone. Pierre Jean de Volder's *La bataille de Jena* (1806) includes trumpet calls, cavalry charges, cannonades, and laments, and monumentalizes the figure of Napoleon on the battlefield through its Maestoso setting of the "*Arrivée de l'empereur*" and sections titled "*Vive l'empereur.*" After dramatizing the French victory over the Prussian army, the symphony concludes with a musical representation of imperial conquest: *Pas redouble: L'Armée*

---

fest gegründet seyn, denn man bemerkt nicht die mindeste Abnahme des Luxus weder in Kleidern, noch in Equipagen, noch an den Tafeln, und wo es auf Beförderung wohlthätiger Zwecke, auf Unterstützung Hülfsbedürftiger und auf Ermunterung des Verdientes ankommt, da giebt der Wiener mit vollen Händen und ohne Ansprüche. Wir haben heuer früher als sonst gelinde Witterung und alle Vorboten des Frühlings. Da strömt die ganze schöne Welt zu Fuß nach der Bastey, und im Wagen nach dem Prater; das Gedränge und Gewühl so vieler froher und wohlgekleideter Menschen aus allen Classen, verdient unter allen Schauspielen Wiens vielleicht die erste Stelle." "Theatre und Musik in Wien in den letzten Wintermonaten 1806. Wien den 16. April 1806," *Journal des Luxus und der Moden* (May 1806): 284–91, 291.

26. James Allen Vann, "Habsburg Policy and the Austrian War of 1809," *Central European History* 7, no. 4 (December 1974): 291–310, 301.

27. "La situation politique du cabinet de Vienne est celle d'un corps débile, échappé à une destruction totale, espérant regagner ses forces dans le calme et la tranquillité et redoutant à tout instant une nouvelle secousse qui pourrait l'accabler et l'anéantir." Count Andrey Razumovsky, diplomatic cable of March 20, 1806, quoted in Aleksandr Alekseevich Wassiltchikow, *Les Razoumowski*, trans. Alexandre Brückner, 3 vols. (Halle: Tausch and Grosse, 1893–4), vol. 2, part 2, 318.

française marche sur Berlin.[28] Meanwhile, Abbé Georg Joseph Vogler celebrated German nationalism from a regional, populist standpoint, appending a chorus to an existing symphony in C major and creating his *Bayerische nationale Sinfonie* (1806). Bavaria was something of a special case during the Napoleonic wars, and Vogler's symphony stands in open defiance of French presence in the region.[29] With great patriotism, its chorus proclaims: "Ich bin ein Baier, ein Baier bin ich!" (I am a Bavarian, a Bavarian am I!).[30]

The battles of Jena and Auerstadt took place on October 14, at which time Beethoven was in Silesia under the aegis of his patron Prince Lichnowsky.[31] The region was visibly war-torn, and although Beethoven's reaction to the new military campaign is largely undocumented, it was after the French victories at Jena and Auerstadt that he reportedly said about Napoleon, "It's a pity that I do not understand the art of war as well as I do the art of music. I would conquer him!"[32] It seems likely that for Beethoven, as for many German intellectuals and artists, this was a time of ideological uncertainty. Napoleon, regarded throughout Europe as a military genius, continued to command admiration and respect from those sympathetic to the democratic ideals represented by the French Revolution. But as the idealism of the Revolution faded into the reality of a new empire, his symbolic status as liberator deteriorated. Beethoven's already ambivalent attitude toward Napoleon—encapsulated in his decision to compose a "Bonaparte" Symphony followed by his destruction of the symphony's title page and suppression of explicit references to Napoleon in the title itself—could only have been further complicated by the events of 1806.

Whatever Beethoven's private feelings, the French occupation of Vienna effectively put an end to one of his major projects of 1803–5: his preparation for a career in Paris.[33] It is not that the occupation rendered a career in French service impossible (after all, Napoleon's brother Jerome Bonaparte would entice Beethoven with a position at the court of Westphalia in 1808), but rather that 1806 seems to mark the end of Beethoven's "multifront campaign" to plan

28. See Richard Will, *The Characteristic Symphony in the Age of Haydn and Beethoven* (Cambridge: Cambridge University Press, 2002), 198, 290.

29. Unlike Vogler, Bavaria's prince-elector Maximillian Joseph had great sympathy for the ideals of the French Revolution and was one of Napoleon's strongest allies. As a result of the Peace of Pressburg, he was granted the title King of Bavaria and was rewarded for his faithfulness with important territorial acquisitions. Bonaparte further cemented the alliance in 1806 through the marriage of his stepson Eugène de Beauharnais to Joseph's eldest daughter.

30. The text was adapted from an earlier Lied by Vogler. See Will, *Characteristic Symphony*, 238 and 289.

31. Beethoven left Vienna for Silesia on July 5 and returned before November 1.

32. Quoted in Thayer/Forbes, vol. 1, 403.

33. In August 1803, Ries told Simrock, "Beethoven will remain here [in Vienna] at most another year and a half. Then he is going to Paris, which I am extraordinarily sorry about." Ferdinand Ries to Nikolaus Simrock, August 6, 1803, in Albrecht, ed. and trans., *Letters to Beethoven*, vol. 1, no. 65, 110.

for relocation to the French capital.[34] This campaign appears to have involved several strategic decisions, including the dismissal of Schikaneder's libretto *Vestas Feuer* in favor of Bouilly's *Leonore*, the dedication of the Violin Sonata in A Major to the Parisian virtuoso Rodolphe Kreutzer, the composition of a triple concerto of the kind popular in Paris, the purchase of a French piano from the Parisian firm of Erard (see chapter 5), and, most strikingly, the decision to compose a symphony "*auf Bonaparte.*" While Napoleon's self-proclamation as Emperor in May 1804 caused Beethoven to change his mind about the former First Consul, the final performances of *Leonore* in the spring of 1806 provided a more formal end to the French project. To be sure, Beethoven would still contemplate leaving Vienna and even use this prospect as leverage, both in his petition of December 1807 to the directors of the Imperial and Court Theaters and in the "annuity contract" of early 1809. But in the wake of the 1805 occupation, there is no longer evidence of an active plan to seek a position in France— politically, the tide had turned.[35] Indeed, it is telling that in both the 1807 petition and the 1809 contract (the latter drawn up just months before Napoleon's troops would occupy Vienna a second time), Beethoven emphasizes that "the patriotism of a German" and "patriotic feelings for his second fatherland" are among the reasons he wishes to remain in the Austrian capital.[36]

A STYLISTIC TURN

Discouraged by his foray into opera and disillusioned by the political situation, Beethoven remained resolved to build an international reputation. He now pivoted toward more familiar territory, instrumental music, completing an impressive series of orchestral and chamber works between early 1806 and early 1807. See Table 1.2. The pivot seems to have been in part strategic: with the exception of the Violin Concerto, each of these works was in a genre with which Beethoven was highly experienced (and in which he was already an acknowledged master). By playing to his strengths, he knew he stood a greater chance of commercial success. However, acquaintances new and old—all of

34. I borrow this turn of phrase from Jan Swafford, *Beethoven: Anguish and Triumph* (Boston and New York: Houghton Mifflin Harcourt, 2014), 330.

35. Plantinga has observed that Beethoven's responses to political events were often governed by pragmatism and self-interest; the end of the French project in early 1806, I would suggest, is best understood in this light. See Leon Plantinga, "Beethoven, Napoleon, and Political Romanticism," in Jane F. Fulcher, ed., *The Oxford Handbook of the New Cultural History of Music* (Oxford and New York: Oxford University Press, 2011), 484–500.

36. See *Briefwechsel*, vol. 1, no. 302, pp. 333–5 (Anderson, vol. 3, appendix I, no. 1, pp. 1444–6), and Anderson, vol. 3, appendix F, no. 4, pp. 1420–2. The latter translation is based on the German text of the annuity contract in Hermann Deiters and Hugo Riemann, eds., *Ludwig van Beethovens Leben von Alexander Wheelock Thayer nach dem Original-Manuskript*, 3rd ed., 3 vols. (Leipzig: Breitkopf & Härtel, 1917–23), vol. 3, 123–4.

TABLE 1.2 Beethoven's compositions of 1806 and 1807.

No.	Title	Composition	Publication	Dedicatee
Op. 72	*Leonore* (second version, incl. Overture "Leonore No. 3")	1805–6	Leipzig, 1810	
Op. 58	Piano Concerto No. 4 in G Major	1805–6	Vienna, 1808	Archduke Rudolph
Op. 59	Three String Quartets, F Major, E Minor, and C Major	1806	Vienna, 1808	Count Razumovsky
Op. 60	Symphony No. 4 in B-flat Major	1806	Vienna, 1808	Count Oppersdorff
Op. 61	Violin Concerto in D Major	1806	Vienna, 1808; London, 1810	Stephan von Breuning
WoO 80	Thirty-Two Variations on an Original Theme for Piano	1806	Vienna, 1807	
WoO 83	Six Ecossaises for Piano	c. 1806	Vienna, 1807	
WoO 132	Als die Geliebte sich trennen wollte	1806	*AMZ*, xii (1809–10)*	
WoO 133	In questa tomba oscura	1806–7	Vienna, 1808	Prince Lobkowitz (ded. by publisher)
Op. 138	Overture in C Major ("Leonore No. 1")	1807	Vienna, 1838	
Op. 61a	Violin Concerto in D Major, arr. for piano	1807	Vienna, 1808; London, 1810	Julie von Breuning
Op. 62	Overture to Collin's *Coriolan* in C Minor	1807	Vienna, 1808	H. J. von Collin
Op. 86	Mass in C Major	1807	Leipzig, 1812	Prince Ferdinand Kinsky

*Also published as "Empfindung bei Lydiens Untreue"

them either Austrian by birth or sympathetic to the Austrian cause—also played an important role in determining the compositional program for the year. The string quartets were commissioned by and dedicated to the Russian ambassador to Austria, Andrey Razumovsky; the new symphony (or a new symphony, at any rate) by the imperial count and Silesian nobleman, Franz von Oppersdorff.[37] The piano concerto may have been intended for performances

---

37. On Oppersdorff and his chamber orchestra (about which few details survive), see Mark Ferraguto, "Beethoven's Fourth Symphony: Reception, Aesthetics, Performance History" (PhD diss. Cornell University, 2012), 18–20 and 125–7.

by Beethoven's influential patron and pupil (as well as the work's dedicatee), Archduke Rudolph of Austria. Meanwhile, the violin concerto and overture would not have come into being if not for Beethoven's collaborations with the violinist and music director at the Theater an der Wien, Franz Clement, and the playwright, Heinrich von Collin (both Viennese natives), respectively.

While the five major opuses of 1806–7 (nos. 58 through 62) cover a wide array of genres and styles, there are compelling reasons to consider them as a group. For one thing, Beethoven himself conceived of them this way beginning in 1807. Following Haydn's business model, he planned to publish all five works (plus his transcription of the Violin Concerto as a piano concerto, Op. 61a) simultaneously in France, Great Britain, and the German-speaking lands—the three most significant markets of the day. This was still uncharted territory for him, and despite his best efforts, his plan did not succeed. He managed to strike a deal with the Viennese publisher Bureau des Arts et d'Industrie (Kunst- und Industrie-Comptoir), which purchased the rights to all six works for 1,500 gulden.[38] But the firms Pleyel in Paris and Simrock in Bonn (both representing France) apparently did not agree to Beethoven's terms, and the London firm Clementi—despite agreeing to publish all six works in a contract dated April 20, 1807—only partially fulfilled its end of the deal.[39] Nevertheless, the fact that Beethoven packaged these six opuses together is significant from the perspective of reception; these represented not only his most recent compositions but also a conspectus of his achievements in the wake of *Leonore*. By marketing these works as a set, he offered a fresh basis on which publishers, and by extension consumers, could evaluate his compositional aims.

---

38. Opp. 59 and 62 were available in print by January 1808, Opp. 58 and 61 (piano version) by August 1808. Opp. 60 and 61 (original version) were not advertised as being for sale until April 1809 but were probably also available in 1808, given their plate numbers. See Kurt Dorfmüller, Norbert Gertsch, and Julia Ronge, eds., *Ludwig van Beethoven: Thematisch-bibliographisches Werkverzeichnis*, 2 vols. (Munich: G. Henle, 2014), vol. 1, 315–16.

39. Muzio Clementi obtained the British rights to these six works directly from Beethoven—the two drew up a contract during Clementi's stay in Vienna in 1807. Beethoven's friend Baron von Gleichenstein drew up the official document, signed by both parties (Anderson, vol. 3, pp. 1419–20). But Clementi's firm never published the Fourth Symphony, the Fourth Piano Concerto, or the Overture to *Coriolan*. Perhaps the manuscripts never reached the island. The remaining three opuses lay unpublished until 1809–10 (at which point pirate editions of the quartets had already been produced). When Clementi visited Beethoven in Vienna for a second time in September 1808, he was surprised to discover that his firm had also failed to pay the composer. Despite all this, the two went on to have a productive business relationship. See Alan Tyson, *The Authentic English Editions of Beethoven* (London: Faber and Faber, 1963), 51–2; Barry Cooper, "The Clementi-Beethoven Contract of 1807, a Reinvestigation," in Roberto Illiano, Luca Sala, and Massimiliano Sala, eds., *Muzio Clementi: Studies and Prospects* (Bologna: Ut Orpheus, 2002), 337–53; David Wyn Jones, "Some Aspects of Clementi's Career as a Publisher," in B. M. Antolini and C. Mastroprimiano, eds., *Muzio Clementi. Compositore, (Forte)pianista, editore* (Lucca: Lim Editrice, 2006), 3–19; and Rudolf Rasch, "Muzio Clementi, the Last Composer-Publisher," in Illiano et al., eds., *Muzio Clementi: Studies and Prospects*, 355–66.

What were these aims? To be sure, it is difficult to generalize about works in such diverse genres as symphony, string quartet, overture, and concerto. That said, modern critics have suggested that the orchestral works of 1806 (the Fourth Piano Concerto, Fourth Symphony, and Violin Concerto) share a unified aesthetic. These works have been understood as a departure from the heroic impulse that so strongly characterizes the music of the preceding years. Maynard Solomon, for instance, maintains that they signal a "temporary retreat from exalted rhetoric into a more lyrical, contemplative, and serene style," one that possesses "certain qualities of a magnified chamber music." "What [Paul] Bekker wrote of the Fourth Piano Concerto," he continues, "holds in some measure for the Violin Concerto and the Fourth Symphony as well, that they are 'characterized by quiet, reflective gravity, by a latent energy, capable from time to time of expressing intense vitality, but usually preserving the mood of tranquility.'"[40] William Kinderman, who treats the years 1806 to 1809 as a subperiod in its own right, likewise notes that a "spacious, lyrical serenity characterizes several of the works from this time, including the Fourth Piano Concerto."[41] And Donald Francis Tovey conjures similar terms—"gigantic," "spacious," and "serene"—to describe the Violin Concerto, noting that its "most famous strokes of genius are not only mysteriously quiet, but mysterious in radiantly happy surroundings."[42] In other words, despite the expansive scope of these works, scholars have viewed them as expressively distinct from the music written in Beethoven's so-called heroic style. In this sense, they are among those major works that challenge the heuristic utility of the "heroic" as a catch-all for this decade in Beethoven's career.

While no single epithet suffices to describe the orchestral works of 1806, they exhibit expressive and structural characteristics that suggest a post-*Leonore* stylistic turn. These include (in no particular order): a general preference for the major mode, both within and across movements; reduced scoring (but an appreciably soloistic treatment of the timpani); a predilection for quiet but distinctive openings and lyrical primary themes; an avoidance of fugue and learned counterpoint, whether as fleeting topic, developmental strategy, or expressive culmination; an absence of descriptive titles or other programmatic texts; and a tendency to build musical drama through moments of "suspended time" (often

40. Maynard Solomon, *Beethoven*, rev. ed. (New York: Schirmer, 1998), 261–2.

41. William Kinderman, *Beethoven*, 2nd ed. (Oxford: Oxford University Press, 2009), 135.

42. Donald Francis Tovey, *Essays in Musical Analysis: Concertos and Choral Works* (London: Oxford University Press, 1981), 71. For Plantinga, writing about Op. 61, "Beethoven's music engages us not in heroic drives toward musical climax, nor in any ongoing mental exercise in measuring implication against realization, or (at the other extreme) in a passive presence in a motionless landscape, but rather in a quiet act of contemplation and assent to what we had expected all along." Leon Plantinga, *Beethoven's Concertos: History, Style, Performance* (New York and London: W.W. Norton & Company, 1999), 225–6.

involving a decrease in volume and texture and a slowing of harmonic rhythm). Several of these characteristics appear in other works, both earlier and later, and not all of them appear in equal measure in the three large-scale works of 1806. However, they constellate in these works in ways that deserve to be explored. In what follows, I turn to matters of musical design, examining three of these characteristics in detail: (1) reduced scoring and soloistic use of the timpani, (2) quiet but distinctive openings, and (3) moments of "suspended time." As I will suggest, the works of 1806 have significant stylistic affinities with each other, despite the fact that they respond to different generic and performative concerns.

Reduced Scoring and Soloistic Use of the Timpani

One element that fosters the sense of a "magnified chamber music" in the orchestral works of 1806 is reduced scoring. The Fourth Symphony is perhaps most noteworthy in this regard, since it is the only one of Beethoven's nine symphonies to call for a single flute instead of the typical pair, a scoring sometimes called for in the symphonies of Haydn and Mozart. Moreover, unlike Beethoven's Third, Fifth, Sixth, and Ninth Symphonies, it does not require any instruments beyond the standard Viennese complement of the 1790s and early 1800s (violins, violas, cellos, contrabasses, and pairs of flutes, oboes, clarinets, bassoons, horns, trumpets, and timpani). Both the Fourth Piano Concerto and Violin Concerto also call for a single flute; however, this is somewhat less remarkable in the context of Beethoven's concertos, of which only the Third and Fifth Piano Concertos require the pair. More striking is the extent to which, in the Fourth Piano Concerto, particularly, the winds and brass remain tacet. Not only are trumpets and drums completely withheld from the first movement, but the entire complement of winds, brass, and timpani is also omitted from the second movement Andante con moto, allowing for a sparse dialogue between piano and strings (a unique orchestration among the concertos). The second-movement Larghetto of the Violin Concerto, though far removed from the astringent quality of the Andante con moto, is also modestly scored. Against the rhapsodic concertante violin part, the strings are marked *con sordini* throughout (except for the last few measures), while horns, clarinets, and bassoons contribute evocative horn calls, long-breathed melodies, and delicate accompaniments.

Coupled with this reduced scoring is—in the Violin Concerto and Fourth Symphony—an appreciably soloistic approach to timpani writing. Beethoven had already experimented with the use of the timpani as a soloistic element in earlier works. In the ballet *The Creatures of Prometheus*, a bombastic timpani solo introduces the "Danza eroica" of Bacchus and the Bacchantes. In the Introduction to *Christ on the Mount of Olives*, a tapping motive in the kettledrums, *pianissimo*, foretells Christ's doom. And in the Introduction to Act II of *Leonore*, Beethoven asks the timpanist to tune the drums to the interval of a tritone— one of the first uses of this interval in the history of the instrument—to depict the sense of foreboding in Florestan's dungeon cell.[43] The orchestral works of 1806, however, are among his earliest attempts at heightening the timpani's role within a purely instrumental (that is, not theatrical, sacred, or otherwise pro- grammatic) context. The Violin Concerto, famously, opens with five strokes of the timpani—a motive that governs much of the ensuing thematic material. In the Fourth Symphony, the first movement includes an extended passage scored primarily for timpani and strings (mm. 281–332), while the second movement is governed by a persistent drumbeat-like alternation of tonic and dominant pitches, a motive that is presented on the timpani at key moments in the form (most notably the coda).[44]

The timpani, their sonic product somewhere between distinct tone and indistinct noise, added a new dimension to orchestral writing in the late eigh- teenth and early nineteenth centuries. They offered not just another orchestral color but also a way of evoking extramusical ideas by drawing on familiar musi- cal topics, both pastoral and martial. These topics had developed over the course of several decades in cantatas, ballets, and operas, as well as on the battlefield. The frightening roll of thunder and thunderous noise of the cannon, however, overlapped in the soundworld of the time, and the timpani often brought to mind different associations depending on who was listening.[45] At least two of Beethoven's contemporaries—A. B. Marx and Ludwig Rellstab—described the long timpani rolls in the Fourth Symphony as representations of rolling thun- der.[46] Conversely, Beethoven himself emphasized the timpani's warlike associa- tions in his first-movement cadenza for the Violin Concerto arranged as a piano concerto. Scored as a duet for piano and timpani, the lengthy cadenza was most likely composed in 1809 for Archduke Rudolph, in whose library it belonged. It begins typically of Beethoven's piano cadenzas, but after an extensive series of chromatic runs in the piano's right hand (underpinned by the opening

43. Salieri had earlier called for timpani tuned to a tritone (C and G-flat) in his opera *La grotta di Trofonio* (1785). See Jeremy Montagu, *Timpani and Percussion* (New Haven and London: Yale University Press, 2002), 99.

44. Beethoven's inclusion of timpani in this symphony is itself unusual, given its key of B-flat major; Haydn's "London" Symphonies Nos. 98 (1792) and 102 (1794) perhaps served as models in this respect. See chapter 4. For more on Beethoven's use of timpani, see Paul Mies, "Die Bedeutung der Pauke in den Werken Ludwig van Beethovens," *Beethoven-Jahrbuch* 8 (1975): 49–71.

45. For Burke, "The noise of vast cataracts, raging storms, thunder, or artillery, awakes a great and awful sensation in the mind, though we can observe no nicety or artifice in those sorts of music." Edmund Burke, *A Philosophical Enquiry into the Origin of Our Ideas of the Sublime and Beautiful*, ed. Adam Phillips (Oxford and New York: Oxford University Press, 1999), 75. My thanks to Damien Mahiet for bringing this passage to my attention.

46. Ludwig Rellstab, "Reiseberichte von Rellstab. No. 4, Wien," *Berliner allgemeine musikalische Zeitung* 3 (May 18 and 25, 1825): 161–3, 169; Marx, *Leben und Schaffen*, vol. 2, 10.

five-note motive in the left hand), the timpani suddenly intrude with the five-note motive on A, initiating an unexpected new passage. Labeled "*Marcia*" in the autograph, the passage is a miniature movement of its own, a sixteen-measure march in symmetrical binary form with internal repeats of both halves, beginning and ending in A major. Dotted rhythms, trills, and alternations of fifths and thirds in the piano's right hand further emphasize the military character. After this surprising intrusion, a short drumroll gives way to more fantasizing in the piano, leading up to further exchanges between piano and timpani, a statement of the main theme in the piano, and, at length, the return of the orchestra. With the composition of this cadenza-*cum*-march in 1809 (the year of the second French occupation), Beethoven arguably drew out an already latent aspect of militarism in the Violin Concerto, making explicit what had previously been an implicit musical topic.[47]

Quiet but Distinctive Openings

Each of the orchestral works of 1806 begins with a quiet but distinctive opening gesture. The Fourth Piano Concerto opens with the piano alone on a lush G-major chord, marked *piano* and *dolce*; the Violin Concerto starts with the unaccompanied strokes of the timpani, also marked *piano*; and the Fourth Symphony begins with an arresting, five-octave-deep unison B-flat, marked *pianissimo* in the winds and *pizzicato* in the strings. Each of these gestures defies expectations in its own way: the piano concerto's opening subverts genre conventions by beginning with the soloist rather than the orchestra; the violin concerto's opening is unusual for according the timpani a prominent thematic role; and the symphony's opening, taking a page from Haydn's book (see chapter 4), establishes the atmosphere of suspense and harmonic ambiguity that characterizes the slow introduction (in B-flat minor) and serves as a foil for the Allegro to follow (in B-flat major).

Beyond these arresting opening gestures, however, the works of 1806 show Beethoven's continued interest in harmonically expansive opening strategies, strategies that establish the ambitious scope of these works and sometimes complicate the notion of what constitutes the tonic. One such strategy involves the tonicization of the mediant (iii or III♯) within the context of a movement's

47. Maiko Kawabata touches on this aspect of the Violin Concerto in her article "Virtuoso Codes of Violin Performance: Power, Military Heroism, and Gender (1789–1830)," *19th-Century Music* 28, no. 2 (Fall 2004): 89–107, 93–5. For more on the piano arrangement, see Wilhelm Mohr, "Beethovens Klavierfassung seines Violinkonzerts op. 61," in Carl Dahlhaus et al., eds., *Bericht über den internationalen musikwissenschaftlichen Kongress Bonn 1970* (Kassel: Bärenreiter, 1970), 509–11, and "Die Klavierfassung von Beethovens Violinkonzert," *Österreichische Musikzeitschrift* 27, no. 2 (February 1972): 71–5; see also Alan Tyson, review of "Beethoven, Ludwig van; Klavierkonzert nach dem Violinkonzert, op. 61," *Musical Times* 111, no. 1530 (August 1970): 827.

opening theme. The tonicization of this key area has the effect not only of creating an unusual and memorable opening but also of implying a broad harmonic canvas for the movement to follow. A pre-1806 example, useful as a point of comparison, appears in the Rondo alla Polacca of the Triple Concerto. Here, the concertante cello leads what appears to be an antecedent-consequent period consisting of two four-measure phrases. The first phrase remains in the tonic C major (over a pedal point), but the second takes a surprising turn, via a German augmented sixth chord, toward B major as the dominant of E minor. After a pause, the concertante violin responds with a miniature antecedent-consequent phrase of its own, beginning in an unexpected E major (III♯) and modulating back to C major over the course of eight measures. The whole sixteen-measure complex is a large-scale antecedent-consequent period in its own right, and the fact that this period both begins and ends in the tonic ensures a sense of harmonic stability in spite of the presence of the remote III♯.

A similar gravitational pull toward the mediant can be observed in the opening themes of the first movement of the Fourth Piano Concerto and the second movement of the Violin Concerto. See Table 1.3. In the first movement of the Fourth Piano Concerto, the piano leads a five-measure opening phrase, moving from the tonic G major to a half-cadence on D Major. The strings respond, strikingly, in the remote key of B major (III♯); in contrast to the Triple Concerto's finale, however, this key's arrival is unprepared. As if to correct for this overreach, the strings lead a nine-measure response that gradually restores the tonic through a descending $_{3-3}^{6-5}$ sequence, culminating in a cadence in the home key. As in the Triple Concerto, Beethoven uses the unexpected appearance of III♯ as a means of intensifying the sense of dialogue and difference, whether between soloists or between soloist and ensemble.

The opening theme of the romance-like Larghetto of the Violin Concerto also pulls expressively toward the mediant, though in this case without actually reaching it. Like the Triple Concerto theme, it is a parallel antecedent-consequent period (here, plus a codetta) in which the antecedent phrase moves from the tonic to the dominant of iii and the consequent phrase gradually restores the tonic. The consequent phrase, rather than beginning in the mediant key, starts on its dominant (F-sharp major) and proceeds to reestablish the preeminence of

TABLE 1.3 Beethoven's use of the mediant in three opening themes.

Theme	Phrase model	Harmonic outline
Triple Concerto, Op. 56 (1804), iii, mm. 1–16	Antecedent-consequent period ([4+4]+[4+4])	I–V/iii | III♯–I
Fourth Piano Concerto, Op. 58 (1806), i, mm. 1–14	Antecedent-consequent period ([3.5+1.5]+[6+3])	I–V | III♯–I
Violin Concerto, Op. 61 (1806), ii, mm. 1–10	Antecedent-consequent period plus codetta ([1+1+2]+[1+3]+2)	I–V/iii | V/iii–I

G major via a sequence. The coloristic lingering on the remote F-sharp major (V/iii) contributes to what Leon Plantinga has called the theme's "invocation of antiquity"; as he notes, the theme is built on a descending ground bass pattern reminiscent of the chaconne and makes use of a distinctly sarabande-like rhythmic impulse (despite being in duple meter).[48]

The mediant plays an equally important role in the opening theme of the Kyrie of the Mass in C (1807), the first large-scale vocal work Beethoven composed in the wake of *Leonore*. The theme is sentential rather than periodic, its expressive climax coinciding with the appearance of the remote E major in measure 9. In this case, however, the mediant is not tonicized, functioning instead as the dominant of A minor. Nevertheless, its presence here is significant: not only does it receive special emphasis (it is marked *forte* and occurs following a crescendo) but it also has significant structural implications. It anticipates both the key of the "Christe eleison" section (E major, mm. 37–68) and the use of third-related harmonic juxtapositions throughout the mass (most notably, the use of A major for the Sanctus movement and, within this movement, F major for the Benedictus). In a broader sense, Beethoven's use of the mediant in these various local contexts relates to his interest in harmonic movement by thirds as an alternative to the tonic-dominant polarity.[49]

The slow introduction of the Fourth Symphony includes a similar harmonically expansive strategy, but on a larger scale. Here, rather than moving toward the mediant, part of the opening paragraph originally on the dominant of B-flat minor is repeated a step higher on the dominant of C-flat minor (the Neapolitan key, notated enharmonically as B minor). From here, Beethoven works his way (again via a sequence) to A major as the dominant of D minor, and this leads through an unmediated third-related juxtaposition to an F major seventh as the dominant of B-flat major. Hence, while the introduction clearly begins and ends in the home key, it passes through several far-flung keys in the interim, establishing early on the movement's ambitious tonal program. A similar repetition of opening materials in the Neapolitan key characterizes the opening themes of the "Appassionata" Sonata, composed in 1804–5, and the Second "Razumovsky" Quartet (1806).

"Suspended Time"

Another distinctive aspect of Beethoven's approach in 1806 is his tendency to build drama through passages that seem to interrupt or suspend the musical discourse. The first and third movements of the Fourth Piano Concerto present numerous examples,

---

48. Plantinga, *Beethoven's Concertos*, 226. Owen Jander has explored these issues in depth in "Romantic Form and Content in the Slow Movement of Beethoven's Violin Concerto," *The Musical Quarterly* 69, no. 2 (Spring 1983): 159–79.

49. See Charles Rosen, *The Romantic Generation* (Cambridge, MA: Harvard University Press, 1998), 240–6.

some of which will be discussed in chapter 2. In the present context, I will focus on a handful of representative passages in the Violin Concerto and Fourth Symphony.

Consider the way Beethoven handles the end of the solo exposition in the Violin Concerto's first movement. By this point, the movement's main thematic ideas have been heard twice, first by the orchestra alone and then again with the solo violin leading or embellishing. In measure 178, the closing theme, newly decorated by the solo violin, is stated in the dominant key, as one would expect in a movement of this kind. Whereas in the orchestral exposition, this theme (in D major) led to a brief transition and the appearance of the solo violin's cadenza-like opening statement on the dominant, here it leads to a grand cadential progression preparing A major. Again adopting a cadenza-like rhetoric (mm. 195ff.), the solo violin punctuates each change in harmony with a two-measure triplet fill, after which it extends the cadential $^6_4$ for another four measures. This leads to a trill on a high b[2] (over an implied cadential $^5_3$), strongly suggesting much-awaited cadential closure. But the cadence is postponed: instead, the timpani's five-note motive intrudes, divided between the first violins (on e[1]) and the cellos and basses (on F) and marked *pianissimo*, ushering in a moment of formal and harmonic ambiguity. This marked interruption of a conventional cadential progression creates a sense of stasis that is heightened by the continuous trill, sparse texture, and quiet dynamic. Within a few measures, the ambiguous tritone B-natural / F-natural is reinterpreted as part of a dominant chord with G in the bass, leading to C major and then through a sequence to D minor and (via German augmented sixth) to a restatement of the dominant $^6_4$ in the key of A major (m. 213). In other words, this interruption not only derails our sense of harmony and form, it also requires a resetting of the cadence, a second attempt at the $^6_4-^5_3$ progression aimed at confirming A major. This brief passage hence builds drama not only through surface-level ambiguity but also through the suspension and deferral of a goal-oriented musical process. (Beethoven further confounds our expectations when the long-awaited arrival in measure 225 confirms the "wrong" key of F major.)

The Fourth Symphony contains more extensive instances of this approach, particularly in the first movement's development section. As shown in Figure 1.3, this highly unusual development section alternates between dynamic and static stretches of harmonic activity, with measures 241–56 acting as a kind of transition.[50] The opening sixteen bars consist of a codetta-like progression in which harmonic rhythm speeds up slightly toward the cadence in bar 203.

50. This figure is adapted from Jan LaRue, "Harmonic Rhythm in the Beethoven Symphonies," *Journal of Musicology*, 18, no. 2 (Spring 2001): 221–48. A slur indicates no change in root or harmony; a dotted slur indicates a root arpeggiation with the harmony unchanged; and a bracket indicates different harmonies with a common root. As LaRue notes, the Third and Fourth Symphonies seem to treat harmonic rhythm in reverse fashion: "where the *Eroica* punctuated its basic irregularity with contrasting regular sections, the Fourth, which is extremely regular in its harmonic rhythm, employs irregularity as the source of its punctuation" (243).

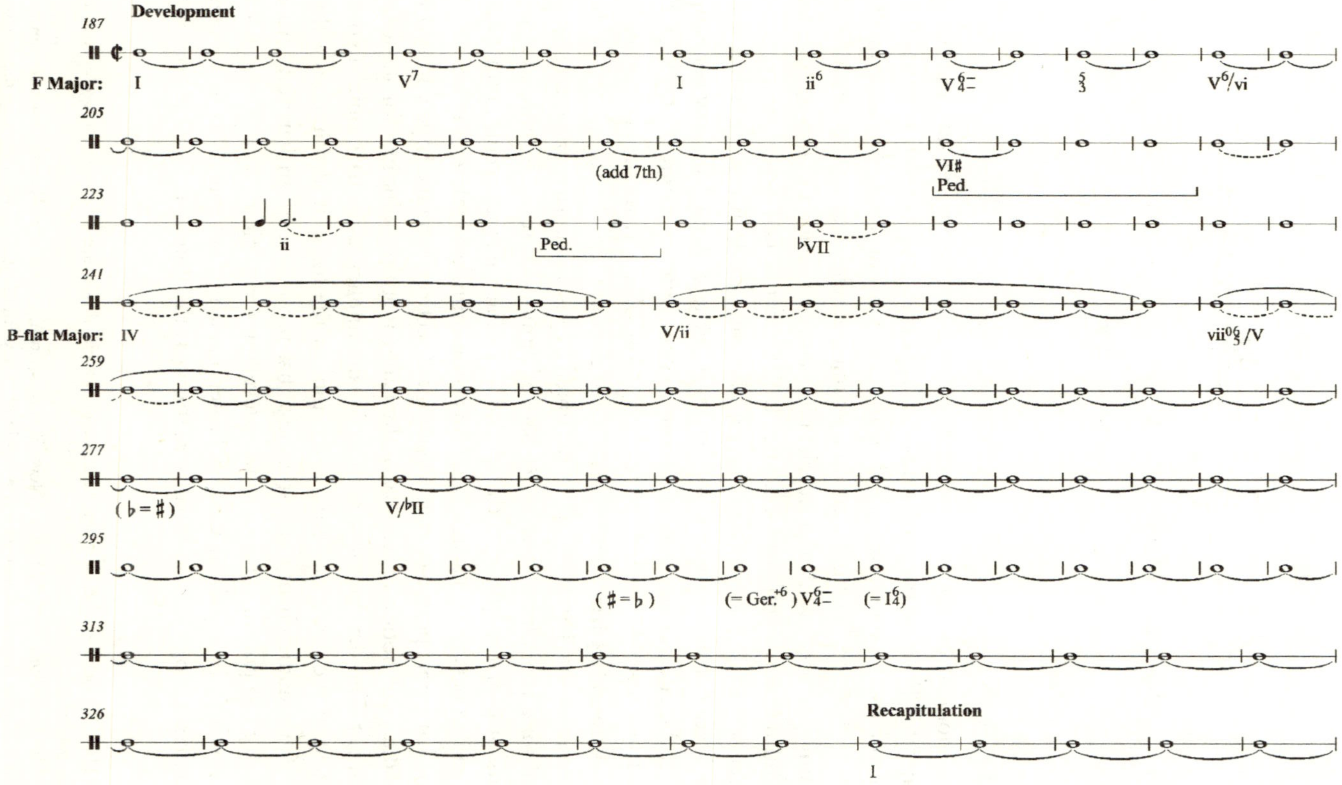

FIGURE 1.3. Harmonic rhythm in Beethoven, Symphony No. 4, i, mm. 187–334.

FIGURE 1.4. Prolonged harmonies in Beethoven, Symphony No. 4, i, development, showing functional reinterpretations.

At the moment of cadential arrival, however, the unexpected substitution of A major for F major triggers a lapse in harmonic activity—for a remarkable fourteen bars, the symphony stands frozen on A major. When D major finally arrives in bar 217, harmonic motion resumes, accelerating to the rate of one harmony per bar.[51] With this acceleration comes a sequence, driven forward by slight harmonic anticipations. After E-flat is confirmed as temporary tonic, another sequence follows (mm. 241ff.), this time made up of eight-bar segments. Here, harmonic rhythm decelerates to the rate of one harmony per eight bars, yet the rate of change remains regular. The sequence progresses through G major to an unstable diminished seventh, upon which harmonic activity again ceases, here for 24 bars. Indeed, starting in measure 257, the remainder of the development—76 bars in total—is occupied by just three harmonies, each prolonged for a monolithic stretch: 24 bars of diminished seventh (mm. 257–80), 24 bars of G-flat major seventh (spelled as F-sharp major seventh, mm. 281–304), and 28 bars of B-flat in second inversion (mm. 305–32); see Figure 1.4.

The harmonic profile of this development section is strange largely in that it contradicts our notion of what typically happens at this point in a sonata-form movement. The development section usually implies faster harmonic rhythm than that of the more stable outer sections of the form. It also implies a fluidity of harmonic change, a restlessness that prevents a given harmony from becoming too prominent. In a typical development section, "The modulations must not only be rapid," as Charles Rosen explains, "but must also never give the impression of a second tonality as strong as the dominant."[52] This does not

51. There are occasional root arpeggiations and a single, almost imperceptible change occurring within a bar (225).

52. Charles Rosen, *Sonata Forms* (New York: Norton, 1988), 272. Rosen describes several instances of "static moments that generate tension" in development sections, including the ten-bar drone bass and continuous *forte* preceding the recapitulation of Haydn's "Emperor" Quartet in C Major, Op. 76, no. 3.

seem to hold for the first movement of the Fourth Symphony. Although the dynamic middle part cycles through keys in the manner one would expect of a development section, the static passages surrounding it overemphasize remote harmonies. The dominant of C-flat major (= B major), in particular, takes up so much space that it seems to rival the true dominant—itself notably absent from the retransition—in tonal strength.

Theodor W. Adorno noted that this development section seems to create the impression of "suspended time," an aspect of Beethoven's art that he felt merited special attention. Beethoven's moments of suspended time, he suggested, are "most emphatically distinct from the 'floating' passages to be found in Romanticism," and seem to be generated "entirely spontaneously."[53] For Adorno, the significance of these moments lay not merely in the fact that they seem to threaten the unfolding of musical time, but rather in that they engender a metaphysical conflict, a dialectical tension between subjective and objective modes of existence. What is "subjectively produced" seems, "just as it is about to be dynamically unfolded, to cut itself off from the source of its production. The subjective force, within its 'productive process', that is, technically speaking, in the course of its modulation, becomes alien to itself, confronting itself as a non-human objectivity." In these moments of alienation, "symphonic time seems to stand still: as they swing back and forth, the passages become the pendulum of time itself."[54]

Amending his remarks many years later, Adorno specifically compared this development section to Hegel's *Phenomenology of Spirit*, writing, "It is as if the objective unfolding of the music were steered by the subject, as if the subject were balancing the music."[55] According to Hegel, the subject is never effaced during the dialectical process; rather, it comes into being precisely through this process of self-abnegation and reinstatement. The subject "is only truly realized in the process of positing itself, or in mediating with its own self its transitions from one state or position to the opposite." It is, in its essence, "pure and simple negativity."[56] See Table 1.4.

Adorno's interpretation may be applied to several moments in the development section; perhaps the most obvious of these is the fourteen-bar prolongation of A major in first inversion (mm. 203ff.). Here, the sudden, marked deceleration in harmonic rhythm and the constant tick-tock motif in the cellos seem to evoke, even enact, the sense of time's standing still ("the pendulum of time itself"). The *tirade* figure in the first violins, too, seems stuck in a loop,

53. Theodor W. Adorno, *Beethoven: The Philosophy of Music*, ed. Rolf Tiedemann, trans. Edmund Jephcott (Stanford: Stanford University Press, 1998), 99.

54. Ibid., 99.

55. Ibid., 107. This fragment (No. 239) dates from 1953; the other (No. 228) from 1938. See the "Comparative Table of Fragments" in Adorno, *Beethoven: The Philosophy of Music*, 253ff.

56. G. W. F. Hegel, *Phenomenology of Mind*, trans. J. B. Baillie (Mineola, NY: Dover, 2003 [1910]), 10.

TABLE 1.4 Adorno's Hegelian interpretation of the development section of Beethoven, Symphony No. 4, i.

Subjective production	→ Objective unfolding	→ Reification of subjective production
Alienation through stasis, repetition; music "cuts itself off from the source of its production"	Confrontation; "symphonic time stands still"	Subject "steers" music; return to dynamism

and the addition of the dominant seventh to the triad in bar 213 only intensifies the music's curious state of paralysis. But time cannot remain suspended forever—the flute intervenes at last, steering the music toward D major. The unity of the musical form restates itself as a duality, only to emerge once again as a unity. Similar moments of "suspended time" appear in the symphony's second and fourth movements, in both cases—as in the first movement retransition—occurring in central episodes involving the descending minor second motive G-flat—F (ii, mm. 54–64; iv, mm. 161–81). In these passages, the symphony's slow introduction is recalled on multiple simultaneous levels, not only through motivic and harmonic reminiscence, but also through a return to the slow harmonic rhythm first encountered there.[57] (See chapter 4.)

On the surface, these moments of intense stasis seem to set the Fourth Symphony apart from Beethoven's so-called heroic symphonies, in which the drama often arises out of an amplification of techniques associated with the *Sturm und Drang* or *Tempesta* style.[58] And yet, following Adorno,

57. These "suspended" passages are novel not only in the way they refer to earlier events but also in the way they contradict typical formal functions. As William Caplin indicates, the development's "core" is generally the most unstable part of a sonata movement: "The core of the development typically projects an emotional quality of instability, restlessness, and dramatic conflict. The dynamic level is usually forte, and the general character is often one of *Sturm und Drang*. The core normally brings a marked increase in rhythmic activity projected by conventionalized accompanimental patterns. Polyphonic devices—imitation, canon, fugal entries—can contribute further to the complexity of the musical texture. In short, the core is that part of the development in which the traditional aesthetic sense of a 'working out' of the material is most prominently expressed" (William Caplin, *Classical Form: A Theory of Formal Functions for the Instrumental Music of Haydn, Mozart, and Beethoven* [Oxford: Oxford University Press, 1998], 142). In the symphony's first movement's core section, Beethoven almost systematically disregards these generalizations: harmonic rhythm decelerates, the texture becomes simpler, and the overall dynamic decreases, all the way to a rare *pianississimo* (m. 281). A similar observation may be made regarding the central episode of the second movement and the finale's development section; in both cases, Beethoven creates a sense of drama by contradicting sonata norms—rather than "working out" his material through rhythmic instability, modulations, and polyphonic textures, he does so through a marked suspension of these elements.

58. On this style and its problematic terminology, see Clive McClelland, "*Ombra* and *Tempesta*," in Danuta Mirka, ed., *The Oxford Handbook of Topic Theory* (New York: Oxford University Press, 2014), 279–300.

one might suggest that the Fourth Symphony's passages of suspended time—paradoxically—are those most strongly marked as heroic: they exemplify what has come to be understood as this style's fundamental aesthetic concern—the emergence through dialectic of a sense of subjectivity, of "presence."[59] This idea identifies a link between the Fourth Symphony and, say, the Third and Fifth.[60] To whatever extent these three symphonies occupy diverse points on a stylistic axis, their underlying sense of dramatic expression, in this view, is alike. Put differently, "subjectivity" in Beethoven's music—if one subscribes to such a notion—takes on multiple forms, not necessarily correlating with the musical markers of the heroic style.

The "Razumovsky" Quartets and the Stylistic Turn

In many ways, the "Razumovsky" Quartets stand apart from the orchestral works of the year and hence complicate the idea of a unified aesthetic outlook for 1806. For one thing, they include a greater number of movements in minor keys (five out of twelve movements in the quartets versus one out of ten in the orchestral works). And whereas the orchestral works mostly eschew fugue and learned counterpoint, the quartets celebrate them (see chapter 3). In fact, one might argue that a significant aspect of Beethoven's compositional process in 1806 was a more deliberate differentiation of musical materials into the chamber and orchestral spheres. The minor mode, learned style, and fugue now found their primary outlets in the string quartet, generically a more appropriate venue for sophistication and complexity. The orchestral works, meanwhile, evince a more overtly "public" style, one calculated to appeal to a broader and more diverse audience.

---

59. In the most influential recent book on the heroic style, *Beethoven Hero*, Scott Burnham characterizes Beethoven's music as the ideal expression of Hegel's philosophy: "The feeling provoked by this music is one of transcendent individuality, of merger with a higher world order in the name of Self. This effect is identical to that enunciated in the Idealist trajectory of Hegel's phenomenology, with one overwhelmingly important exception: Beethoven's music is heard and experienced; it is a concretion with a degree of compression and concentration that Hegel's philosophy could never hope to reach" (Burnham, *Beethoven Hero* [Princeton: Princeton University Press, 1995], 121). The idea of the dialectic is fundamental to Burnham's conception of the heroic style, since it is the dialectic that is seen to generate the music's "ironic self-consciousness," and by extension, its powerful impression of "presence."

60. Karol Berger has drawn attention to similar instances of suspended time in Beethoven's oeuvre, arguing that they signal a retreat from the "real world" into one of "contemplation," the object of which is "either the interiority of the individual mind or God—either the world within or the world beyond." Karol Berger, *Bach's Cycle, Mozart's Arrow: An Essay on the Origins of Musical Modernity* (Berkeley and Los Angeles: University of California Press, 2007), 293–352, 333.

That said, the "Razumovsky" Quartets have also been understood as a turn away from the "heroic." As Solomon notes, despite their expansive, symphonic quality, the quartets "in another sense represent a withdrawal from the heroic impulse, with its insistence upon strength and virtue, its 'public' style and affirmative outlook. If the symphonies of 1804 to 1812 are, in Bekker's phrase, 'speeches to the nation, to humanity,' then these quartets are interior monologues addressed to a private self whose emotional states comprise a variegated tapestry of probing moods and sensations."[61] Recently, Nancy November has offered an alternative way of conceptualizing these quartets with respect to the heroic paradigm and the public-private divide. In her view, Beethoven's middle-period quartets (including Opp. 59, 74, and 95) are best understood in terms of a "perceived rapprochement between the chamber and theater styles c. 1800"; they elevate or exaggerate intimate musical gestures and idioms in ways that suggest a wide array of dramatic modes, from the lyrical and melancholy, to the stoic and resigned, to the joyous and triumphal. The metaphor of the theater is especially compelling, she suggests, because of Beethoven's sustained engagement with theatrical works and concepts during this period in his career.[62]

Despite the differences in tone, there are stylistic similarities between the "Razumovsky" Quartets and the orchestral works of 1806 that further suggest a post-*Leonore* stylistic turn. One such similarity involves the significance of "traditional" musical elements, particularly in the Fourth Symphony and the Third "Razumovsky" Quartet. These two works have been thought especially reminiscent of Haydn and Mozart, the Fourth Symphony through its orchestration, proportions, and character, among other aspects, and the quartet through its use of forms such as the third-movement minuet (in place of the scherzo) and fugal finale, again among other aspects.[63] But it is not merely references to tradition but also—and more importantly—the reimagining of tradition that these works have in common. Consider as an illustration Beethoven's use of off-tonic openings, a striking example of which occurs in the finale of the Fourth Piano Concerto.[64] Here, the opening theme begins on the subdominant C major, winding its way back to the tonic G major over the course of ten measures. Beethoven takes a similar approach in the finale of the second "Razumovsky" Quartet, which begins on the submediant C

61. Solomon, *Beethoven*, 260.

62. November, *Beethoven's Theatrical Quartets*, 5.

63. See James Webster, "Traditional Elements in Beethoven's Middle-Period String Quartets," in Robert Winter and Bruce Carr, eds., *Beethoven, Performers, and Critics: The International Beethoven Congress, Detroit, 1977* (Detroit: Wayne State University Press, 1980), 94–133, esp. 103–16.

64. Burstein identifies four strategies for approaching off-tonic returns; this movement, remarkably, uses all of them. L. Poundie Burstein, "The Off-Tonic Return in Beethoven's Piano Concerto No. 4 in G Major, Op. 58, and Other Works," *Music Analysis* 24, no. 3 (2005): 305–47.

major rather than the E minor to which it eventually gives way.[65] This technique has numerous precedents in Haydn's instrumental music. But as James Webster has observed, Beethoven did not merely adopt this technique but rather transformed it to suit new expressive ends, "creating a finale tradition of his own in 1805 and 1806."[66]

A C-MINOR CONCLUSION

Alongside the stylistic turn of 1806, Beethoven continued to cultivate expressive and technical elements that more closely relate to his so-called heroic style. The two C-minor compositions of 1806–7—the Thirty-Two Variations on an Original Theme, WoO 80, and the *Coriolan* overture, Op. 62—epitomize at least three elements of this style: the noble but restless general mood, the pervasiveness of the minor mode (and C minor in particular), and the influence of French composers and aesthetic trends.[67] In the case of the *Coriolan* overture, composed as an introduction to Collin's eponymous tragedy, the heroic nature of the material also imbues the work with extramusical significance, and it is no surprise that, like the Third and Fifth Symphonies, the overture has often been interpreted in programmatic or narrative terms (see chapter 6). At the same time, both Op. 62 and WoO 80 deviate from the heroic paradigm in its narrow sense of representing a journey from struggle to transcendence (or darkness to light), for the simple reason that neither work ends joyously. If these works are indeed "heroic," then, they probe different aspects of the heroic style, aspects that seem to have little to do with the "unmistakable ethical aura" and sense of a "psychological journey or growth process" associated most strongly with Symphonies Nos. 3, 5, 6, 7, and 9.[68] In fact, the work composed in 1806–7 that hews most closely to this ideal is a vocal one—the Mass in C. In the mass's final movement, Beethoven juxtaposes C-minor penitence ("Agnus Dei, qui tollis peccata mundi, Miserere nobis"; Poco Andante, 12/8) with C-major reconciliation ("Dona nobis pacem"; Allegro ma non troppo, common time). This

---

65. The finale of Op. 59, No. 1 also has a modulating theme (based on a Russian folksong), but it proceeds in reverse, modulating from the tonic F major to the submediant D minor and necessitating a "course correction" at the end of each statement. It seems plausible that Beethoven's interest in modulating themes was piqued by his experience with the Lvov-Pratsch collection, the volume of Russian folksongs he perused in preparation for fulfilling Razumovsky's commission.

66. Webster, "Traditional Elements," 118.

67. The overture strongly suggests the influence of Méhul and Cherubini; see Michael Broyles, *Beethoven: The Emergence and Evolution of Beethoven's Heroic Style* (New York: Excelsior Music Publishing, 1987), 154ff. On French influences in WoO 80, see chapter 5 of this book.

68. Joseph Kerman et al., "Beethoven, Ludwig van." In *Grove Music Online*, http://www.oxfordmusiconline.com/subscriber/article/grove/music/40026pg14.

tonal and expressive move resonates not only with the affective trajectory of the Fifth Symphony but also with the other "affirmative" vocal works of the middle period: *Christus am Oelberge* (1803), *Leonore*, and the Choral Fantasy (1808).[69] It represents one of several stylistic continuities amid Beethoven's exploration of a range of aesthetic ideals in 1806–7.

69. See Joseph Kerman, "Beethoven's Minority," in *Write All These Down: Essays on Music* (Berkeley: University of California Press, 1994), 217–37, 228–9.

CHAPTER 2

MUSIC FOR A VIRTUOSO

Opuses 58 and 61

As a professional pianist, Beethoven was no stranger to virtuoso display. Piano duels with the Abbé Gelinek in 1793, Joseph Wölffl in 1799, and Daniel Steibelt in 1800 provided forums for him to demonstrate his ingenuity and athleticism, visually as well as musically. Tia DeNora has likened these duels to sporting events, noting that "piano contests provided not only 'good music,' but also the drama of combat."[1] Like any virtuoso, Beethoven had a repertoire of impressive tricks up his sleeve—one specialty was the so-called Beethoven trills, involving the playing of a melodic line while trilling with the same hand.[2] A talented improviser, Beethoven sometimes made a dramatic point of besting his rivals. On one occasion, after Steibelt played a "carefully prepared" improvisation on a theme from Beethoven's Op. 11 trio (which he had heard eight days earlier), Beethoven snatched the cello part from a Steibelt quintet that had just been performed, turned the page upside down and placed it on the music rack, and improvised on the upturned theme "in such a manner that Steibelt left the room before he finished, would never again meet him and, indeed, made it a condition that Beethoven should not be invited before accepting an offer." This, at least, is the account of Beethoven's pupil Ferdinand Ries.[3]

Beethoven's piano concertos provide perhaps the clearest evidence of his skills as a virtuoso. Rather than being designed for amateur consumption, concertos were typically conceived as showpieces in which a composer-virtuoso

---

1. Tia DeNora, *Beethoven and the Construction of Genius: Musical Politics in Vienna, 1792–1803* (Berkeley: University of California Press, 1995), 150. As she further notes, "[T]he piano contest was a place where pianistic athletes were tested, where reputations were raised and lowered, where musical fashions were put on display, and where different types of taste could be compared and pitted against each other. In addition, it was a place where the identities of patrons could be asserted, reaffirmed, and undercut" (152).

2. See William S. Newman, *Beethoven on Beethoven: Playing His Piano Music His Way* (New York and London: W. W. Norton & Company, 1988), 214–16.

3. Quoted in Thayer/Forbes, vol. 1, 257.

could publicize his or her own distinctive style of playing. Publishing one's concertos was not typically the priority, in part because there were distinct disadvantages to putting them into print. On the one hand, broadcasting one's signature techniques meant that they could more easily be imitated by other virtuosos, a prospect of which Beethoven was ever wary; on the other hand, few amateur performers possessed the skills or resources needed to perform a concerto, so the market was small. And yet, as Simon McVeigh notes, most composer-virtuosos of the era "sought to maximize their international reputation and income" by publishing concertos, even if this sometimes involved toning down the technical difficulties.[4] Published concertos thus not only offer a glimpse of a virtuoso's playing style, but also reflect a complicated web of relationships between the virtuoso and his or her audience, comprising not only the ticketed concertgoers, but also other prospective performers (both professional and amateur), as well as patrons, publishers, and critics.

While Beethoven's two concertos of 1806—the Fourth Piano Concerto and Violin Concerto—were written for different instruments and with different soloists in mind, they are similar in that both challenge the conventional notion of the concerto as a vehicle for virtuosic display. The first movement of the Fourth Piano Concerto, according to Leon Plantinga, represents a "conundrum": "the piano as leader, show[s] occasional fine bursts of virtuosity, but remain[s] all the while devoted to the cause of tranquil and nuanced reflection, a curb on the orchestra's propensity for energetic motion, for direct action."[5] Beethoven's pupil Carl Czerny portrayed the movement in similar terms; acknowledging that it makes considerable demands on the performer, he nonetheless described its character as "calm, simple and agreeable, almost in the pastoral style," noting that a successful performance of the solo part "must partake considerably more of delicate lightness and fluency, than of actual *bravura*."[6] For Joseph Kerman, "this is a concerto movement unusually low on virtuoso writing, and our final memory of it is likely to be of its mild, retiring lyricism."[7] Nor is this lyrical impulse restricted to the first movement; the entire concerto, writes Lewis Lockwood, "sustains a plateau of quiet beauty from beginning to end."[8] The Violin Concerto has evoked similar descriptions. Lockwood, for instance, describes an affect of "quiet serenity and love," which he relates to

4. Simon McVeigh, "Concerto of the Individual," in Simon P. Keefe, ed., *The Cambridge History of Eighteenth-Century Music* (Cambridge: Cambridge University Press, 2009), 583–612, 597.

5. Leon Plantinga, *Beethoven's Concertos: History, Style, Performance* (New York and London: W. W. Norton & Company, 1999), 204.

6. Carl Czerny, *On the Proper Performance of All Beethoven's Works for the Piano: Czerny's Reminiscences of Beethoven and Chapters II and III from Volume IV of the* Complete Theoretical and Practical Piano Forte School, *Op. 500*, ed. Paul Badura-Skoda (Vienna: Universal Edition, 1970), 99, 100.

7. Joseph Kerman, "Representing a Relationship: Notes on a Beethoven Concerto," *Representations* 39 (Summer 1992): 80–101, 87.

8. Lewis Lockwood, *Beethoven: The Music and the Life* (New York: Norton, 2003), 242.

the A-major trio in *Leonore*, in which Rocco and Leonore offer the suffering Florestan a sip of wine ("You will be rewarded in better worlds").[9]

Critics have thus appreciated the lyricism and serenity of these two concertos while also expressing a sense of uncertainty about the diminished role of virtuoso brilliance in these works, especially their first movements. The minimization of bravura writing in these concertos has often been explained in relation to the idea of aesthetic dualism discussed in the introduction to this book; that is, it is seen as evidence of Beethoven's supposed desire to suspend or bracket his "heroic style" in 1806. While this narrative subsumes the concertos within a large-scale concept of style, it overshadows their uniqueness and historical specificity. Concertos, then as now, were not merely showpieces; they also served as vehicles through which the concept of virtuosity was celebrated—and contested. Reexamining the two concertos of 1806 through a historical lens, this chapter will first investigate the concept of virtuosity as it featured in contemporary writings and debate in Beethoven's day. As I will illustrate, by the early 1800s virtuosity connoted not only technical proficiency and exceptional showmanship but also what might be termed the self-conscious performance of interiority—a notion in which Beethoven was himself invested. I will then examine a handful of musical passages in the Fourth Piano Concerto and Violin Concerto, showing how these works both topicalize and elevate interiority, and in so doing, celebrate salient aspects of Beethoven's "musical persona."[10] But concertos are mutable texts, ever subject to further mediations in performance. In the last part of this chapter, I examine Beethoven's unpublished revisions to the solo part of his Fourth Piano Concerto, showing how they further intensify the contrast between competing conceptions of virtuosity in the work.

DEFINING THE VIRTUOSO

By 1800, the term "virtuoso" had acquired a range of meanings. Quite apart from its applications outside of music (beautifully explored in Paul Metzner's book *Crescendo of the Virtuoso*), the term was used to describe a range of musical occupations, skills, attitudes, and behaviors.[11] At the most basic level, it could connote simply a musical professional. As David Wyn Jones has observed, Johann Ferdinand Schönfeld's alphabetical listing of "Virtuosen und Dilettanten in Wien" (*Jahrbuch der Tonkunst von Wien und Prag* [1796]) uses the term in this sense, and the virtuosos Schönfeld lists include both composers and performers.[12]

9. Ibid., 245.

10. Philip Auslander, "Musical Personae," *The Drama Review* 50, no. 1 (Spring 2006): 100–19.

11. Paul Metzner, *Crescendo of the Virtuoso: Spectacle, Skill, and Self-Promotion in Paris during the Age of Revolution* (Berkeley: University of California Press, 1998).

12. David Wyn Jones, *Music in Vienna: 1700, 1800, 1900* (Woodbridge: The Boydell Press, 2016), 107.

This relatively broad definition of the musical virtuoso hearkens at least as far back as the late seventeenth century, when the term was applied equally in German-language writings to composers, theorists, and performers of exceptional skill. According to Erich Reimer, it was not until 1730 that the term "virtuoso" began to be regularly applied in a narrower sense, referring specifically to practicing musicians, whether instrumentalists or singers.[13] But, as the Schönfeld example implies, this narrow definition was not universally adopted even by the beginning of the nineteenth century, and it was not until the 1830s and 1840s that virtuosity came to be associated exclusively with performers.[14]

As the term "virtuoso" gained widespread usage, theorists and critics sought to legislate its meaning. Already as early as 1700, Johann Kuhnau, Bach's predecessor at the Thomaskirche in Leipzig, attempted to distinguish the true virtuoso from the mere pretender in his satirical novel *Der musikalische Quacksalber* (The Musical Charlatan).[15] Kuhnau begins by noting that the term "virtuoso" may refer to artists, scholars, and poets, but it is especially reserved for musicians. Like many later authors, he maintains that the term is often misapplied and that many who would call themselves virtuosos are in fact not destined for a seat "among the Muses."[16] Furthermore, "the word *virtuoso* is understood by most people not in its moral sense where it signifies a person who is accustomed to leading his life according to the rules of honesty and also constantly intends to do good and to refrain from evil. . . . Rather, here it has a political meaning and means as much as an excellent, noble, and famous artist knowledgeable in his art."[17] The virtuoso must not only be proficient on their instrument but also have a strong knowledge of music theory, composition, and singing. Even so, it is ultimately the moral qualities of the virtuoso that distinguish them from the charlatan. "[The virtuoso] strengthens his title not through his art alone, but also through his conduct and his virtuous way of living. He follows the admonition of St. Augustine: *Cantet vox, cantet vita, cantent facta.* That is, one's life and deeds must come out as nicely as the vocal or instrumental music."[18] The virtuoso should not boast or be arrogant, should not use their music for "voluptuousness and lust" or to "lure women's hearts," and should act with a higher spiritual purpose in mind.[19]

---

13. Erich Reimer, "Der Begriff des wahren Virtuosen in der Musikästhetik des späten 18. und frühen 19. Jahrhunderts," *Basler Jahrbuch für historische Musikpraxis* 20 (1996): 61–72, 61.

14. There is, of course, a substantial literature on virtuosity in this period. An excellent overview is given in Žarko Cvejić, *The Virtuoso as Subject: The Reception of Instrumental Virtuosity, c. 1815–c. 1850* (Newcastle upon Tyne: Cambridge Scholars Publishing, 2016), 6–17.

15. See Johann Kuhnau, *The Musical Charlatan*, trans. John B. Russell with an introduction by James Hardin (Columbia, SC: Camden House, 1997), 153–63.

16. Ibid., 153.

17. Ibid., 153.

18. Ibid., 161.

19. Ibid., 162.

Although Kuhnau's conception of the virtuoso was influenced by his experience as a church musician in Leipzig, his discussion is in many respects congruent with later eighteenth-century attempts to define the virtuoso. As Reimer has shown, authors such as Johann Abraham Peter Schulz (1774), Christian Friedrich Daniel Schubart (1784, published 1806), Johann Heinrich Georg Heusinger (1797), and Johann Karl Friedrich Triest (1802) similarly attempted to distinguish the true virtuoso (*ächte* or *wahre Virtuos*) from the pretender. Like Kuhnau, they emphasized the idea that the virtuoso must be not only an exceptional performer but also a composer and improviser. But these later authors also ascribed qualities and behaviors to the true virtuoso that reflect changing attitudes toward both virtuosity and instrumental music in general. Schubart, for example, links virtuosity to genius, creativity, and originality, making special reference to the genre of the free fantasy. The virtuoso must be capable not only of improvising his own fantasies but also of executing the works of others in a transformative way:

> If I want to play a sonata by [C. P. E.] Bach, I must immerse myself so much in the spirit of this great man that my ego vanishes and becomes Bach's idiom. Even factoring out all mechanical skills—the ear, the winged fist [i.e., the ability to play rapidly], the fingering, the steady tempo, the understanding of the instrument, the ability to read, and the rest—no solo player should dare to appear on stage if he does not possess creative power; if he does not know how to transform the notes into so many sparks; if he cannot petrify the accompanying voices around him, as he does the listeners; and—alas, if he is incapable *of commanding the spirit* to burn in all ten fingers.[20]

Schubart's account posits a tension in the role of the virtuoso. On the one hand, the virtuoso's creative power (*Schöpferkraft*) allows him to transcend the realm of the mechanical; on the other hand, his individuality must be suppressed in order to allow another composer's idiom to emerge.[21] Schubart hence defines virtuosity as a function of the work concept—the true virtuoso understands

---

20. "Will ich eine Sonate von [C. P. E.] *Bach* vortragen, so muss ich mich so ganz in den Geist dieses grossen Mannes versenken, dass meine Ichheit wegschwindet, und Bachisches Idiom wird. Alle mechanischen Fertigkeiten: Ohr, geflügelte Faust, Fingersatz, Tactfestigkeit, Verständnis des Instruments, Lesekunst, und dergleichen weggerechnet; so wage sich nur kein Solospieler auf den Schauplatz, wenn er nicht Schöpferkraft besitzt; wenn er nicht die Noten in eben so viel Feuerflocken zu verwandeln weiss; wenn er nicht die begleitenden Stimmen um ihn, wie die Zuhörer versteinern kann, und—ach, wenn er unfähig ist, *dem Geiste zu gebiethen* in allen zehn Fingern zu brennen." Christian Friedrich Daniel Schubart, *Ideen zu einer Ästhetik der Tonkunst* (Vienna: J.V. Degen, 1806), 295.

21. Mary Hunter has called attention to the fact that early Romantic definitions of performance, in contrast to Enlightenment-era ones, frequently center on the "miraculous merging of [the performer's] own self with that of the composer to represent a new subjectivity." Mary Hunter, "'To Play as if from the Soul of the Composer': The Idea of the Performer in Early Romantic Aesthetics," *Journal of the American Musicological Society* 58, no. 2 (Summer 2005): 357–98, 370.

how to move the listener through creative intervention but remains faithful to the musical work and its composer.[22]

Schubart's opposition of the mechanical with the creative or expressive is a trope in eighteenth-century writings about virtuosity. In his *Versuch über die Wahre Art das Clavier zu spielen*, C. P. E. Bach inveighed against technicians who "overwhelm our hearing without satisfying it and stun the mind without moving it."[23] Leopold Mozart, similarly, chided performers who could play "with uncommon dexterity the most difficult passages in various concertos or solos" but who could not execute simple minuets or adagios with the correct expression.[24] In a letter to his father, Wolfgang Amadeus Mozart famously described Clementi as "simply a *mechanicus*," writing that apart from his good right-hand technique and ability to play parallel thirds, "he has not a kreutzer's worth of taste or feeling."[25] For Schulz, writing in Sulzer's *Allgemeine Theorie der schönen Künste*, it was "expression" (*Ausdruck*) that separated the master from the pupil and the great virtuoso from the middling one.[26]

Several of these critical strands—including the multiple skills required of the virtuoso, the moral imperative of virtuosity, and the opposition of the mechanical with the expressive—come together in what is perhaps the most sophisticated account of virtuosity from the late eighteenth and early nineteenth centuries, Johann Karl Friedrich Triest's essay "On Traveling Virtuosos" (1802).[27] Published in the *Allgemeine musikalische Zeitung* in three installments, Triest's essay has received relatively little attention from scholars, but it deserves close exploration. First, Triest, though he had no direct connection to the Viennese scene, had emerged as a major voice in music criticism with his eleven-part series, published in the *Allgemeine musikalische Zeitung* in 1801, on

22. As Cliff Eisen has observed, the term "virtuoso" was also used in the seventeenth and eighteenth centuries to signify the collector or curator, whether of *objets d'art* or of scientific specimens and data. This relates to the idea that the musical virtuoso was increasingly seen as a "conservationist, a guardian of traditional, authorial values." Cliff Eisen, "The Rise (and Fall) of the Concerto Virtuoso," in Simon P. Keefe, ed., *The Cambridge Companion to the Concerto* (Cambridge: Cambridge University Press, 2005), 177–91, 189.

23. Carl Philipp Emanuel Bach, *Essay on the True Art of Playing Keyboard Instruments*, trans. and ed. William J. Mitchell (New York and London: W. W. Norton & Company, 1949), 147.

24. Leopold Mozart, *Treatise on the Fundamental Principles of Violin Playing*, trans. Editha Knocker (London: Oxford University Press, 1951), 215–16.

25. The remark appears with slightly different wording in two subsequent letters from Mozart to his father. Emily Anderson, ed., *The Letters of Mozart and His Family*, 3 vols. (London: Macmillan, 1938), vol. 3, no. 440 (January 12, 1782) and no. 441 (January 16, 1782). Quoted version on p. 1180.

26. See the quoted passage from Schulz's article on execution (*Vortrag*) in Reimer, "Der Begriff des wahren Virtuosen," 63.

27. Johann Karl Friedrich Triest, "Abhandlung: Ueber reisende Virtuosen," *Allgemeine musikalische Zeitung* 4, no. 46 (August 11, 1802): cols. 737–49, no. 47 (August 18, 1802): cols. 753–60, and no. 48 (August 23, 1802): cols. 769–75.

the development of German music in the eighteenth century.[28] Second, he is one of few contemporary authors to address the topic of virtuosity in detail, and his essay, as Dana Gooley has noted, "in many respects set the terms of the debate" about the status of virtuosity in the mid-nineteenth century.[29] Third, the publication of Triest's essay coincides with both the beginning of the last phase of Beethoven's career as a public performer and the period in which he was most heavily invested in the concerto (four of the five piano concertos, the triple concerto, and the violin concerto were composed between 1796 and 1810). It provides a window into conceptions of the virtuoso as Beethoven attempted to navigate the shift from performer to composer and redefine his own relationship with virtuosity.

Triest defines the virtuoso more thoroughly than any other contemporary author. When he comes to this definition well into his essay, he immediately complicates matters by drawing an implicit distinction between the true virtuoso and the impostor: "what is a virtuoso?—what should he really be?" (*was ist ein Virtuos?—was soll er eigentlich seyn?*). He begins with the following working definition:

> I understand *virtuoso* to mean a *performing* (musical) artist who is in command of his art (whether singing or playing an instrument); that is, who has brought this art so far that it is reliably at his disposal for attaining *every artistic goal* with *certainty*—most of all the consummate representation of artistic products.[30]

Triest thus starts by defining the musical virtuoso in its narrow sense, as a performer as opposed to a proficient musician of any kind. Like Schubart, he relates virtuosity to the concept of the musical work, arguing that the realization of the work—rather than merely exceptional musicianship—represents the virtuoso's highest goal. He then goes on to enumerate four characteristics that are necessary for one to call oneself a virtuoso. The first two—"*proficiency* with *neatness* and *precision*" (Fertigkeit *mit* Reinheit *und* Präzision) and "merely *correct execution*" (*blos* richtige Vortag)—belong to the domain of the mechanical and do not yet raise the musician beyond the level of "craftsman" (*Handwerker*). The third characteristic, "beautiful execution" (schöne *Vortrag*), elevates the musician to "the rank of the *artist*" (*im Rang des* Künstlers). It arises through "*individual*

---

28. For an English translation, see Johann Karl Friedrich Triest, "Remarks on the Development of the Art of Music in Germany," trans. Susan Gillespie, in Elaine R. Sisman, ed., *Haydn and His World* (Princeton: Princeton University Press, 1997), 321–94.

29. Dana Gooley, "The Battle against Instrumental Virtuosity in the Early Nineteenth Century," in Christopher H. Gibbs and Dana Gooley, eds., *Franz Liszt and His World* (Princeton: Princeton University Press, 2006), 75–111, 82.

30. "Unter einem *Virtuosen* verstehe ich einen *praktischen* (Ton-) Künstler, der seiner Kunst (des Gesanges oder eines Instruments) *mächtig* ist, d. h. der es darin so weit gebracht hat, dass sie ihm zur Erreichung *jedes Kunstzwecks* (möglichst vollkommener Darstellung der Kunstprodukte) mit *Sicherheit* zu Gebote steht." Triest, "Ueber reisende Virtuosen," part 2, cols. 758–9.

judgment, disposition, and invention, from a culture of sensibility, briefly, from *free inner* activity and genius" (*hier kommt es auf eigne Beurtheilung, Anordnung und Erfindung, auf Kultur des Gefühlsvermögens, kurz, auf* freye innere *Thätigkeit und Genie an*). Beautiful execution also relates to the idea that the virtuoso's productions "are not only unusual and excellent in themselves, but also should *appear* as self-conceived, as original, even if in fact he used nothing but foreign works for this purpose" (*dass seine Produktionen nicht nur an sich ungewöhnlich und excellirend seyn, sondern auch als selbst erdacht, als originell* erscheinen *sollen, wenn er auch in der That nur fremde Arbeiten dazu gebraucht*). But the virtuoso is accomplished only when he possesses a fourth characteristic; namely, that he

> is *certain* never to miss his artistic goals, that is, the impact of these goals on the spirit of the listeners (who are receptive to it), and therefore never to transgress against the rules of *subordination* of these goals [to this higher purpose]. Thus he must not only know how to appreciate the *character* of his performed pieces in both the *whole* and the *individual* parts, but also to never leave unheeded the impression which they *can* and *should* create on the intellect and soul of educated listeners.[31]

In order to achieve this goal of moving the listener, the virtuoso must also possess a

> *fundamental* knowledge of the theory of music and of composition in particular; further, a clear view of aesthetics and psychology, which—because [this view] should work with *certainty*—must not be the mere result of routine and of natural understanding, but of study, in a word, of an—even if not learned—yet finer *inner* cultivation than one generally encounters in our virtuosos.[32]

Triest then takes the opportunity to censure virtuosos who lack a strong basis in musical fundamentals:

> [All virtuosos] have for the most part only one artistic goal (the least important one) in sight, namely: to arouse admiration and astonishment. Thus, they need not fear missing it once they possess an exquisite degree of proficiency (that is, mechanical power). But it does not occur to them that with their witches' leaps and roulades, if *these* are their *greatest* art, they stand below even the clever prestidigitator [. . .] [A]nd when most traveling virtuosos (not excluding *Kapellisten*) are thus examined,

---

31. "*sicher* ist, seine Kunstzwecke, d. h. die Würkung derselben auf den Geist der (NB. dafür empfänglichen) Zuhörer, nie zu verfehlen, und mithin nie wider die Regeln der *Unterordnung* dieser Zwecke zu verstossen. Deshalb muss er nicht nur den *Charakter* seiner vorzutragenden Stücke sowohl im *Ganzen* als in den *einzelnen* Theilen zu würdigen wissen, sondern auch den Eindruck nie unbeachtet lassen, den śie auf den Verstand und das Gemüth der gebildeten Zuhörer hervorbringen *können* und *sollen*." Ibid., part 2, cols. 759–60.

32. "*gründlichen* Kenntnis der Theorie der Musik und der Komposition insbesondre; ferner, eines hellen Blicks in die Aesthetik und Psychologie, der—weil er mit *Sicherheit* würken soll—nicht blos Folge der Routine und des natürlichen Verstandes, sondern des Studiums seyn muss, mit Einem Wort, einer, wo nicht gelehrten, doch feineren *innern* Bildung, als man gemeinhin bey unsern Virtuosen antrift." Ibid., part 2, col. 760.

when at least two-thirds are found among them who lack the most necessary school knowledge, and who are total ignoramuses beyond their dexterity with the throat or on their instrument (what they usually call art); then the opinion of a famous philosopher [. . .] "that the musician is generally unsuited to other occupations," cannot be regarded as unfair.[33]

The lack of schooling is not the worst problem among putative virtuosos; rather, it is immorality. Hearkening back to Kuhnau, Triest maintains that the virtuoso must indeed be virtuous, and that many so-called virtuosos have ruined their finances and reputations through drinking, gambling, and philandering. Many also project an inappropriate attitude, whether it be a "lack of humility and proper comportment, out of which come meddlesomeness, defiance, belittling of other artists, and unrefined conduct," a "stubborn mood," or a "penchant for sensuous excesses."[34] While virtuosos can usually get away with bad behavior in large cities, it is a problem in small cities and towns where there is a more direct connection between the performer and the audience.

Triest is unique for the way he justifies the need for morality among virtuosos. This need arises, he argues, from the fact that the virtuoso performer is inseparable from the artwork he or she performs:

The *person* of the painter, sculptor, and poet (as well as the composer) is separated from their works. Not so that of the *performing* musician (as of the orator and actor), which one is reluctant to lose sight of and, for psychological-aesthetic reasons, may not even completely lose [sight of]. And this maxim is scarcely or not at all subject to the accusation of unfairness once one considers the *inner*, rather than the *outer man*. Only with difficulty will the finely sensitive listener resist asking the question: "Does the outer harmony that issues from the tones of this virtuoso, does his flow of ideas, whose magic power only arises because it [the flow of ideas] is a *true symbol of more*

---

33. "Diese haben mehrentheils nur Einen Kunstzweck (den geringsten) vor Augen, nämlich: Bewunderung und Erstaunen zu erregen. Da darf ihnen freylich nicht bange seyn, dass sie ihn verfehlen, sobald sie nur einen vorzüglichen Grad von Fertigkeit (d. h. mechanischer Kraft) besitzen. Aber dass sie mit allen ihren 'Hexensprungen' und Rouladen, wenn *darin* ihre *grösste* Kunst besteht, noch unter dem geschickten Taschenspieler stehen,—fällt ihnen darum nicht ein, weil der Mensch von einseitiger Kultur, der aber in diesem Fache weit gekommen ist, (der Pedant) alle andre Arten von Kentnissen und Beschäftigungen gegen die seinige gering zu schätzen pflegt.—Dafür gebührt ihnen gegenseitige Verachtung; und wenn man so die mehresten reisenden Virtuosen—(die Kapellisten nicht ausgeschlossen)—mustert, wenn man da weingstens zwey Drittheile unter ihnen findet, die von den nöthigsten Schulkenntnissen entblösst, und ausser ihrer Gewandheit mit der Kehle oder auf ihrem Instrument (was sie Kunst zu nennen pflegen), totale Ignoranten sind; so wird man das—vermutlich hiervon abstrahirte—Urtheil eines berühmten Philosophen, 'dass die Tonkünstler gemeinhin zu andern Geschäften nichts taugen', wohl nicht für unbillig halten können." Ibid., part 2, col. 760.

34. "*Mangel an Bescheidenheit* und richtiger Selbstschätzung, woraus denn unverschämte *Zudringlichkeit* und *Trotz, Verkleinerung* andrer Künstler und überhaupt ein unfeines (oft ungesittetes) Betragen entsteht, dessen verdiente Züchtigung nur hier und da durch die Rücksicht auf das seltene Talent verhindert wird . . . *Eigensinnige Laune . . . Hang zu sinnlichen Auschweifungen.*" Ibid., part 3, col. 773.

tender and therefore nobler feelings, also correspond to the *inner* disposition of his soul? Or does he merely feign this?"[35]

For Triest, not only is it impossible to separate the identity of the virtuoso from the music he or she performs, but for such a performance to be genuine, the performer's moral character (the "*inner* disposition of his soul") must be congruent with the music (the "outer harmony"). Especially striking here is the way in which Triest's conception of the virtuoso cuts against the idea of the autonomous musical work, an idea that was rapidly gaining traction around the turn of the century. In terms that prefigure recent critical discourses on musical performance, Triest maintains that a performance is a social act as much as an aesthetic one, and that the identity of the performer, far from being incidental, mediates the musical work in crucial ways. A lack of congruence between the performer's identity and the performance itself, he suggests, results in an aesthetic breakdown. Indeed, when the virtuoso feigns expression or feeling, he or she "sinks to the level of a mere skilled craftsman, one who inspires *amazement* more than *admiration*"; it is as if one is looking at a "deceptively reproduced wax figure"—a simulacrum of the true virtuoso.[36]

Triest's emphasis on synchronizing the inner and outer aspects of the virtuoso is a theme that runs through his essay. This notion relates to Kantian philosophy, with which Triest was well-versed and in which the "inner sense"—the temporally ordered states of the mind—is contrasted with the "outer sense"— the spatial world of material objects. Equally relevant in this context is Moses Mendelssohn's theory of the sublime and naïve in the fine sciences, in which Mendelssohn argues that one's inner character is reflected in one's outer appearance: "Facial features, looks, and gestures of people are signs of their inclinations and sentiments, while each facial feature signifies an inclination and each expression a corresponding movement of the heart. . . . Nothing is so tasteless as affected naiveté or outer simplicity that we recognize is intentional and

35. "Die *Person* des Mahlers, Bildhauers, Dichters (auch des Komponisten) ist von ihren Werken getrennt. Nicht also die des *ausübenden* Tonkünstlers (wie des Redners und Schauspielers), welche man ungern aus den Augen verliert und sogar (aus psychologisch-äesthetischen Gründen) nicht ganz verlieren darf. Auch trifft der Vorwurf der Ungerechtigkeit jene Maxime nur wenig oder gar nicht, sobald man hierbey nicht an den *äussern*, sondern an den *innern Menschen* denkt. Nur mit Mühe wird also der fein empfindende Zuhörer sich der Frage erwehren: 'Entspricht die äussere Harmonie, welche aus den Tönen diese Virtuosen hervordringt, entspricht sein Ideengang, dessen magische Kraft nur dadurch entsteht, dass er ein *treues Symbol zarter, mithin edler, Gefühle* ist, auch der *innern* Stimmung seiner Seele? oder heuchelt er diese nur?'" Ibid., part 3, col. 769.

36. "Mit der Ueberzeugung, dass der letztere hier der Fall sey, sinkt zugleich der Virtuos in der Vorstellung des Zuhörers zum blos geschickten Handwerker herab, über den man sich mehr *verwundern*, als ihn *bewundern* müsste. Dies bewürkt eine widerliche Empfindung, derjenigen ähnlich, die uns beym längern Betrachten einer täuschend nachgebildeten Wachsfigur ergreift." Ibid., part 3, col. 770.

pretentious."[37] "What should go to the heart," Triest writes, "must come from the heart, may it be words or musical tones." (Years later, Beethoven would present the autograph of the *Missa Solemnis* to Archduke Rudolph with the similar inscription "From the heart—may it go back—to the heart!")

Triest's essay hence provides something of a summary of earlier attempts to define the virtuoso while adding to this discourse the idea that the identity of the virtuoso—his or her performed attitudes, behaviors, and sensibilities— mediates the musical work in complex ways. In modern terms, he might be understood to posit a conception of "musical persona," a notion Philip Auslander has described as a third term capable of bridging the work/performance dichotomy:

> [W]hen we see a musician perform, we are not simply seeing the "real person" playing; as with actors, there is an entity that mediates between musicians and the act of performance. When we hear a musician play, the source of the sound is a version of that person constructed for the specific purpose of playing music under particular circumstances. . . . What musicians perform first and foremost is not music, but their own identities as musicians, their musical personae.[38]

While Triest may not have agreed that musicians perform their identities "first and foremost," he acknowledges that the virtuoso's musical persona plays a significant role in the way his or her music is received. This notion has intriguing implications for thinking about the concerto, the genre most closely associated with the virtuoso. As Simon McVeigh has noted, the concerto was "not only an extension of [the virtuoso's] artistic personality but also an embodiment of the product on offer—in modern parlance, his intellectual property."[39] As such, concertos may be read for the ways in which they reflect or articulate a virtuoso's (constructed) identity. In Bourdieusian terms, the goal of the composing virtuoso was to transform his or her cultural capital—acquired through training and experience—from its "embodied" state (the habitus of the virtuoso, i.e., his or her learning, talents, and mystique) into an "objectified" one (the salable musical work, or more ephemerally, the ticketed concert).[40] While any musical work in some sense represents its author, the concerto is especially bound up with the habitus of the composer-performer. Viewing Beethoven's two concertos of 1806 through the lens of his musical persona (as well as that of Clement) can help to illuminate the particular character of these works.

37. Moses Mendelssohn, "On the Sublime and Naive in the Fine Sciences," in Daniel O. Dahlstrom, ed. and trans., *Moses Mendelssohn: Philosophical Writings* (Cambridge: Cambridge University Press, 1997), 192–232, 226–7.

38. Philip Auslander, "Musical Personae," *The Drama Review* 50, no. 1 (Spring 2006): 100–19, 102.

39. McVeigh, "Concerto of the Individual," 595.

40. Pierre Bourdieu, "The Forms of Capital," in J. Richardson, *Handbook of Theory and Research for the Sociology of Education* (Westport, CT: Greenwood Press, 1986), 241–58.

COMPOSING THE VIRTUOSO

How, then, does the habitus of the virtuoso—and of Beethoven in particular—mediate these two concertos? To begin to answer this question, it is helpful to observe some of the ways in which Beethoven's reputation as a pianist—a central aspect of his musical persona—was constructed by his contemporaries (and indeed by himself). As is well known, Beethoven spent the early part of his career as a touring virtuoso, and he was capable of remarkable technical feats. But accounts of his pianism also suggest that his playing could be rugged, even imprecise. While his technique was certainly praiseworthy, it was often his manner of playing "expressively" that earned special plaudits. In 1791, Carl Ludwig Junker compared Beethoven's improvisations to those of Abbé Vogler, noting that "in addition to being extraordinarily skilled, Bethofen is more eloquent, more significant, and more expressive; in short, he is more for the heart: therefore, a good Adagio as well as Allegro player."[41] The author of a 1799 account of the most famous keyboard players in Vienna voiced a similar opinion when comparing Beethoven to Josef Wölffl:

> [Beethoven] demonstrates his greatest advantage in improvisation. And here it is really quite extraordinary with what ease and yet steadiness in the succession of ideas B. does not just vary the figurations of any given theme on the spot (by means of which many a virtuoso makes his fortune and—bluster [*Wind*]) but really performs it. Since the death of Mozart, who for me still remains the *non plus ultra*, I have never found this kind of pleasure anywhere to the degree provided to me in Beethoven.[42]

According to this author, there was a kind of expressive authenticity in Beethoven's playing—he made music and not just "*Wind*"; while rival pianists merely vary the figurations of a theme, Beethoven "really performs" it. Czerny, too, praised Beethoven's manner of playing expressively, again in comparison to other pianists. While Hummel's "purling, brilliant style, well calculated to suit the manner of the time, was much more comprehensible and pleasing to the public . . . Beethoven's performance of slow and sustained passages produced an almost magical effect on every listener and, so far as I know, was never surpassed."[43] "His execution," Czerny writes elsewhere, "did not possess the pure and brilliant elegance of many other Pianists; but on the other hand it was energetic, profound, noble, with all the charms of smooth and connected cantabile and particularly in the Adagio, highly feeling and romantic."[44]

---

41. Wayne M. Senner, ed., and Robin Wallace, trans., *The Critical Reception of Beethoven's Compositions by His German Contemporaries*, 2 vols. (London and Lincoln: University of Nebraska Press, 1999 and 2001), vol. 1, 25.

42. Ibid., 28.

43. Quoted in Newman, *Beethoven on Beethoven*, 78.

44. Ibid., 79.

Of course, all of these descriptions have something of the commonplace about them. They draw on the same rhetorical opposition between mechanical and expressive playing that figured into contemporary discussions of the virtuoso. While these commentators were doubtless responding to something they heard as special in Beethoven's personal style, they were also adopting conventionalized language to describe it. By contrasting Beethoven's "expressive," "highly feeling," and "romantic" manner of playing with the brilliant but essentially vapid manner of other pianists, they sought to place him, as it were, on the right side of music history. Beethoven identified himself in similar terms. In a letter to Streicher, he remarked that in hearing other pianists "one often believes one hears only a harp, and I am glad that you are one of the few who understand and feel that, if one can feel, one can also sing on the piano."[45] The implication is that he, like Streicher, understands how to be expressive on the instrument. He likewise told publisher Nikolaus Simrock that he greatly preferred the "modesty and natural behavior" of violinist Rodolphe Kreutzer to "*all the exterior* without *any interior*, which is characteristic of most virtuosi."[46] This remark, made two years after the publication of Triest's essay, resonates with Triest's explicit thematization of "inner" and "outer" virtuosity.[47]

That Beethoven engaged this discourse is by no means surprising. Indeed, his remarks underscore that expressiveness was much more than an abstract ideal; it represented a particular kind of cultural capital for the virtuoso. It is no accident that Schönfeld turned to the same discourse in his laudatory account of the sixteen-year-old Clement, writing, "His tone is soulful, entrancing, and melting, his passagework clear, poised, and pure; *at times one believes his own soul resides in the violin, and dissolves in tones.*"[48] Here, Clement is described not just

---

45. Anderson, vol. 1, no. 18, pp. 25–6 (probably August/September 1796) (*Briefwechsel*, vol. 1, no. 22, pp. 31–2). Streicher himself used similar language in his booklet of 1801: "[The good player] knows how to let every tone *sing* without straining his instrument, *because he touches every key appropriately.*" Quoted in Tilman Skowroneck, *Beethoven the Pianist* (Cambridge: Cambridge University Press, 2010), 74.

46. Anderson, vol. 1, no. 99, pp. 119–20 (October 4, 1804). "dieser ist ein guter lieber Mensch, der mir bey seinem hiesigen Aufenthalte sehr viel vergnügen gemacht, seine Anspruchlosigkeit und Natürlichkeit ist mir lieber als *alles Exterieur* ohne *Interieur* der Meisten Virtuosen." *Briefwechsel*, vol. I, no. 193, pp. 224–5, 224.

47. Later, the notion of interiority would feed more explicitly into Beethoven's published compositions: the first movement of Op. 101 (composed around 1815) bears the indication "Etwas lebhaft, und mit der innigsten Empfindung," and the third movement of Op. 109 (composed 1820) is marked "Gesangvoll, mit innigster Empfindung." It is interesting to note that both movements begin similarly to the Fourth Piano Concerto, with hushed opening statements in the piano's middle register, beginning on major chords with the third on top (both in E major). For a different perspective on Beethoven's interiority, see Janet Schmalfeldt, *In the Process of Becoming: Analytic and Philosophical Perspectives on Form in Early Nineteenth-Century Music* (Oxford and New York: Oxford University Press, 2011), 133–57.

48. Emphasis mine. "Sein Ton ist seelenvoll, hinreissend und schmelzend, seine Passagen klar, schwebend und rein, man glaubt zuweilen seine eigne Seele liege in der Violine, und löse sich in Töne auf." Schönfeld, *Jahrbuch*, 11.

as a skillful player but also as a profoundly expressive one: via the medium of the violin, his playing synthesizes "outer harmony" with the "inner disposition of the soul" (to quote Triest). The discourse of expressiveness, Schönfeld recognized, was the quickest and surest way to distinguish the true virtuoso from the mere pretender.[49] While writers resorted to the idea of expressiveness to bolster (or diminish) a virtuoso's reputation, the concerto offered the virtuoso a means of turning his or her particular brand of expressiveness into a marketable commodity. Of course, the showcasing of expressiveness had long been de rigueur in concerto slow movements. What differentiates Beethoven's two concertos of 1806, however, is the degree to which the expressive impulse infuses the entire conception from beginning to end. Expressiveness offers a valuable hermeneutic window into these works.

One way in which Beethoven telegraphs the importance of expressiveness in these concertos is through the use of expressive markings like *dolce, cantabile, espressivo,* and their variant forms. While such markings were designed to be read not by concertgoers but by performers (as well as by consumers of the printed parts, both sets of which were published by 1808), they serve as evidence of a new approach to the concerto in two respects. First, the concertos of 1806 contain a significantly greater number of these expressive markings than Beethoven's earlier concertos (with one exception). The first three piano concertos contain remarkably few such markings, with only one in the Second Piano Concerto (premiered 1795; published 1801), five in the First Piano Concerto (premiered 1795; published 1801), and three in the Third Piano Concerto (premiered 1803; published 1804). The Fourth Piano Concerto, by contrast, includes twenty-five of these markings, and the Violin Concerto twenty-seven—the vast majority pertaining to the solo parts.[50] The exception to the rule is the Triple Concerto (likely premiered 1804; published 1807), which also includes a preponderance of expressive markings. But this leads to the second point: unlike in the Triple Concerto, in which markings such as *espressivo* and *dolce* are used more or less interchangeably (even haphazardly), in the concertos of 1806 Beethoven is more intentional in his use of

---

49. Ironically, later critics found that Clement's playing—initially celebrated for its lightness, elegance, and finesse—lacked expressiveness in comparison to the more powerful manner of Viotti, Rode, Kreutzer, and others of the French school. While the playing of these French violinists was characterized in terms of the "beautiful" and the "sublime," Clement's playing was often described as merely "pleasurable" (*angenehm*). Wiebke Thormählen, "Franz Clement, Violin Concerto in D Major (1805), ed. Clive Brown," *Eighteenth-Century Music* 5, no. 2 (2008): 255–7, 256. See also Robert Haas, "The Viennese Violinist, Franz Clement," *The Musical Quarterly* 34, no. 1 (January 1948): 15–27. For more on Clement's playing and composing styles and their possible influences on Beethoven's Violin Concerto, see Robin Stowell, *Beethoven: Violin Concerto,* Cambridge Music Handbooks (Cambridge: Cambridge University Press, 1998), 20–9.

50. For present purposes, I leave out markings such as "*leggieramente*" and "*delicatamente*," although these could also be construed as having expressive connotations.

these markings, often coordinating their appearance with special effects in the music. This is not to say that he is entirely systematic, but his use of expressive markings in these works is both more consistent and more illuminating from an analytical standpoint. Beethoven would continue this trend toward greater frequency and precision in his use of expressive markings in the Fifth Piano Concerto (premiered 1811; published 1810).

In the Fourth Piano Concerto, the expressive indications *dolce* and *espressivo* (and related terms) frequently coincide with a particular constellation of musical features in the solo part, which I have termed "Expressive Topic 1" in Table 2.1. This topic asserts itself in the first and third movements and involves some or all of the following features: the sudden appearance of a remote key area; a soaring lyrical melody played by the right hand, often in an extremely high register; a simple, often arpeggiated, left-hand accompaniment; a sense of harmonic stasis, brought about by the use of a pedal point; and a quiet dynamic level. Its variant forms correlate with different expressive markings: in the first movement, the version involving sudden plunges to ♭III and ♭VI (Expressive Topic 1a) is marked *espressivo* while the diatonic version (Expressive Topic 1b) is marked *dolce e con espressione*; in the finale, the most tonally stable form of the topic (Expressive Topic 1c) is marked simply *dolce*. (As I shall argue in chapter 5, this topic, with its widely spaced treble and bass voices, likely emerged out of Beethoven's experimentations with his Erard piano.) A second topic, related but distinctive enough to merit its own label (Expressive Topic 2), is also tonally stable but occurs at the farthest possible remove from the tonic (C-sharp minor); it is also marked *dolce*.

Danuta Mirka has defined topics as "musical styles and genres taken out of their proper context and used in another one."[51] This definition is useful in thinking about these contemplative, lyrical, and introspective passages, passages which are atypical of, even incongruous with, the rhetoric of a concerto's outer movements. They are, of course, more suggestive of Beethoven's slow movements, most notably the Adagio un poco mosso of the Fifth Piano Concerto, in which the piano's first two phrases (mm. 16ff. and 28ff.) are essentially identical to what I have called "Expressive Topic 1." Here, in the key of B major (remote with respect to the concerto's E-flat major), the piano enters with the quality of a revelation, on an F-sharp three octaves above middle C over a low BB in the left hand. Beethoven marks both phrases *espressivo* and *pianissimo*. A more evocative term also appears in the margin of the autograph score near the piano's entrance: *dämmernd*, dawning (or fading into night).

---

51. Danuta Mirka, "Introduction," in Danuta Mirka, ed., *The Oxford Handbook of Topic Theory* (New York: Oxford University Press, 2014), 1–60, 2. Mirka's definition builds on Leonard Ratner's original conception of topics in *Classic Music: Expression, Form, and Style* (New York: Schirmer, 1980).

TABLE 2.1 *Espressivo, dolce,* and *cantabile* markings in the Fourth Piano Concerto.

Measure	Key	Marking	Comments
Movement I: Allegro moderato (G major)			
1	I	*dolce*	Opening theme (solo)
105	♭III	*espressivo*	Expressive Topic 1a (solo)
123	V	*dolce*	(solo)
170	on V$_5^6$ of V	*dolce e con espressione*	Expressive Topic 1b (solo)
			Expressive Topic 2 (solo) "far
231	♯iv	*dolce*	out point"
256	I	*dolce*	(solo)
270	I	*dolce*	(solo)
275	♭VI	*espress.*	Expressive Topic 1a (solo)
290	I	*dolce*	(solo)
337	V$_5^6$	*dolce e con espressione*	Expressive Topic 1b
347	V$_5^6$	*dolce*	Expressive Topic 1b
356	I	*espressivo*	Closing theme (solo)
Movement II: Andante con moto (E minor)			
6	V→i	*molto cantabile*	Piano Entrance (solo)
19	VII♯–i	*molto espressivo*	Variant of above
Movement III: Rondo: Vivace (G major)			
25	I	*dolce*	(solo)
80	V	*dolce*	Expressive Topic 1c
184	I	*dolce*	(solo)
300	I	*dolce*	Expressive Topic 1c
370	♭VI	*dolce*	(violas)
			Expressive Topic 1c (solo) "far
460	VII♯	*dolce*	out point"
468	IV	*dolce*	Expressive Topic 1d (solo)
476	I	*dolce*	Expressive Topic 1c (cellos)
511	(I)	*dolce*	
518	(I)	*dolce*	
547	I	*dolce*	

In the slow movement of the Fifth Piano Concerto, style and context match—the soloist deploys slow movement rhetoric within a slow movement. In both the Fourth Piano Concerto and the Violin Concerto, by contrast, there is a disjunction between style and context; expressiveness thus becomes "top-icalized." This is made still clearer by the ways in which Beethoven frames the appearance of the expressive topic in the outer movements of these concertos. Indeed, one could conceivably justify the presence of this style in an outer movement if it were to appear in a formal location typically marked as lyrical—the secondary key area, for instance. But Beethoven's use of this style—particularly in the Fourth Piano Concerto—is neither localized nor strictly tied to formal considerations. Moreover, he dramatizes its emergence at virtually every turn. The brilliant and expressive styles do not exist on equal footing; rather, the brilliant gives way to the expressive, accords it pride of place.

As examples, consider two parallel moments in the development sections of these concertos' first movements. In the Violin Concerto, following a closing ritornello (and repetition of the closing theme) in C major (mm. 272ff.), the strings settle into a dominant seventh sonority. The solo violin starts what appears to be a new rotation of thematic material, but on the dominant of C major (analogous to the cadenza-like entrance on the dominant of D major in m. 89). As in the earlier passage, the rest of the orchestra remains silent as the violin's falling eighth-note triplets give way to rising sixteenth notes. Whereas in the entrance cadenza, this brilliant-style figuration prepared a cadence on the tonic and, following the intoning of the timpani's five-note motive, the arrival of the lyrical main theme, here the figuration is extended an extra two measures, with the violin pausing on a high f^3 (see Example 2.1a). The brilliant style comes to a dramatic halt, as the violin crescendos, the bass enters quietly on G, and both parts resolve not to the expected C major, but outwardly to F-sharps (the dominant seventh G–F is reinterpreted as the augmented sixth G–E-sharp). The five-note motive sounds in the cello, *pianissimo*, and the harmony is finally filled in a measure later, at which point we are at the doorstep of B minor, remote with respect to C major. Over a dominant pedal, the solo violin sounds a melancholy rendition of the main theme, marked *espressivo*, in the extreme high register that is so characteristic of this concerto, leading to a sequential passage more typical of development sections. Over the course of this remarkable transition, Beethoven intensifies the progression from brilliant style to expressive style that originally occurred at the solo's violin's first entrance. Here, not only is the transition between the two styles unbroken but the harmonic juxtaposition of C major and B minor also creates a marked sense of contrast between the soloist's extroverted, cadenza-like material and the introverted, lyrical melody that follows.[52]

52. In the Violin Concerto, Beethoven repeats the move from brilliant to expressive at another important juncture in the development section—the transition into the famous "G-minor episode" (mm. 331ff.). The sense of contrast, here, is often heightened beyond even what Beethoven seems to have intended, insofar as many violinists take this episode "out of time." In a paper delivered at the New Beethoven Research conference in Vancouver, BC (November 2–3, 2016), Johannes Gebauer suggested that it was Fritz Kreisler who globalized this tradition, following Eugène Ysaÿe. My thanks to the author for discussing his paper with me over e-mail. On the early performance history of the Violin Concerto (including documentation of several previously unknown performances), see Gebauer's article "Zur Entstehung eines Klassikers: Die Aufführungen von Beethovens Violinkonzert op. 61 von der Uraufführung bis 1844," *Bonner Beethoven-Studien* 12 (2016): 9–26.

EXAMPLE 2.1. Parallel Appearances of the "Expressive" Topic.

a. Beethoven, Violin Concerto in D Major, Op. 61, i, mm. 297–304

b. Beethoven, Piano Concerto No. 4 in G Major, Op. 58, i, mm. 228–34

Similarly, the expressive topic appears at the crux of the development section of the Fourth Piano Concerto's first movement (see Example 2.1b). Here, the sense of contrast between brilliant and expressive styles is even more striking. Joseph Kerman offers the following apt description of this development section:

> In brief: the solo picks up very notably during these portions of the concerto. At the beginning of the development section, it converts its tentative entry into an eloquent new theme with rich modulatory energy; it rides the orchestral wave that develops out of this theme; and it breaks free of the orchestra in the most brilliant passage in the entire movement—fifteen bars of tense bravura preparing a remote new key and yet another new solo theme. What the bravura prepares is not so much a theme as a somnolent searching for a theme: a moment of high mystery, the one uncanny place in the whole concerto.[53]

Indeed, beginning with the surprising arrival on the inverted Neapolitan ($\natural$II in C-sharp minor) in m. 216, the piano asserts itself in a way hitherto unpredicted. In an almost frantic state, it drives toward C-sharp minor—the movement's "far out point"—using a variety of brilliant figurations: rapid sixteenth-note triplets, interlocking left- and right-hand dotted figures, gargantuan sixteenth-note arpeggios, and finally a dizzying chromatic run of sixteenth-note sextuplets in the piano's uppermost register, *sempre fortissimo*. All of this culminates in two thrilling half-note trills, *sforzando*, on d-sharp^3 and g-sharp^3 respectively, the latter of which drops down an octave for a final, climactic whole-note trill on g-sharp^2 to prepare the new key. But then the remarkable happens: the trill's energy dissipates, its dynamic decreasing from *fortissimo* to *pianissimo* over the course of a single measure. When C-sharp minor arrives, a stylistic transformation has taken place: the piano ruminates on a new idea, marked *dolce* and spanning the descending fifth g-sharp^2–c-sharp^2 while the orchestra returns with a solemn, now quiescent, accompaniment.

Kerman's use of the word "uncanny" to describe this passage is fitting: although there is nothing else quite like it in the concerto, it draws on the solo part's by-now-familiar tendency to veer away from the brilliant style toward the expressive. In the exposition, these moments are occasion for a kind of sublime suspension of the musical discourse: for example, the dramatic triple trill in measures 168–9, analogous to the trill in the development section, gives way to the soloist's ravishing restatement of mm. 157ff. in D major, *dolce e con espressione* (Expressive Topic 1b). As James Hepokoski and Warren Darcy observe about this earlier passage, "the soloist, at first plunging efficiently toward Ritornello 2, undergoes a change of mind, seeking now to stop linear time, reluctant to bring such beauty to an end and wishing to back up for one

---

53. Joseph Kerman, "Representing a Relationship: Notes on a Beethoven Concerto," *Representations* 39 (Summer 1992): 80–101, 88.

more statement of R1:\S$^{1.3}$ [mm. 157ff.] in a wondrous recovery ('Wait! Did you hear that theme? Did you realize what it meant?')."[54] In the development, by contrast, the expressive style emerges not out of a pleasurable caprice but out of a troubling recognition: we have finally arrived, but nothing looks as it should. This singular moment—and the sense of interiority that it implies—is the unsettling but ineluctable outcome of the exhilarating bravura episode that precedes it.

The repeated turns inward in these two concertos, whether joyous or tragic, distinguish these works from typical works in the genre. More than this, they respond in a sophisticated way to the contemporary valorization of expressiveness as the hallmark of the true virtuoso. What is significant about these works is not merely that the brilliant and expressive comingle, but rather that the brilliant serves as a foil to the expressive, both preparing it and heightening its significance. These concertos not only reflect the musical capacities of Beethoven and Clement as players, then, but also serve to elevate the ideal of the true virtuoso through the medium of Beethoven's post-*Leonore* style. By positing the dramatization of *Innigkeit* as its own special form of spectacular display, Beethoven upends the conventions of the genre while "objectifying" a celebrated aspect of his own musical persona.

PERFORMING THE VIRTUOSO

If the written-out concerto represents an objectified form of the virtuoso's habitus, then this frozen habitus is ever subject to reanimation—and transformation—through new acts of performance. Beethoven appears to have been eager to surprise his audiences as much as possible, often elaborating the solo parts of his concertos over the course of successive performances. The Fourth Piano Concerto offers a revealing instance of this tendency. Because no autograph score survives, the principal sources are a copyist's manuscript (primarily in the hand of Joseph Klumpar) with corrections and additions by Beethoven (A-Wgm, A 82 B) and the first printed edition of the parts, published in 1808 by the Vienna firm Bureau des Arts et d'Industrie. While these two sources are in most respects analogous, the former is unique in that it contains more than one hundred measures of variants for the soloist, sketched in Beethoven's hand on or near the staves for the keyboard part. These variants pertain to the first and third movements (the second movement manuscript is a much later copy). Many of the sketches are difficult to discern or simply illegible—Gustav Nottebohm, Willy Hess, and Paul Badura-Skoda all struggled

---

54. James Hepokoski and Warren Darcy, *Elements of Sonata Theory: Norms, Types, and Deformations in the Late-Eighteenth-Century Sonata* (New York: Oxford University Press, 2006), 546.

to decipher them. Barry Cooper has more recently transcribed and completed them, and with some adaptations, the variants have been incorporated into a working edition by Hans-Werner Küthen.[55]

The purpose of these variants has been the source of debate.[56] Küthen has argued that they correspond to a string quintet arrangement of the concerto allegedly prepared by Franz Alexander Pössinger and authorized by Beethoven in early summer 1807. Pössinger is said to have worked from the copyist's score in which the variants appear; however, the solo part that would have theoretically incorporated the variants is lost, making it impossible to definitively link them to the arrangement.[57] Cooper, following Nottebohm and others, has suggested that these variants more likely relate to Beethoven's public premiere of the concerto at the Theater an der Wien on December 22, 1808. As we know from Czerny, who was present at the premiere, Beethoven's performance did not adhere strictly to the written solo part (already published by this point); rather, he played "mischievously," adding "many more notes" to the passage-work.[58] This seems an enticing clue, but there is little else to link the variants to this particular performance.

Whether the sketched variants correspond to the chamber arrangement, the concerto's public premiere, or both (or neither), they underscore some of the ways in which Beethoven's performances could differ from the texts that have been handed down to us as authentic. If one accepts that Beethoven's "musical persona" is somehow inscribed in the Fourth Piano Concerto, then we must content ourselves that this inscription is only a partial one, and tantalizingly so. The C-sharp-minor episode described earlier is one of several places in the concerto where Beethoven apparently chose to depart drastically from the written solo part in performance. As shown in Example 2.2, the revised

55. My thanks to Mike Cheng-Yu Lee for allowing me to consult his personal copy of this score.

56. See Barry Cooper, "Beethoven's Revisions to His Fourth Piano Concerto," in Robin Stowell, ed., *Performing Beethoven* (Cambridge: Cambridge University Press, 1994), 23–48; Hans-Werner Küthen, "The Newly Discovered Authorized 1807 Arrangement of Beethoven's Fourth Fortepiano Concerto for Fortepiano and String Quintet: An Adventurous Variant in the Style of the Late Cadenzas," *Beethoven Journal* 13, no. 1 (Summer 1998): 2–11; Barry Cooper, "Beethoven's Fourth Piano Concerto Revisited: A Response to Hans-Werner Küthen," *Beethoven Journal* 13, no. 2 (Winter 1998): 70–2; and Hans-Werner Küthen, "Die authentische Kammerfassung von Beethovens Viertem Klavierkonzert für Klavier und Streichquintett (1807)," *Bonner Beethoven-Studien* 1 (1999): 49–90 (an expanded version of his earlier article in *Beethoven Journal*).

57. Jonathan Del Mar has recently disputed the claim that the quintet version was an authorized arrangement based on the copyist's score, arguing that it in fact post-dates (and is based on) the first edition. As he notes, there is no evidence connecting Beethoven to the arrangement. In addition, the increased range of the revised solo part in the copyist's score (up to f^4—not f^3 as stated in Del Mar) would seem to imply a later date for this solo part than the 1807 date suggested by Küthen. Jonathan Del Mar, *Beethoven: Concerto No. 4 in G Major for Pianoforte and Orchestra, op. 58: Critical Commentary* (Kassel: Bärenreiter, 2015), esp. 14–15.

58. Gustav Nottebohm, *Zweite Beethoveniana: Nachgelassene Aufsätze*, ed. Eusebius Mandyczewski (Leipzig: Peters, 1887), 75.

EXAMPLE 2.2. Beethoven, Piano Concerto No. 4 in G Major, Op. 58, i, mm. 226–31, published solo part (top) versus sketched variant (bottom).

version reaches even greater heights of virtuoso display, with the addition of a rapid sixty-fourth-note chromatic run in place of thirty-second-note arpeggiations (m. 226), a second, more rhythmically complex run spanning two octaves from c-sharp^2 to c-sharp^4 (a note that requires the resources of a six-octave piano—was this an impetus for the revision?, m. 228), and most dramatically of all, a beat-long caesura in the right hand (accompanied by bass notes in the left) preparing a difficult sequence of eighth-note trills on d-sharp^2, g-sharp^2, and g-sharp^3 (mm. 228–9). A final, longer trill on g-sharp^2 then introduces the *dolce* theme as before. But while Beethoven reaches newly spectacular heights in this revision, he also plumbs more profound depths, calling for a *ritardando* at the moment of the *dolce* theme's arrival.[59] By pointing up the disjunction between brilliant and lyrical registers in this improvisatory variant, Beethoven opens up an opportunity to reclaim the published Fourth Piano Concerto as his "intellectual property" in performance. In so doing, he both reasserts and elaborates his musical persona in ways that further attest to his reputation as a true virtuoso.

<hr/>

59. This *ritardando*, along with similar instances in measures 172 and 336, appears in the Henle Urtext edition of the concerto; however, as Del Mar notes, they do "not belong to the finished work as Beethoven signed off and published it" but rather pertain to the variant solo part. See Del Mar, *Critical Commentary*, 26, 28.

CHAPTER 3

MUSIC FOR A DIPLOMAT

Opus 59

> Well then, what do you say of this finale, the host asked me
> as soon as the piece had ended.—I say that this poor Russian
> theme, manipulated as it has been here by Beethoven, drowned
> in floods of German erudition, gives me the impression of
> one of our peasants who has been decked out in the coat and
> powdered wig of a professor, but is left with his unkempt beard,
> his shoes of bark, and his haircut *à la moujik* protruding from
> underneath the wig. It lacks sense and taste. You know Glinka's
> *Kamarinskaia*: this is how one should treat Russian themes.[1]

For Alexandre Oulibicheff, writing in 1857, the Russian theme in the finale of Beethoven's Opus 59, no. 1 was caught between two worlds. A serf at heart—complete with unruly beard, bowl-style mujik (Russian peasant) haircut, and bast shoes—the lowly theme has been forced to don the elevated garb of a *docteur*. The result is a grotesque blend of Muscovite and Teuton, peasant and professor. Nor was Oulibicheff alone in the judgment he shared with his colleagues at a quartet party in St. Petersburg. As he reports, "I was not lambasted. Far from it, M. Louis Maurer, the skilled composer, M. [Berthold]

---

1. "Eh bien, que dites[-]vous de ce finale, me demanda le maître du logis, lorsque le morceau fut achevé.—Je dis que ce pauvre thème russe, manipulé comme il l'a été ici par Beethoven, noyé dans des flots d'érudition allemande, me fait l'effet d'un de nos paysans qu'on aurait affublé d'un manteau et d'une perruque de docteur, en lui laissant sa barbe inculte, ses souliers d'écorce et sa coiffure à la moujik, débordant la perruque. Ça manque de sens et de goût. Vous connaissez la *Kamarinskaia* de Glinka. Voilà comme on doit traiter des thèmes russes." Oulibicheff, *Beethoven, ses critiques et ses glossateurs* (Leipzig and Paris: F. A. Brockhaus & Jules Gavelot, 1857), 265–6.

Damcke, the knowledgeable critic, and . . . three virtuosi agreed that my observation was right."[2]

Oulibicheff's caricature of the *thème russe* in Opus 59, no. 1 is perhaps the earliest in a series of critiques regarding Beethoven's treatment of the two Russian themes in Opus 59.[3] Writing in the early 1940s, Gerald Abraham, a specialist in Russian music, felt compelled to apologize for Beethoven's settings, writing that "we must not blame him . . . the sympathetic treatment of folk-music was unthought of in his day; his business was musical composition, not musical ethnology."[4] In his review of Abraham's book, the British composer Ernest Walker went further: "Democrat though he was, Beethoven had not the slightest regard for the Rights of the People where folk music was concerned."[5] More recent commentators, too, have felt that the Russian themes remain at odds with the rest of the musical conception, though for different reasons. The finale of Opus 59, no. 1, Joseph Kerman suggests, "strikes a tone wrongly scaled to the quartet as a whole."[6] In this instance, "Beethoven was writing at the very top of his form, but his instinct for the larger coherence faltered."[7] More extreme is Kerman's critique of the fugal treatment of the Russian tune in Opus 59, no. 2: "This does not sound as though the composer inserted the Russian tune as an urbane compliment to his Russian patron. . . . It sounds as though Count Razumovsky had been tactless enough to hand Beethoven the tune, and Beethoven is pile-driving it into the ground by way of revenge."[8]

In a collection of essays on Russian music, Richard Taruskin has argued that Beethoven's treatments are best understood as parodies. Drawing on work

2. "Je ne fus pas lapidé. Loin de là, M. Louis Maurer, l'habile compositeur, M. Damcke, le savant critique et MM. Maurer fils et Albrecht, les trois virtuoses, tombèrent d'accord sur ce que mon observation était juste." Ibid., 266.

3. A close friend of Glinka's, Oulibicheff was influenced by the so-called Russian nationalist movement in music. In this context, his mention of *Kamarinskaia* takes on something of a didactic tone, as if he is trying to demonstrate the value of the Russian nationalist approach against the backdrop of Beethoven's contrapuntally laden (and hence fatally Germanic) settings. Wilhelm von Lenz, himself of Russian and Baltic German descent, defended Opus 59 against Oulibicheff's criticisms in a footnote spanning four pages of his *Beethoven: Eine Kunst-Studie*. He refuted the logic of Oulibicheff's comparison: "To accuse Beethoven of not being as Russian as Glinka, to require of a universal genius that he nevertheless should be a Russian, is to confuse basic concepts" (Beethoven vorwerfen, nicht so russich zu sein wie Glinka, von einem Universalgenie verlangen, daß er auch noch ein Russe sein solle, heißt Grundbegriffe konfundiren); *Beethoven: Eine Kunststudie*, 5 vols. (Cassel: Ernst Balde, and Hamburg: Hoffmann & Campe, 1855–60), vol. 3, 21. I thank Lewis Lockwood for bringing this passage to my attention.

4. Gerald Abraham, *Beethoven's Second-Period Quartets* (London: Oxford University Press, 1942), 28.

5. E[rnest] W[alker], "*Beethoven's Second-Period Quartets* by Gerald Abraham," *Music and Letters* 24, no. 2 (April 1943): 112–13, 112.

6. Joseph Kerman, *The Beethoven Quartets* (New York: Norton, 1979), 114.

7. Ibid., 115.

8. Ibid., 130.

EXAMPLE 3.1. "Ah, Whether It's My Luck, Such Luck" (Akh! talan li moi, talan takoi), in Lvov-Pratsch Collection (LPC), 1806.

by Abraham, he notes that Beethoven altered the key, tempo, and affect of the Russian folksongs as they appear in the well-known Lvov-Pratsch Collection (LPC, first ed. 1790), an anthology to which Beethoven had access.[9] He suggests that Beethoven's transformation of the *protyazhnaya* "Ah, Whether It's My Luck, Such Luck" from a lament—marked "Molto andante" in LPC—into an Allegro finale is a deliberate misreading (see Example 3.1).[10] By speeding

9. Nottebohm reports that Beethoven possessed a copy of the LPC in which he made some annotations. Gustav Nottebohm, *Zweite Beethoveniana: Nachgelassene Aufsäze* (New York: Johnson Reprint Corporation, 1970), 90. See note 14 later.

10. The term *protyazhnaya* encompasses a wide variety of slow and lyrical Russian folksongs. In contrast to faster dance songs, *protyazhnye* often contained many verses with long individual lines, and included "retarding devices" such as repetitions of words, phrases, and whole lines. A common

up the tempo, he maintains, Beethoven ignores or contradicts the folksong's melancholy character. Taruskin goes on to read the movement's coda—in which the Russian tune is at last played slowly—in ironic terms: "Near the end [Beethoven] allows the melody's first phrase one adagio statement, with juicy harmonies that suggest the original affect, but immediately mocks it with a silly fanfare of a coda, Presto. As if Russians could have real feelings!"[11] He similarly describes the fugal treatment of the "Slava" hymn in Opus 59, no. 2 in parodistic terms, interpreting its "learned brainlessness" as a satirical send-up of Russian imperial might.

On one hand, then, Beethoven's seemingly odd choices of character and tempo have been viewed as inappropriate or even demeaning to his Russian source material (as presented in its already mediated form in the LPC). On the other hand, his unabashedly erudite treatments have seemed incompatible with the tunes' folklike simplicity.[12] To be sure, one would not want to dismiss such criticisms. On the contrary, they point to a peculiar tension in Beethoven's handling of the Russian folksongs, one whose aesthetic and cultural implications have not yet been fully explored. In this chapter, I suggest that a closer look at the relationship between folk- and learned-style elements in Opus 59 has the potential to illuminate both this tension and the cycle as a whole. Furthermore, it presents an opportunity to reconsider the circumstances of the commission, in particular the relationship between Beethoven and his Russian patron, Count Andrey Razumovsky. Reconsidering Beethoven's approach to the Russian themes also opens up new ways of thinking about the use of folk materials in Western art music more generally.

I will begin by reexamining the finale of Opus 59, no. 1 with an eye (and ear) to the ways in which Beethoven juxtaposes folk- and learned-style elements. I will then turn my focus to the trio of Opus 59, no. 2, suggesting—in contrast to recent readings—that the trio's collision of high and low elements is less a parody of Russianness than a self-conscious critique of the highbrow Viennese style. Indeed, the allegedly parodistic intent of both movements is not only difficult to prove (as is often the case in musical works) but also makes little sense in light of Beethoven's relationship with Razumovsky. His idiosyncratic

theme was the difficulties and sorrows of the soldier's life, the topic of "Ah, Whether It's My Luck, Such Luck." See Elizabeth A. Warner and Evgenii S. Kustovskii, *Russian Traditional Folk Song* (Hull, UK: Hull University Press, 1990), 55–7.

11. Richard Taruskin, *On Russian Music* (Berkeley: University of California Press, 2009), 347.

12. See, for further examples, Joseph de Marliave, *Beethoven's Quartets* (Mineola, NY: Dover, 2004), 62; Robert Haven Schauffler, *Beethoven: The Man Who Freed Music* (Garden City, NY: Doubleday, Doran, & Co., 1929), 179; Daniel Gregory Mason, *The Quartets of Beethoven* (New York: Oxford University Press, 1947), 98–9; Philip Radcliffe, *Beethoven's String Quartets* (London: Hutchinson, 1965), 68; and William Kinderman, *Beethoven*, 2nd ed. (Oxford and New York: Oxford University Press, 2009), 133–5.

treatment of the two Russian themes is better understood as a creative response to a pair of independent but interrelated stimuli, the German reception of Russian folksong around 1800 and the cosmopolitan persona of Razumovsky himself. In the final part of this chapter, these conclusions will be brought to bear on the third and final quartet in the opus, the only one that lacks a labeled *thème russe*. Beethoven appears to have concealed a Russian folksong within the opening theme of the Andante movement, blurring the boundary between folk and art music, and fulfilling his pledge—as reported by Czerny—to weave a Russian melody into each of the Opus 59 quartets.[13]

"AH, WHETHER IT'S MY LUCK, SUCH LUCK"

Before turning to the finale of Opus 59, no. 1, it seems important to address the claim that Beethoven misrepresented (either accidentally or deliberately) the folksong on which it is based. We do not know which edition of the LPC Beethoven knew or when it came into his possession; he could have had access either to the original edition printed in 1790 or to the revised and expanded second edition of 1806.[14] The LPC was designed to appeal to a class of "Westernized" Russians, primarily noblemen and aristocrats living in urban environments. As such, the compilers made every effort to adapt their materials to the particular demands of European amateur music making. The melodic and rhythmic idiosyncrasies have largely been ironed out, and Pratsch's harmonizations overwhelmingly prefer applied dominants and modulations to any kind of modal treatment. (Looking at Example 3.1, for instance, one doubts that the F-sharp in measure 6 would have been at all idiomatic, since the melody otherwise suggests G Aeolian—but the raised leading tone permits Pratsch to cadence firmly in G minor.)

In working with the LPC, Beethoven had access not only to the harmonized melodies, but also to the Russian-language texts and the Italian-language tempo markings. Thus, whether or not he was familiar with the text of "Ah, Whether It's My Luck, Such Luck" (Akh! talan li moi, talan takoy)—a soldier's lament—he certainly would have seen the tempo marking "Molto Andante"

13. Carl Czerny, *On the Proper Performance of All Beethoven's Works for the Piano: Czerny's Reminiscences of Beethoven and Chapters II and III from Volume IV of the* Complete Theoretical and Practical Piano Forte School, *Op. 500*, ed. Paul Badura-Skoda (Vienna: Universal Edition, 1970), 13.

14. Nottebohm does not specify which edition contained Beethoven's annotations. A copy of the LPC in its third edition (1815) survives in the Gesellschaft der Musikfreunde, but this could not have been the source for Opus 59. See Malcolm Hamrick Brown, ed., *A Collection of Russian Folk Songs by Nikolai Lvov and Ivan Prach* (Ann Arbor: UMI Research Press, 1987), xii, note 9. It is generally assumed that Beethoven had access to the first edition, though it remains possible that the second edition reached him (perhaps through Razumovsky) while he was composing in 1806. On the chronology of Opus 59, see Alan Tyson, "The 'Razumovsky' Quartets: Some Aspects of the Sources," in Alan Tyson, ed., *Beethoven Studies 3* (Cambridge: Cambridge University Press, 1982), 107–40, 107–9.

printed at the top of the page. Why, then, did he choose an Allegro tempo for his finale? One answer is that the term "Molto Andante" is ambiguous; indeed, in Beethoven's day it may well have indicated faster than andante, not slower as some commentators have suggested.[15] Beethoven himself expressed concern about the arbitrary nature of middle-of-the-road tempo markings in an 1813 letter to George Thomson, for whom he arranged many Scottish, Welsh, and Irish folksongs:

> If among the airs that you may send me to be arranged in the future there are Andantinos, please tell me whether Andantino is to be understood as meaning faster or slower than Andante, for this term, like so many in music, is of so indefinite a significance that Andantino sometimes approaches . . . [an] Allegro and sometimes, on the other hand, is played like Adagio.[16]

Additionally, though Lvov and Pratsch included tempo markings for all the songs in their collection, we cannot know how these songs were performed in their original contexts. As the compilers themselves indicated in the preface to LPC, even the most familiar folk melodies were subject to widely varying performance practices.[17] Beethoven's choice of tempo may have reflected performance traditions that differed from those notated in LPC. He could well have developed a sense of how these songs sounded through his interactions with Razumovsky, an accomplished amateur string player with strong familial ties to Russian and Ukrainian musical culture.[18]

---

15. In his definition of "molto," Koch observes that in addition to using molto to qualify Allegro and Adagio; "Some composers also use it with the word *Andante*; however, the term [molto] thereby becomes uncertain, so that one cannot exactly determine whether the movement of the Andante should be faster or slower." (Einige Tonsetzer brauchen es auch bey dem Worte *Andante*, wo aber der Begriff dadurch schwankend wird, so daß man nicht ganz genau bestimmen kann, ob dadurch die Bewegung des *Andante* geschwinder oder langsamer werder soll.) Heinrich Christoph Koch, *Musikalisches Lexikon* (Frankfurt am Main: August Hermann dem Jüngern, 1802), col. 979. Scholars of performance practice have continued to debate the meaning of "Andante" and "Molto Andante." See Clive Brown, *Classical and Romantic Performing Practice 1750–1900* (Oxford: Oxford University Press, 2004), 357–8. See also "Andante," in Don Michael Randel, ed., *The Harvard Dictionary of Music*, 4th ed. (Cambridge, MA: Harvard University Press), 43; and David Fallows, "Andante," in *Grove Music Online* (*Oxford Music Online*), http://www.oxfordmusiconline.com/subscriber/article/grove/music/00854 (accessed October 3, 2011).

16. Quoted and trans. in Thayer/Forbes, vol. 1, 555 (translation modified).

17. "How difficult it was to gather the unwritten melodies of the songs, scattered over the vast expanse of Russia, and to take them down in notation, often from the out-of-tune singing of unskilled singers, can easily be imagined by anyone; but no less difficulty was faced in how not to spoil the folk melody, yet to accompany it with a correct bass, which itself would be in folk character." Brown, *Collection of Russian Folk Songs*, 82.

18. Razumovsky's father, Kirill Grigorievich (1728–1803), and uncle, Aleksey Grigorievich (1709–71), had gained fame, wealth, and political importance as singers at the Russian court and as favorites of the Empresses Elizabeth Petrovna and Catherine II. Kirill maintained his own private chamber ensemble of forty Russian and foreign singers, "the likes of which could not be equaled by any other private person in Russia" (dergleichen noch bey keiner Privat-Person in Rußland

Therefore, the claim that Beethoven misrepresented the folksong by setting it as an Allegro is far from clear-cut. In any case, the adaptation of folksongs—whatever their origin or nationality—to the context of European art music often, perhaps necessarily, implied changes to the source material. Indeed, the measure of a successful folksong adaptation traditionally had less to do with the preservation of the folksong's original character than with the degree to which it was "artfully" reworked into the new context.[19] One of the goals of the LPC's editors was to present this collection of Russian folksongs in such a manner that the songs could live on not merely within the Russian tradition, but also within the tradition of European art music, through precisely such artful cultivation: "One would hope that this collection will serve as a rich source for the musically gifted and for opera composers, who, making use not only of the motives but also of the strangeness itself of certain Russian songs, will afford by means of their gracious art new pleasures to the ear and new delights to music lovers."[20] From this perspective, Beethoven's adaptation of "Ah, Whether It's My Luck, Such Luck" was in keeping with the spirit in which this collection and others like it were compiled.

RUSSIAN FOLKSONG AND LEARNED STYLE IN THE FINALE
OF OPUS 59, NO. I

Nonetheless, the finale of Opus 59, no. 1 has little in common with contemporary folksong arrangements, even those of a more sophisticated bent.[21] To be sure, there were precedents for a full-blown instrumental finale based on a folksong or popular tune: the finales of Haydn's Symphonies nos. 103 and 104, to take two well-known examples, are both said to be based on Croatian folksongs. Beethoven had employed a folk idiom—if not a specific folksong—in

zu finden gewesen war). Stählin, "[Fortsetzung der] Nachrichten von der Musik in Rußland," *Musikalische Nachrichten und Anmerkungen* 4, no. 23 (June 4): 175.

19. Stählin, for instance, praised the Italian composer Domenico Dall'Oglio for the way he reworked the Russian folksongs in his *Sinfonia alla Russa* (c. 1766–7): "Namely, he selected several of the most common folk tunes or country songs, and worked them as themes into an Allegro, Andante and Presto, after the best Italian taste." (Er hatte nähmlich etliche der gemeinsten Landsmelodien oder Baurenlieder erwählt, und sie mit immer vorkommenden Passagen derselben, nach bestem italiänischen Geschmack, in einem Allegro, Andante und Presto ausgeführt.) A pair of sonatas by Madonis on Ukrainian themes, as well as contredanses on Russian melodies and an "Italian-Russian ballet" by Fusano (Stählin, "Nachrichten," 4, no. 22 [May 28]: 173) further highlight the fashion for "artful" adaptations of Russian music to suit existing European genres, forms, and styles. This attitude would continue to gain traction throughout the nineteenth and early twentieth centuries, culminating in the ideal (most often associated with Bartók) of folk music's "sublimation" into art music.

20. Brown, *Collection of Russian Folk Songs*, 82.

21. Beethoven had already written a number of variation sets on popular or folk tunes, including one for piano on a Russian folksong (WoO 71, composed 1797). The melody, popularized in Vienna by Wranitzky's ballet *Das Waldmädchen* (1796), also appears in the LPC. See Appendix 3.1.

the finale of the Triple Concerto, marked "alla polacca" (in the Polish style). The finale of the *Eroica* Symphony also makes extensive use of a "borrowed" tune (though not necessarily a folklike one)—a lively contredanse from Beethoven's own *Prometheus* ballet. Hence, Beethoven was already well acquainted with the effect of evoking a familiar melody or style at the close of a large-scale work, a strategy that would continue to serve him well throughout his career.[22]

As in the Triple Concerto (and later the Violin Concerto and *Pastoral* Symphony), the finale of Opus 59, no. 1 emerges directly out of the previous movement, creating a run-on movement pair. The third and fourth movements are linked by a cadenza-like passage culminating on a lengthy trill in the first violin part. The linkage creates a sense of expectancy, placing dramatic significance on what follows, the Russian folksong played by—surprisingly—the cello. As is well known, this unusual opening "rhymes" with that of the first movement, the opening theme of which also occurs in the cello and uses the same ambitus of c to f. By foregrounding the folksong's initial appearance in this way, Beethoven not only reminds listeners and performers of the quartet's opening bars but also creates the impression that the Russian tune (presented here in F major/D minor) dispels the darkness of the preceding *Adagio molto e mesto*, a weighty F-minor lament for which the finale is the F-major foil. (He would later pursue a similar tonal and expressive strategy in the *Pastoral* Symphony, the F-minor storm movement of which leads directly into an F-major song of thanksgiving.)

But the finale of Opus 59, no. 1 differs from its counterparts in the Triple Concerto, Violin Concerto, and *Pastoral* Symphony. Though by no means a fugal movement, it is a contrapuntal tour de force, a spirited demonstration of the art of *ingenio*. Indeed, Beethoven seems deliberately to obviate the folk idiom implied by the finale's source material in favor of a conspicuously high-brow approach. The aesthetic implications of this stylistic entanglement require unpacking; I shall begin by examining several of the most distinctive moments in detail.

Beethoven's learned approach to the *thème russe* is already apparent within the first twenty bars (see Example 3.2). The finale opens with the Russian tune in the cello against a countermelody in the first violin. In measure 8, after the tune has reached its final note, it begins again as the cello descends from d to c. Rapid diminutions in the inner parts lead into a second statement of the theme in measures 9–16. Here, Beethoven places the melody in the first violin

22. He would further pursue this strategy in a number of works, including the Violin Concerto (1806) and *Pastoral* Symphony (1808), both of which culminate in finales based on folklike themes. The Choral Fantasy (1808) and Ninth Symphony (1824) also conclude with the celebration (both instrumental and vocal) of elemental and nobly simple melodies, a phenomenon Nicholas Mathew has recently described as an "aggrandizement of the folk ideal." See Mathew, *Political Beethoven* (Cambridge: Cambridge University Press, 2013), chap. 4, esp. 156–67 and 172–3.

EXAMPLE 3.2. Beethoven, String Quartet No. 7 in F Major, Op. 59, no. 1, iv, mm. 1–19.

and the countermelody in the cello, inverting their relationship. When the melody again reaches completion in measure 16, the bass part cadences deceptively to the subdominant; a third statement of the Russian tune ensues, this time in canon between the viola and first violin, breaking off just before measure 22. This elaborate opening paragraph—all of which unfolds over a mere twenty seconds or so—forecasts that the movement will be neither an ordinary finale nor an ordinary folksong setting, but rather a movement in which opposing styles and registers coexist.

Perhaps the most striking example of such stylistic coexistence is found near the end of the movement, where the Russian theme is treated as both subject and countersubject of a fugato (see Example 3.3a–3.3c). By isolating two segments of the Russian theme (marked x and y in Example 3.3a), reversing them, and transposing the second segment down a minor third, Beethoven creates an independent theme that, unlike the original Russian theme, is tonally closed (shown in D minor as Example 3.3b). Not only this, the new theme functions vertically as well as horizontally, since each segment may be contrapuntally combined with the other. The brief fugato, immediately following a grand pause, explores these contrapuntal combinations while ratcheting up the rhetoric through its sudden shift to a *piano* dynamic, its turn to G minor (rather than the expected F major), and its overt sophistication (Example 3.3c). The passage—witty to be sure, but hardly parodistic in the pejorative sense—points up the disjunction between low and high registers through its conspicuously ingenious treatment of the Russian theme.

The finale's secondary theme (mm. 45–62) offers a parallel example of Beethoven's intricate approach (see Example 3.4a–3.4c). In the same way that he crafts new motives from fragments of the Russian tune, here he fashions a contrasting lyrical theme out of fragments of the Russian theme's countermelody (mm. 1–8, first violin). As in the case of the fugato, he isolates two segments of the countermelody (marked a and b in Example 3.4a), reverses them, and transposes one segment to create an independent melody (Example 3.4b). In this case, the new melody (minus the thirty-second-note embellishments) acts as the four-bar antecedent to a longer phrase. The phrase first appears in the major mode; when it appears in the minor mode, Beethoven ups the ante, placing it in free canon at the twenty-second (Example 3.4c).

In addition to these contrapuntal treatments, Beethoven quasi-systematically explores the different harmonic implications of the Russian tune.[23] In the

---

23. As Gelbart points out, Beethoven would go on to experiment with a variety of such methods in his harmonizations of modal tunes for George Thomson, often trying the strangest effects to maintain a sense of folk otherness while creating a coherent and fresh accompaniment. Matthew Gelbart, *The Invention of "Folk Music" and "Art Music": Emerging Categories from Ossian to Wagner* (Cambridge: Cambridge University Press, 2007), 208. For an excellent treatment of Beethoven's approach to modal melodies, see Nicole Biamonte, "Modality in Beethoven's Folk-song Settings," *Beethoven Forum* 13, no. 1 (Spring 2006): 28–63.

recapitulation, for instance, he presents the *thème russe* in an unexpected light (see Example 3.5a). After a stepwise sequence descending from D minor through C minor to B-flat major, the tune begins to emerge from the inner parts in measure 177. The melody itself appears two measures later in the first violin, but here it has been altered to work in B-flat, the subdominant key. Tonic harmony remains absent until the tune's third measure, where a new counter-melody appears in the cello. The lack of dominant preparation and the subtle transformation of the folksong initially obscure the sense of thematic return. But the rise and fall of the melody soon give the game away: the moment is both a return and a metamorphosis.[24] The same holds for the final appearance of the Russian melody in the coda, with its "juicy" chromaticism (Example 3.5b).[25] Here, in the new tempo (Adagio ma non troppo), Beethoven offers a further reharmonization, this time beginning over a tonic pedal. Hymnlike in character, the passage trails off after about five bars, *perdendosi*, before the closing flourish. Far from mocking the theme, this recomposition offers a newly transfigured glimpse of it, one that sets into relief the rhythmic intensity and dense contrapuntal work from earlier in the coda.

Clearly, Beethoven has dressed up the *thème russe* and taken it into town. To this extent, Oulibicheff's caricature of it as a poor serf in expensive raiment may not be so far off the mark. But to interpret the finale as an exercise in erudition for its own sake (or as an exercise in German cultural hegemony) is to miss the larger point. By using the Russian folksong as the basis for an extended

EXAMPLE 3.3. Derivation of fugato theme from *Thème russe* (mm. 267–84).

a. *Thème russe* (mm. 1–8)

b. Fugato theme (mm. 267–70, transposed for ease of comparison)

c. Fugato (mm. 266–84), showing contrapuntal combinations of x and y

24. As Kerman observes, "Altering one of the notes, Beethoven now wants us to hear the modal melody—which is really in D Minor, which he has previously always pressed into F—as beginning in a third tonality, B-flat" (*Beethoven Quartets*, 113–14). Alternatively, it might be suggested that the substitution of E-flat for E in m. 179 indicates a modal reinterpretation of the Russian theme (in Phrygian rather than the expected Aeolian).

25. Taruskin, *On Russian Music*, 347.

EXAMPLE 3.3. (CONT.)

(c)

finale in the learned style, Beethoven explores fruitful incongruities between low and high registers while making a point of emphasizing the Russian theme's preeminence. In this regard, one might read this movement in much the same way that Maynard Solomon reads Beethoven's "Diabelli" Variations. As Solomon explains, "by virtue of its ordinariness, not to be mistaken for triviality," Diabelli's lowbrow waltz tune is especially "suited to unpacking issues of firstness and lastness and their interchangeability."[26] The "vernacular beginning" leads not only to "variation and metamorphosis" but also (and more importantly) to "transvaluation and reversal."[27] In the Variations, Beethoven uses "an image drawn from the German vernacular as a point of departure for a metaphysical exploration."[28] While the means of expression are different in the finale, the underlying concept is similar: Beethoven begins with a folk melody, constructs an elaborate movement using it as the compositional cornerstone, and then breaks down the façade (in the coda) to reveal the simple melody in all its hitherto unexpected significance. The Russian folksong is literally transported from low (in the cello) to high (in the first violin's upper reaches) over the course of the finale, its "register" thereby elevated in both senses of the term.[29] The stratospheric final statement, Adagio ma non troppo, might be

EXAMPLE 3.4. Derivation of secondary theme from *Thème russe* countermelody (mm. 45–61).

a. *Thème russe* countermelody, mm. 1–8

b. New four-bar antecedent phrase

c. Secondary theme (mm. 45–61), in both major- and minor-mode versions; Beethoven places the latter in free canon

26. Maynard Solomon, "The End of a Beginning: the 'Diabelli' Variations," in *Late Beethoven: Music, Thought, Imagination* (Berkeley: University of California Press, 2003), 11–26.

27. Ibid., 21.

28. Ibid., 20.

29. On the structural function of register (in the sense of pitch) throughout the movement, see Malcolm Miller, "Peak Experience: High Register and Structure in the 'Razumovsky' Quartets, Op. 59," in William Kinderman, ed., *The String Quartets of Beethoven* (Urbana: University of Illinois Press, 2006), 60–88, 70.

EXAMPLE 3.4. (CONT.)

EXAMPLE 3.5. Reharmonizations of *Thème russe* in Recapitulation and Coda.

a. Recapitulation, showing newly harmonized *Thème russe*, beginning and ending on subdominant, with E-flat (modal?) melodic alteration

b. Coda, showing final iteration of *Thème russe*, now in the tonic key and fading to **ppp**

understood as the goal and fulfillment of the entire movement, perhaps even of the entire quartet.[30] At the same time, this moment marks the final waypoint in the Russian tune's journey, one marked by major structural junctures in the finale. The dominant-anchored statement in the exposition, with its lengthy trill, creates a strong sense of anticipation; the subdominant-tinged statement in the recapitulation provides a sense of respite; and the tonic-anchored statement in the coda stabilizes, marks an arrival home.[31] The galloping tonic flourish, Presto, acts as a paratactic gesture of conclusion, closing the curtain on this journey and on the quartet as a whole.

Ultimately, it is impossible to know whether or to what extent Beethoven—who neither spoke nor read Russian himself—took into account the text of "Ah, Whether It's My Luck, Such Luck." To be sure, the movement's playful juxtapositions of high and low seem to depend less on the folksong's original character than on its status as emblematic of a generic folk type. But one need not discount the possibility that Beethoven had a more specific interpretation in mind. One might even consider the notion that the folksong text finds its realization not in the finale per se, but in the final pair of movements. The F-major finale emerges out of one of Beethoven's most emotionally charged lament movements, the F-minor *Adagio molto e mesto*. The text of "Ah, Whether It's My Luck, Such Luck" describes a soldier lamenting his long years of service to the Tsar, which has caused him to grow old far away from his family and friends (a topic that would surely have appealed to Razumovsky). One wonders if perhaps Beethoven's reading of the text suggested to him the notion of pairing a lament of his own design with a finale based on the Russian tune. In any case, the finale need not be dismissed on the grounds that it complicates or even contradicts the original character of the tune. Indeed, it is precisely by recontextualizing the tune that Beethoven creates the sense of playfulness and ingenuity on which the movement turns.

30. Lockwood has suggested that Beethoven's decision to use the Russian folksong as the basis for the finale may have been the "compositional starting point" for the entire quartet, as was the case with the contredanse tune in the finale of the *Eroica*. As he notes, the theme has "strong intervallic relationships" to the first themes of movements 1 and 3 (*Beethoven: The Music and the Life* [New York: Norton, 2003], 318).

31. This process recalls the treatment of the first movement's main theme. First presented in the cello in an unstable configuration (under the pulsating third and fifth of the tonic triad), the theme undergoes several transformations (including a transposition to the subdominant as a part of a sequence, beginning in m. 111), culminating in a final presentation in the first violin over a tonic pedal (beginning in m. 348). As Greene suggests, until the coda, the theme of the first movement is essentially "ambiguous": "its melodic and rhythmic contours and the phrase structure they imply have been unequivocally theme-like, while the persistent six-four chords harmonizing it have made it relentlessly and, what is perhaps even more disturbing, uniformly unstable" (David B. Greene, *Temporal Processes in Beethoven's Music* [New York: Gordon & Breach, 1982], 88–9).

RUSSIAN FOLKSONG AND LEARNED STYLE IN THE TRIO
OF OPUS 59, NO. 2

Beethoven further explored the expressive interplay of folksong and learned style in the third movement of Opus 59, no. 2. The movement's trio is based on the fortune-telling song turned Tsarist hymn of praise "Uzh kak slava Tebe Bozhe" (Just as there is glory to thee, O God on high)—a tune later used by Musorgsky, Rimsky-Korsakov, and Rachmaninov. Whether Beethoven knew of either the folksong's original function during Yuletide games or its later political connotations remains unknown.[32] In any case, he again chose to transform the folksong as it appears in the LPC, in this instance changing the meter and tempo from a 3/8 Andante to a 3/4 Allegretto, and the key from A major to E major. If the change from Andante to Allegretto implies only a slight increase in tempo, then Beethoven's metronome marking for the movement ($\bullet$. = 69) is on the faster side. Abraham concedes that "Beethoven has certainly not maltreated this dignified and virile tune as badly as Rimsky-Korsakov did in *The Tsar's Bride* where it is tortured into 2/4 time; but he has, to say the least, disguised it, like the theme of the finale of the F-major Quartet, by taking it too quickly; indeed his markings for the whole movement suggest that there was something wrong with his metronome."[33]

For most commentators, the tempo change has proven less of a problem than the treatment itself. Indeed, critics have tended to read the quasi-fugal setting of the "Slava" tune—with its occasionally crunchy counterpoint—in parodistic terms. Michael Steinberg calls attention to Beethoven's "dissonant roughhousing" with the folksong, and his "mocking sweeping of its shards out of the door" in the codetta.[34] Philip Radcliffe maintains that the tune, "originally a solemn hymn, is robbed of its ecclesiastical associations and made to take part in a lively fugue."[35] William Kinderman suggests that Beethoven "showed little regard for the stately character and moderate tempo of the preexisting theme. . . . The theme is stripped of its solemn, ecclesiastical associations and

---

32. On the early meanings of the "Slava" tune, see Richard Taruskin, *Musorgsky: Eight Essays and an Epilogue* (Princeton: Princeton University Press, 1993), 300–6.

33. Abraham, *Beethoven's Second-Period Quartets*, 37. Beethoven's metronome marking (dotted half note = 69) is brisk, though by no means unplayable; modern performers have tended to prefer a slower tempo for the movement. See Robert Martin, "The Quartets in Performance: A Player's Perspective," in Robert Winter and Robert Martin, eds., *The Beethoven Quartet Companion* (Berkeley: University of California Press, 1994), 111–41, 116–20. There is, of course, much controversy about the accuracy of Beethoven's tempo markings; see, for an overview, Anne-Louise Coldicott, "Performance Practice in Beethoven's Day," in Barry Cooper, ed., *The Beethoven Compendium: A Guide to Beethoven's Life and Music* (London: Thames & Hudson, 1991), 280–9, 282–3.

34. Michael Steinberg, "The Middle Quartets," in Winter and Martin, eds., *The Beethoven Quartet Companion*, 175–213, 187.

35. Radcliffe, *Beethoven's String Quartets*, 68.

treated in a parodistic fugal medley."[36] No critic has been more provocative than Kerman (quoted earlier), for whom the "fatuous entries" and "insane canons" seem to beat the Russian theme into submission.[37] All of these accounts make use of a common rhetoric: the Russian theme is "stripped," "robbed," "made to take part," "mocked," "pile-driven," "roughhoused"—in so many words, abused. Such language has in turn helped to foster speculations about Beethoven's attitude toward Russians in general.[38]

These parodistic interpretations depend on the notion that the trio represents a fugue gone awry. To be sure, the trio draws on the vocabulary of fugue in its use of answers at the fifth, canonic imitation, and even stretto. However, as Warren Kirkendale has noted, "one barely notices the fugal writing . . . the [fugal elements] cannot disguise the general homophonic character of the movement."[39] In its structure, the trio also deviates from standard fugal practice: it has no episodes and no development, insofar as modulations are eschewed in favor of a tug-of-war between tonic and dominant keys.[40] Rather, its form encompasses four distinct treatments of the *thème russe*, each of which may be said to constitute an independent fugal exposition (with successive entries of the tune in all four parts). In this sense, the form is perhaps best described as a set of cantus firmus variations in the fugal style (see Table 3.1).[41]

Following the first presentation of the scherzo—a suave, minor-mode affair replete with syncopation—Beethoven presents the *thème russe* in the parallel major with continuous triplet accompaniment. As the variations progress, each elided with the next, the counterpoint becomes more rigorous. The surface rhythm decelerates from triplets (mm. 52–79), to eighth notes (mm. 80–105), to quarter notes (mm. 106–end). The articulation and dynamics also create an impression of increasing rigidity as they progress from *legato* and *piano*, to *staccato* and *piano*, to *staccato* and *forte*, and eventually to *staccato* and *fortissimo* with accented offbeats. The trio reaches its dynamic and registral climax in the third variation, measures 114–15, where the theme is treated canonically. Following this variation, the dynamic decreases to *piano*, and the articulation softens to *legato*. The canons give way to a stretto, which itself dissolves into a final statement of the Russian tune, more lyrical in character. This last full statement

36. Kinderman, *Beethoven*, 133–5.

37. Kerman, *Beethoven Quartets*, 130.

38. Taruskin goes so far as to suggest that Beethoven may have harbored "condescension toward peasants or Slavs"; *On Russian Music*, 347.

39. Warren Kirkendale, *Fugue and Fugato in Rococo and Classical Chamber Music*, trans. Warren Kirkendale and Margaret Bent (Durham, NC: Duke University Press, 1979), 235.

40. Here, and in the next sentence, I use the terms "episode," "development," and "exposition" in the sense used by Marpurg in "Selections from *Abhandlung von der Fuge*," trans. Alfred Mann in Alfred Mann, ed., *The Study of Fugue* (New York: Dover, 1987), 142–212, 176ff.

41. As James Webster notes, the trio's form is a "direct descendant" of the trio to Haydn's Opus 76, no. 6; "Traditional Elements in Beethoven's Middle-Period String Quartets," in Robert Winter

TABLE 3.1 Diagram of Beethoven, Op. 59, no. 2, iii, trio.

Fugal exposition	Measures	Entries	Harmony	Dynamic level	Variation of Thème russe
1	52–58	viola	I	p	
	58–64	violin 2	V	p	
	64–70	cello	I	p	
	70–80	violin 1	V	p	
2	80–86	viola	I	p	
	86–92	violin 2	V	p	
	92–98	cello	I	p cresc	
	98–104 (alt.)	violin 1	V	f	
3 (canons)	★104–110	cello	I	ff	
	★★106–112	viola	I	ff	
	★★★110–116	violin 2	I	ff	
	★★★★112–118	violin 1	I	ff	
4 (stretto)	★116–117 (inc.)	viola	I	p	
	★★117–118 (inc.)	cello	I	p	
	★★★118–124	violin 1	I	p	
	★★★★119 (inc.)	violin 2	I	p	
Codetta	124–135	—	I–i	p–pp	

of the Russian theme initiates the brief transition back into the minor-mode scherzo, *pianissimo*.

Beethoven marks the treatment of the *thème russe* in canon (mm. 104–16) as the high point of the trio. Yet these thirteen bars, as many commentators have observed, are dissonant, disordered, and even abrasive, not at all what one would expect from a passage in the strict contrapuntal style. To be sure, Beethoven follows the rules here; yet disruptive sforzandi as well as dissonant appoggiaturas and passing tones result in a highly idiosyncratic counterpoint, one without precedent in Beethoven's oeuvre. Is this highbrow German mockery of peasants and Russians or are there other explanations possible here?

To answer this question, it is helpful to turn to Mozart, who had himself embraced such jarringly dissonant counterpoint in a number of works. The finale of the "Jupiter" Symphony, No. 41, based on the famous four-note Fux cantus firmus, offers one salient example. As Elaine Sisman has demonstrated, the finale seems to dramatize a rhetorical confrontation between learned and galant elements, culminating in the fugal presentation in the coda of nearly all of the themes presented in the movement. In the recapitulation, however, Mozart presents the Fuxian theme in an especially bold and unusual manner (see Example 3.6). Rather than following the theme's initial statement with a celebratory tutti repetition (as in the exposition), Mozart here presents a new passage based on the four-note theme, this time built on a scalar ascent and descent by whole tone (beginning first on C, then on D, then on E, and then back down through D to C). He immerses this peculiar sequence in a dissonant contrapuntal web, making reference to some of the procedures employed elsewhere but treating them in a new and arresting way. Sisman characterizes the passage as an instance of the mathematical sublime, noting that "the dissonances seem to increase exponentially to the point of not being aurally comprehensible. . . . The passage is disordered and obscure, massive and repetitious (all terms that appear in discussions of the sublime)."[42] Indeed, one has the impression that Mozart means to push the limits of counterpoint here, creating, through ingeniously placed appoggiaturas and suspensions, sonorities that exceed tonality's traditional bounds. At the same time, the passage might be heard as a send-up of the learned style—the rhetoric is transcendent but overwrought, sublime but exaggerated. The return of a galant-style idiom in measure 254 seems an almost necessary respite, a welcome rejoinder to such a forcefully demonstrated claim.

There may indeed be an element of the sublime in Beethoven's dissonant canons—despite the obvious difference in scale between symphony and string

and Bruce Carr, eds., *Beethoven, Performers, and Critics: The International Beethoven Congress, Detroit, 1977* (Detroit: Wayne State University Press, 1980), 94–133, 120.

42. Elaine Sisman, *Mozart: The "Jupiter" Symphony, No. 41 in C Major, K. 551*, Cambridge Music Handbooks (Cambridge: Cambridge University Press, 1993), 76–7.

EXAMPLE 3.6. Mozart, Symphony No. 41 in C Major ("Jupiter"), K. 551, iv, mm. 233–55.

EXAMPLE 3.6. (CONT.)

EXAMPLE 3.6. (CONT.)

quartet. The striving for registral and dynamic heights, the repetition, the massive sound, the disunity, all of these seem to reach toward, even dramatize, the unattainable. But, as in the Mozart example, one also has the sense that this unorthodox use of counterpoint is somehow self-aware. From this perspective, there is indeed a strong feeling of irony in Beethoven's dissonant canons, though not necessarily in the way critics have tended to suggest. Indeed, the sense of irony here is less pejorative than self-reflexive, a notion of irony that Mark Evan Bonds has explored with respect to Haydn's instrumental music. As he explains, Haydn's music, like the prose of Laurence Sterne, often calls attention to its own structural rhetoric. In so doing, it "takes irony beyond its traditional (and relatively local) status as a rhetorical trope to embrace a wider aesthetic in which artworks overtly call attention to their own techniques of artifice."[43] Such an approach "establishes a quality of aesthetic distance between the artist and his work, which in turn calls into question the basic premises of the traditional relationship between the artist, his work, and his audience."[44] By calling attention to its own artifice, this kind of irony engages the reflexive capacity of the listener: what unfolds at the musical level becomes subject to mediation—and even critique—at a philosophical level.[45] With its progressive emphasis on contrapuntal procedures, culminating in the canons, the trio thus invites the listener to contemplate the disjunction between the naïveté of the folksong and the artificiality of the surrounding context.

From this perspective, the humor of the trio might be understood to lie in its overdetermination to "elevate" the folksong through counterpoint. The issue is not so much that the Russian theme fails to meet the criteria of strict counterpoint, but rather that the criteria themselves become outrageous. The increasingly rigid counterpoint over the course of the trio, at first polite and urbane, borders on the farcical during the canons: seriousness, carried to extreme, threatens to become its exact opposite. At the same time, as in the Mozart example, humor seems to court the sublime—as so often in Beethoven's music, the two are not easily disentangled. (One is reminded of Anton Schindler's paradoxical description of the "Muss es sein?"/"Es muss sein!" motif in Opus 135 as "the master's serious joke, or joking seriousness.")[46]

43. Mark Evan Bonds, "Haydn, Laurence Sterne, and the Origins of Musical Irony," *Journal of the American Musicological Society* 44, no. 1 (Spring 1991): 57–91, 68.

44. Ibid.

45. As Rey M. Longyear notes, this kind of irony parallels "Romantic irony" as articulated by Beethoven's literary contemporaries Friedrich Schlegel and Ludwig Tieck. Beethoven's frequent deliberate highlighting of contrapuntal artifice, as he points out, is analogous to Tieck's "purposely making the audience aware of the machinery of stage effects" ("Beethoven and Romantic Irony," *Musical Quarterly* 56, no. 4 [October 1970]: 647–64, 656).

46. Anton Felix Schindler, *Beethoven as I Knew Him*, trans. Constance S. Jolly, ed. Donald W. MacArdle (Mineola, NY: Dover, 1996), 337. In its merging of the comical and the sublime, the trio

By treating the Russian melody as the unlikely basis for a pair of strict canons, Beethoven is able to call attention to the artifice of counterpoint; in so doing, he opens up new opportunities for the "transvaluation and reversal" of high and low registers. The intermezzo-like trio hence acts as a complement to the longer and weightier finale of Opus 59, no. 1, further exploring the range of expressive possibilities arising from stylistic incongruity. In both movements, the highlighting of artifice brings irony to the fore; however, it is an irony directed not toward the folksongs but rather toward the compositional fabric that encompasses them—this is music about different *kinds* of music, the individual aesthetic premises of which are knowingly called into question and occasionally subjected to radical reversal.

SYNTHESIS VERSUS COSMOPOLITANISM: CULTIVATING RUSSIAN MUSIC

As Walter Salmen has observed, Beethoven's treatments of the two Russian themes from the LPC—while firmly grounded in a tradition of artworks based on popular melodies—go beyond what would have been expected in music of this kind.[47] To be sure, Haydn's finales on folk tunes (or in folklike styles) offered significant models. For inspiration and instruction, Beethoven could also have drawn on the vast number of contemporary instrumental works—variation sets, symphonies, concertos, and other kinds of music—based on Russian and other popular melodies.[48] Yet, as Salmen points out, Beethoven's multifaceted and multilayered settings of the *thèmes russes* depart drastically from the aesthetic of the "episodic, casual quoting of pleasant folksongs" that was the norm.[49] In their persistent emphasis on contrapuntal and other such procedures (fragmentation, reharmonization, rhythmic reinterpretation, etc.), they also differ from comparable pieces by Haydn and Mozart (and even Beethoven himself), pieces that tend to wear their learning more lightly.[50]

also looks forward to the *Grosse Fuge*, a work Stephen Husarik has linked to the aesthetics of the grotesque: "Musical Direction and the Wedge in Beethoven's High Comedy, *Grosse Fuge* Op. 133," *Musical Times* 153, no. 1920 (Autumn 2012): 53–66.

47. Walter Salmen, "Zur Gestaltung der 'Thèmes russes' in Beethovens Opus 59," in Ludwig Finscher and Christoph-Hellmut Mahling, eds., *Festschrift für Walter Wiora zum 30. Dezember 1966* (Kassel: Bärenreiter, 1967), 397–404.

48. For a list of contemporary compositions on Russian themes, see ibid., 399, and note 10.

49. "In den Quartetten op. 59 intendierte [Beethoven] aber mehr als dieses nur episodenhaft beiläufige Zitieren von netten Volksweisen, denn diese werden für mehrschichtige komplizierte Kunstwerke als neu hinzugewonnene Elemente total adaptiert." Ibid., 400.

50. An interesting comparison in this regard is the virtuosic *moto perpetuo* finale of Haydn's Opus 64, no. 5 (1790). Though less varied in its repertoire of learned techniques, it also makes a point of combining folklike "low" material with sublime but exaggerated "high" counterpoint.

To an extent, this high-minded approach to the Russian tunes can be viewed as an example of the new "synthetic" concept of art championed by philosophers such as Johann Gottfried Herder and Friedrich Schiller. Writing in 1779, Herder sought to complicate the traditional binary opposition between nature (as represented by the *Volkslied*—a term that typically referred to song texts rather than the melodies themselves) and art (as represented by art song). He proposed that while the *Volkslied* still represented nature, it was no longer the opposite of art song but rather the "[raw] 'material' for poetic 'art'" (*Materialien zur Dichtkunst*).[51] As Matthew Gelbart has emphasized, this claim represents a shift in the very meaning of "art": "Thus—while the word 'art' occasionally remains in its older usage (meaning artifice, as in Tytler, Gregory, Campbell, and the earlier Herder, etc.)—Herder's later writing also presents a new 'art,' something that is never derogatory. Rather, it is the opposite: a mystical, organic synthesis of natural genius with the old art-as-rules."[52] In this new conception, the artist's role was literally to "cultivate" the *Volkslied* through his individual genius, the object of which cultivation was a "higher" poetic or musical product.

Underlying this view, of course, is the notion that the *Volkslied*—and by extension, the folksong—is a primitive Other in need of cultivation. This idea cuts both ways. On one hand, it could border on cultural imperialism, particularly when the folk music of far-off nations was involved. David Gramit has detailed the ways in which an Orientalist discourse—the counterpart to Western expansionism—pervades the discussions of Indian and Chinese music in German periodicals like the *Allgemeine musikalische Zeitung*. As he explains, cultivation not only represented a form of cultural control, it also "proved a useful standard for defining a musical world in which serious music—the music whose existence increasingly centered on the institution of the concert—occupied the highest level of a hierarchy."[53] On the other hand (and somewhat paradoxically), philosophers from Rousseau and Herder to Kant and Schiller idealized the musics of various "primitive" cultures as reflecting humanity in a kind of prelapsarian state.[54] In his treatise *On Naive and Sentimental Poetry* (1795–6), for instance, Schiller described the forms of nature, from "plants, minerals, animals, and landscapes" to "human nature in children, in the customs of country folk, and . . . the primitive world" as "representations of our highest

51. Gelbart, *Invention of "Folk Music" and "Art Music,"* 198.

52. Ibid., 199.

53. David Gramit, *Cultivating Music: The Aspirations, Interests, and Limits of German Musical Culture, 1770–1848* (Berkeley: University of California Press, 2002), 36–7.

54. The connection in Rousseau and Herder between "primitive" musics and the ideals of "nature" and "folk" also underscores Enlightenment preoccupations about the construction of racial difference; Ronald Radano and Philip V. Bohlman, *Music and the Racial Imagination* (Chicago: University of Chicago Press, 2000), 13–16.

fulfilment in the ideal, thus evoking in us a sublime tenderness."[55] The modern poet, he argued, should seek to recover or reflect on this "natural" state through the playful synthesis of sense and reason, naive and sentimental modes.[56]

Both attitudes are present in the German reception of Russian folksong at least as early as the publication of the LPC in 1790. Johann Nikolaus Forkel, who had already published a series of articles on the music of other cultures (including China and Ancient Egypt), praised the anthology precisely because it seemed to offer a tantalizing window into a lost past. According to Forkel (in correspondence with Pratsch), some of the melodies were allegedly over a thousand years old, making them the oldest then known to Europeans.[57] Hence, the LPC was much more than a collection of Russian national songs; it was a cultural treasure of transnational value, the representation of European civilization in embryo. Travelers bold enough to brave the vast Russian countryside also sent back reports that its music was somehow frozen in time. In a series of "Letters on the Present State of Music in Russia" published in 1802, the correspondent for the *AmZ* called Russia one of the "few singing nations on God's earth."[58] Russia was thus figured as a modern embodiment of the arcadian society propounded by Rousseau, Schiller, and others. At the same time, its folksong was considered exotic, primitive, and inferior. C. F. D. Schubart called it "very wild and rough," comparing it to "the cries of certain birds, the pattern and vocalization of which are very similar to our wild ducks."[59] To cultivate Russian folksong, then, was to cultivate a *bon sauvage*.

55. Friedrich Schiller, "On Naive and Sentimental Poetry," trans. Julius A. Elias, in H. B. Nisbet, ed., *German Aesthetic and Literary Criticism*, vol. 3, *Winckelmann, Lessing, Hamann, Herder, Schiller and Goethe* (Cambridge: Cambridge University Press, 1985), 177–232, 180–1.

56. As Gelbart puts it, "Rather than pitting the sentimental directly against the naïve, Schiller claimed that naïve nature was opposed to reflective *artifice*; and by citing Kant's 'categories' he proposed that the 'sentimental' was actually a reconciliation of these two in a perfected form of poetry, rather than a simple opposite of the naïve" (*Invention of "Folk Music" and "Art Music,"* 201). See Peter Szondi, "Das Naïve ist das Sentimentalische: Zur Begriffsdialektik in Schillers Abhandlung," *Euphorion* 66 (1972): 174–206, from which Gelbart here draws. For discussions of Beethoven's music in reference to Schiller's naive and sentimental modes, see Thomas Sipe, *Beethoven, Eroica Symphony*, Cambridge Music Handbooks (Cambridge: Cambridge University Press, 1998), beginning 86; and Stephen Rumph, *Beethoven after Napoleon: Political Romanticism in the Late Works*, California Studies in 19th-Century Music 14 (Berkeley: University of California Press, 2004), 58–65.

57. Johann Nikolaus Forkel, *Allgemeine Litteratur der Musik* (Leipzig: Schwickert, 1792), x.

58. "Die russische Nation gehört überhaupt zu den wenigen singenden Nationen auf Gottes Erdboden." "Briefe über den jetzigen Zustand der Musik in Russland. Erster Brief," *Allgemeine musikalische Zeitung* 4, no. 21 (February 17, 1802): cols. 346–50, and no. 22 (February 24, 1802): col. 353. This letter is the first in a series of articles on Russian music to appear in the *Allgemeine musikalische Zeitung* between 1802 and 1805, including two further "Briefe" (a continuation on February 24 and another letter on March 3, 1802); and a report, "Darstellung des gegenwärtigen Zustandes der Musik in Russland, vornämlich in St. Petersburg," *Allgemeine musikalische Zeitung* 8, no. 5 (October 30, 1805).

59. "Die russische Nationalmusik hat, wie man leicht erachten kann, sehr viel Wildes und Rauhes. Man bemerkt es in ihren meisten Volksliedern, dass sie das Geschrey gewisser Vögel nachahmen, die

But to view Russian folksong merely as an idealized Other ripe for European cultivation is to ignore its significance as a political resource. For while Russian folksong connoted "ancient Rus," it also represented modern Russia, a nation at pains to establish itself as a European superpower. Indeed, the Russian correspondent for the *AmZ* was well aware of the political significance of an emerging Russian folksong corpus, reminding his German readers that "Only nations in the true sense of the word have folksongs [*Nationalgesänge*] and something national in their musical taste."[60] Russia, precisely because it laid claim to an authentic folk music of its own, could thus be considered a nation "in the true sense of the word," a notion that had important consequences in an era when the question of alliances weighed heavily on the minds of all Europeans.

Therefore, the inclusion of Russian folksongs in Opus 59—a work dedicated to the Russian ambassador to Austria—needs to be understood not just as an effort to merge opposing styles or registers but also as a social gesture and, in effect, a political act. At the center of both gesture and act, of course, is Opus 59's dedicatee. And yet, Count Razumovsky's position as a cultural, political, and musical intermediary between Austria and Russia has not been fully appreciated. In what follows, I shall reexamine Razumovsky's persona through the lens of the "European Russian," with a view toward further elaborating the contemporary meanings—private and public—of the Russian folksong settings in Opus 59.

ANDREY RAZUMOVSKY: COSMOPOLITE, DIPLOMAT, MUSICIAN

As cultural historian Orlando Figes has emphasized, Russians living in Europe around 1800 typically had a split identity: "On one level [the European Russian] was conscious of acting out his life according to prescribed European conventions; yet on another plane his inner life was swayed by Russian customs and sensibilities."[61] Strangers in a strange land, European Russians spent disproportionate amounts of time and treasure on their appearance, manners, and self-fashioning. It is no surprise that they were frequently caricatured in visual art, literature, and theater. A contemporary print, *Le Russe prenant une Leçon de Grace à Paris* (Paris, 1815), for instance, depicts a Russian officer receiving a lesson in deportment from a Parisian noblewoman (Figure 3.1). Standing

<hr>

in Form und Stimme viel Aehnliches mit unsern wilden Aenten haben." Christian Friedrich Daniel Schubart, *Ideen zu einer Ästhetik der Tonkunst* (Vienna: J.V. Degen, 1806), 245.

60. "Nur Nationen im eigentlichen Verstande haben Nationalgesänge und etwas Nationales in ihrem Geschmack an Musik." "Briefe über den jetzigen Zustand der Musik in Russland," *Allgemeine musikalische Zeitung* 4, no. 21 (February 17, 1802): col. 350.

61. Orlando Figes, *Natasha's Dance: A Cultural History of Russia* (New York: Metropolitan Books, 2002), 44.

Le Russe prenant une Leçon de Grace à Paris.

FIGURE 3.1. *Le Russe prenant une Leçon de Grace à Paris.* Paris: Paul André Basset, 1815. Used by permission of the Anne S. K. Brown Military Collection, Brown University Library.

before a mirror in a dancer's pose, the young man gazes over his right shoulder as the woman behind him holds a second mirror to his back. The positioning of the two mirrors creates a mirror tunnel, in which the officer's image (invisible to the viewer) is endlessly reflected—an acknowledgment of Russia's self-conscious presence on the European stage. Opposite the noblewoman sits a second soldier in traditional Cossack garb; spoon in mouth, he looks away, uninterested in the preening display. The dog, meanwhile, mimics his master's pose by standing upright on hind legs, a reminder of the absurdity of training a Russian to behave like a European.[62]

The clever positioning of the two mirrors in the print suggests the self-awareness that was, by 1815, well embedded in the moral upbringing of Russian youth. Its roots lay in *The Honorable Mirror of Youth* (*Iunosti chestnoe zertsalo*, 1717),

62. While the seated figure looks like a servant at first glance, the uniform and arms behind the mirror are those of a Russian artilleryman. The wooden rammer, which the dog holds parallel to the officer's sword, and the sponge on the shelf further suggest that the officer is here accompanied by an artilleryman who has dressed "down" in traditional Russian attire (though still wearing his decorations), in contrast to his Frenchified superior.

a treatise originally written in German but translated into Russian by Peter the Great in an effort to instill Western manners in the Russian nobility.[63] The *Mirror* was a compendium of social graces and proper actions; as Catriona Kelly explains, "Readers were told to stand up straight, rather than 'lolling in the sun like a peasant'; not to interrupt; to be obedient and respectful to their parents; to avoid drunkenness, gaming, spiteful gossip, and fornication. In company . . . one should not belch, cough, eat greedily; swearing and staring at women in church were both to be avoided."[64] The tract also detailed the skills that young Russians would need to master in order to succeed in European society; chief among them were conversing in French and dancing the minuet.

Razumovsky was, by all accounts, the European Russian par excellence.[65] Within the span of a generation, his family had risen from Ukrainian cattle herders to the upper strata of the Russian nobility. The rapid ascent was thanks to Andrey's uncle Alexey, who charmed and morganatically married Tsarina Elizabeth. Through Alexey's influence, Andrey's father, Kirill, also achieved tremendous success, becoming President of the St. Petersburg Academy of Sciences at the age of eighteen—with an annual pension of three million rubles—and later Hetman of the Ukraine. In part, the brothers owed their astonishing rise to music. Alexey's talent as a church singer had gained him recognition from a passing Russian delegation, a chance encounter that resulted in an invitation to St. Petersburg and the boy's eventual admission into the choir of the imperial chapel (and shortly thereafter, into grand-duchess Elizabeth's "small court"). But it was Kirill, Andrey's father, who continued to foster the family's passion for music. He assembled a retinue of forty chamber singers deemed significant

63. The German source, *Liber aureus Erasmi Roterodamis de civilitate morum puerilium; das ist: Ein guldenes Buchlein,* trans. J. W. Pause and reworked by [James] Jacob Bruce (Hamburg, 1678), was itself an adaptation of a classic 1530 treatise by Erasmus of Rotterdam. See Lindsey Hughes, "'The Crown of Maidenly Honour and Virtue': Redefining Femininity in Peter I's Russia," in Wendy Rosslyn, ed., *Women and Gender in 18th-Century Russia* (Aldershot, UK, and Burlington, VT: Ashgate, 2003), 35–50, 48–9.

64. Catriona Kelly, *Refining Russia: Advice Literature, Polite Culture, and Gender from Catherine to Yeltsin* (Oxford: Oxford University Press, 2001), 33. There are numerous parallels between Russian and German self-fashioning during the long eighteenth century, in part because of the cross-cultural impact of *De civilitate morum puerilium* on the development of *civilité* as a concept. See Norbert Elias, *The Civilizing Process,* Vol. 1, *The History of Manners,* trans. Edmund Jephcott (New York: Urizen Books, 1978), 53–9.

65. Biographical accounts include Alexandre Wassiltchikow's extensive family history, *Les Razoumowski,* trans. Alexandre Brückner, 3 vols. (Halle: Tausch & Grosse, 1893–4); Maria Razumovsky, *Die Rasumovskys: Eine Familie am Zarenhof* (Cologne: Böhlau, 1998); J. M. P. McErlean, "Razumovskii, Andrei Kirillovich," in Joseph L. Wieczynski, ed., *The Modern Encyclopedia of Russian and Soviet History,* 60 vols. (Gulf Breeze, FL: Academic International Press, 1982), vol. 30, 210–14; Thayer/ Forbes, vol. 1, 400–2; and Theodor von Frimmel, *Beethoven-Handbuch,* 2 vols. (Leipzig: Breitkopf & Härtel, 1926), vol. 2, 51–4. See also Nadeschda Schukoff and Alexander Schukoff, *Russland in Wien* (Vienna: Österreichischer Rundfunk, 2006), a television documentary in which Maria Razumovsky discusses her family's rise to fame, and which includes some footage of the Razumovsky palace.

enough to receive mention in Jacob von Stählin's seminal account of music in eighteenth-century Russia.[66] The renowned ensemble included the talented Ukrainian singer Gavrila [Marcinkevich], famous for singing "the most difficult Italian operatic arias with the most sophisticated cadenzas and refined embellishments."[67] Its success even encouraged the Empress to order one of the earliest stagings of a full-scale opera in Russian, Francesco Araja's *Tsefal i Prokris* (Cephalus and Procris, 1755).[68]

Into this politically and musically significant family, Andrey was born in 1752. He had access to a thoroughly European education including a stint on an English man-of-war and extensive travels. An early portrait, by the celebrated Swedish painter Alexander Roslin, shows a young man thoroughly in step with modern European fashion, as befit his class and wealth (Figure 3.2). Like many in the foreign service, Andrey learned to play an instrument, the violin, and took an active role in the musical cultures of the locales in which he was stationed. After serving diplomatic posts in several European capitals (including Vienna from 1777 to 1779), he settled in Vienna in 1801, where he embarked on the construction of the magnificent palace that would become his home and the new seat of the Russian embassy (Figure 3.3).[69] With his inherited fortune, he filled its rooms with paintings by the great Dutch masters and newly commissioned sculptures by Antonio Canova. At his own expense, he had a bridge constructed over the Danube River canal to shorten the distance between his home and the Prater. As the lord of his sprawling palace and landscape garden, he became known by the sobriquet "Erzherzog Andreas" (Archduke Andrey). Famously, tragedy would befall him during the Congress of Vienna, when the "*French* heating system" malfunctioned and destroyed a large section of the palace (including many artworks and much of his renowned library).[70] By the time of his death in 1836, he was so much a fixture in Viennese life that his obituary declared: "Prince Razumovsky has effectively become a native of this imperial city."[71]

As Figes observes, European Russians often struggled to maintain a balance between their Russian upbringing and European acculturation, and

66. There is a series of articles by Jacob von Stählin, "Nachrichten von der Musik in Russland," in Johann Adam Hiller, ed., *Musikalische Nachrichten und Anmerkungen* (Leipzig, 1770). Kirill Razumovsky is mentioned in issue no. 23 (June 4): 175.

67. Marina Ritzarev, *Eighteenth-Century Russian Music* (Aldershot, UK: Ashgate, 2006), 53.

68. Ibid., 52–6.

69. For more on Razumovsky's palace and landscape garden, see Mark Ferraguto, "Representing Russia: Luxury and Diplomacy at the Razumovsky Palace in Vienna, 1803–1815," *Music and Letters* 97, no. 3 (August 2016): 383–408.

70. A vivid account of the fire is given in David King, *Vienna 1814: How the Conquerors of Napoleon Made Love, War, and Peace at the Congress of Vienna* (New York: Harmony Books, 2008), 191.

71. *Wiener Zeitung*, October 3, 1836. Quoted in Razumovsky, *Die Rasumovskys*, 296, note 13. Razumovsky was created Prince in 1815.

FIGURE 3.2. *Count Andrey Kyrillovich Razumovsky* (1776). Portrait by Alexander Roslin (Swedish 1718–93, worked throughout Europe 1745–93). Oil on canvas; 63.8 × 52.7 cm. Used by permission of the National Gallery of Victoria, Melbourne. Everard Studley Miller Bequest, 1962.

FIGURE 3.3. *Palais du Prince Rasoumovsky*. [Vienna]: Maria Geissler, [1812?]. Used by permission of the Ira F. Brilliant Center for Beethoven Studies, San José State University.

Razumovsky was no exception.[72] His official *entrée* into Viennese society in 1788—through his marriage to Princess Lichnowsky's sister, Countess Elisabeth von Thun-Hohenstein—offers a telling illustration. The marriage to von Thun—an Austrian and a Catholic—cemented his foothold in Viennese society but jeopardized his identity as a Russian. Upon learning of his son's intent to marry, the former Hetman of the Ukraine warned: "To enter into Austrian service, to forsake your fatherland, to become Austrian and cease to be Russian, to destroy your inheritance . . . all this is not merely difficult, but impossible and ruinous to your reputation; neither I, nor your family, can condone such a decision."[73] Kirill gradually consented to the marriage, but the stern warning tugged at a tension in Razumovsky's very being. To the Countess, he earlier lamented that he had "no fatherland," a thought that disturbed him greatly.[74]

Shifting cultural allegiances also marked the professional life of an ambassador, all the more so in the case of the Russian *corps diplomatique*. As a civil servant, Razumovsky was responsible for delicate and often complex negotiations between the imperial courts of Austria and Russia. After the disastrous Battle of Austerlitz in late 1805, he was charged with helping to establish a new coalition—made up of Russia, Austria, England, and hopefully Prussia—against Napoleon.[75] The difficult negotiations he pursued on behalf of Alexander I in the face of a stolid and often somnolent Austrian cabinet were intensified by his own personal animus toward Napoleon, which he expressed both privately and in the salons held at his home.[76] Despite his dedication to the Russian cause, his intimacy with the Viennese frequently raised suspicions.[77] Indeed, throughout

72. Figes, *Natasha's Dance*, 44–51.

73. Kirill Razumovsky to Andrey Razumovsky, n.d. [spring 1786]. Quoted in Wassiltchikow, *Les Razoumowski*, vol. 1, 231. Translated with reference to Razumovsky, *Die Rasumovskys*, 127.

74. Quoted in Razumovsky, *Die Rasumovskys*, 123. The remark provoked an impassioned response from the Countess; see her letter of November 1, 1785 (ibid.; original French in 277, note 9).

75. On the political and cultural implications of the Battle of Austerlitz in Vienna, see Ferraguto, "Beethoven's Fourth Symphony: Reception, Aesthetics, Performance History," 145–56.

76. Among the Razumovskys' regular guests at this time were three radical anti-Bonapartists, Friedrich von Gentz, Pozzo di Borgo, and Gustaf Armfeldt. Gentz recalls that in 1803, "Pozzo di Borgo was a member of the ladies circle [salon] of Countess Razumovsky, where the cream of good society assembled and Armfeldt, Pozzo and I formed a kind of political three-leaf clover" (Pozzo di Borgo war Mitglied des Damen-Zirkels bei der Gräfin Rasoumoffsky, wo sich die Crême der guten Gesellschaft versammelte, und Armfeldt, Pozzo und ich eine Art von politischem Kleeblatt bildeten") Friedrich von Gentz, *Tagebücher: Mit einem Vor- und Nachwort von K. A. Varnhagen von Ense* [Leipzig: F. A. Brockhaus, 1861], 36). Razumovsky dispatched the memoirs of Gentz and Pozzo to Prince Czartoryski with his enthusiastic recommendation.

77. Czartoryski complained that the Count's "intimate relations" "with various prominent personages at Vienna" often resulted in "inaccuracies" in his reports, stemming from his desire to remain on good terms with the Viennese government; Adam Czartoryski, *Memoirs of Prince Adam Czartoryski and His Correspondence with Alexander I: With Documents Relative to the Prince's Negotiations with Pitt, Fox, and Brougham, and an Account of His Conversations with Lord Palmerston and other English Statesmen in London in 1832*, ed. Adam Gielgud, 2 vols. (New York: Arno Press, 1971), vol. 2, 5.

the spring of 1806—precisely when Beethoven was beginning work on Opus 59—Razumovsky was living in constant fear of being transferred to London. In ill health and with his wife in much worse condition (she would die later that year), he was forced to plead with the Tsar's right hand, Prince Czartoryski, to retain his coveted Viennese post.[78] After a prolonged and tense correspondence, the court finally consented to Razumovsky's wish to stay in Vienna; he would remain there for the rest of his life. At the Congress of Vienna, in which he played a major role, he would be the only one of Alexander's major advisors of Russian parentage, despite the fact that he remained unable to write a dispatch in Russian, successively married two Austrians, and converted to Roman Catholicism before his death.[79]

Razumovsky's European inclinations were most vividly displayed in his patronage of the arts—especially music. Known as one of the city's foremost amateur violinists, he was particularly passionate about instrumental music and derived special pleasure from string quartets.[80] As is well known, he both pensioned and housed members of the Schuppanzigh Quartet, an ensemble he placed at Beethoven's disposal and for which he frequently played second violin.[81] Less well known is that during the first decades of the 1800s, he sought out and commissioned several new works: in addition to subscribing to the first edition of Haydn's *Creation*, Pleyel's complete edition of the Haydn quartets, and Beethoven's Opus 1 trios, he received the dedications to at least seven opuses by five different composers (quartets by Beethoven, Krommer, Spohr, and Weiss, a concerto by Hummel, and—jointly with Prince Lobkowitz—Beethoven's

78. "Nearly thirty years of my life have been consecrated to foreign missions, I dare say, with a constant diligence of work and of implementation in very complex negotiations. [. . .] I was perhaps only listening to my zeal for service and my loyalty to my Sovereign when I believed I could, for still a few more years, merit his trust in the position I occupy. Notwithstanding, my prince, I will say with frankness of honor and of conviction that this post is the only where I have believed it possible to be of some usefulness to the interests of H[is] I[mperial] M[ajesty]. Persuaded of this opinion, I urge him to deign exempt me from all other destinations. The habit of the climate, the care of my health, my establishment here, the ailing state of my wife, all these considerations limit my wishes to fixing my retirement in this country, and it is the one grace that I dare solicit from the goodwill, the humanity, and the justice of my august sovereign." Count Razumovsky to Prince Czartoryski, March 26, 1806. Quoted in Wassiltchikow, *Les Razoumowski*, vol. 2, 334–5.

79. Patricia Kennedy Grimsted, *The Foreign Ministers of Alexander I: Political Attitudes and the Conduct of Russian Diplomacy, 1801–1825*, Russian and East European Studies (Berkeley: University of California Press, 1969), 15.

80. Ignaz von Mosel, "Uebersicht des gegenwärtigen Zustandes der Tonkunst in Wien," *Vaterländische Blätter für den Österreichischen Kaiserstaat* 1, no. 6 (May 27, 1808): 39–44; and no. 7 (May 31, 1808): 49–54, 53.

81. Reichardt, who visited Vienna in 1808, notes that the Quartet performed regularly on Thursdays from 12 to 2 during the winter season; Johann Friedrich Reichardt, *Vertraute Briefe geschrieben auf einer Reise nach Wien und den Österreichischen Staaten zu Ende des Jahres 1808 und zu Anfang 1809*, ed. Gustav Gugitz, 2 vols. (Munich: G. Müller, 1915), vol. 2, 204.

Fifth and Sixth Symphonies).[82] In a letter to the Russian court, he wrote enthusiastically of Haydn's "Apponyi" quartets, and he knew both Haydn and Mozart personally (in fact, through his negotiations, Mozart was nearly sent to work for Prince Potemkin in 1791).[83] Around the time Beethoven completed Opus 59, Razumovsky even applied to him for instruction in music theory and quartet composition. Beethoven recommended his former teacher Emanuel Aloys Förster, who took the Count on as pupil.[84]

Most importantly, by 1808 (if not sooner), the *Palais Rasoumoffsky* had become an invaluable resource for Beethoven, a laboratory for his newest creations.[85] Ignaz von Seyfried, who lived with him at the time, tells us that "[he] was as much at home in the Rasumovsky establishment as a hen in her coop. Everything he wrote was taken warm from the nest and tried out in the frying pan."[86] "Rasumovsky's quartet," Schindler echoes, "became Beethoven's quartet; the musicians were put entirely at his disposal just as if they had been hired expressly for his use."[87] Moreover, if we may believe Schindler (and I see no reason to doubt him here), the Count—"the person most dedicated to the carrying on of the Haydn tradition of the quartet"—contributed his "fine sensitivity to those particular qualities in [Beethoven's] quartets and symphonies that, because they could not be grasped superficially nor conveyed through the usual musical symbols, had escaped other artists."[88] All of this provides ample evidence that Beethoven would have had little incentive indeed to mock Razumovsky or Russians in composing the quartets.

82. Johann Nepomuk Hummel, Concerto for Piano and Violin, Op. 17 (1805); Franz Krommer, Three String Quartets, Op. 68 (n.d.); Ludwig Spohr, Grand String Quartet, Op. 27 (1812); Franz Weiss, Two String Quartets, Op. 8 (1814). Weiss was violist in the Schuppanzigh Quartet.

83. "It took me no trouble, my Prince, to [arrange to] send you the first pianist and one of the ablest composers in Germany—the one named Mozart. Being unhappy here, he would be willing to undertake the voyage. He is in Bohemia now, but will be back soon. Should Your Highness so authorize me, I will engage him, not for the long term, but simply so that you might hear him and then decide whether or not to employ him." Count Andrey Razumovsky to Prince Potemkin, September 15, 1791. Quoted in Wassiltchikow, *Les Razoumowski*, vol. 2, 133–4. Potemkin would die in October and Mozart in December.

84. Beethoven purportedly considered Emanuel Aloys Förster to be the first of all the Vienna teachers of counterpoint and composition; his eldest son told Thayer it was on Beethoven's advice that Förster published the *Anleitung zum General-Bass* in 1805.

85. On the palace's musical life and performance spaces, see Ferraguto, "Representing Russia." I recently had the opportunity to tour the palace and learned about an architectural detail previously unknown to me: in the ceremonial hall of the main wing, one of the palace's best-preserved spaces, there are eleven sets of mirrored windows at the level of the chandeliers (five on the longer garden side and three on each of the short sides). Three of the interior windows open onto the ballroom from the upper level, allowing for musicians to perform from above without interfering with the dancers below. My thanks to Antonis Stachel for bringing this to my attention.

86. Cited in Schindler, *Beethoven as I Knew Him*, 60. Compare Thayer's translation: "as is known Beethoven was, as it were, cock of the walk in the princely establishment; everything that he composed was rehearsed hot from the griddle and performed to the nicety of a hair." Thayer/Forbes, vol. 1, 444.

87. Schindler, *Beethoven as I Knew Him*, 60.

88. Ibid., 59.

Both personally and professionally, then, Razumovsky—like Oulibicheff's well-dressed mujik—was between two worlds. From this vantage point, the inclusion of Russian themes from the LPC in Opus 59—whether of Razumovsky's or Beethoven's own initiative—is more complex than has hitherto been thought. Compositional matters aside, the gesture has multiple overlapping implications: it marks Razumovsky's public continuation of his family's support for Russian musical culture, even recalling the elder Razumovskys' ascent through the medium that facilitated their social mobility—song. It also reflects the personal desire of a Russian émigré to forge a sophisticated, cosmopolitan identity—one in which traditional Russian elements could literally be molded to the modern European context. Moreover, Beethoven's learned treatments seem expressly designed to resonate with a patron who involved himself with the design and aesthetics of Viennese quartet music. More than merely reaching toward a synthesis of folk and learned styles (whether serious or comic, or both), the quartets thus enact an aesthetic program that integrates traditional Russian music within a cutting-edge European musical idiom.[89] The sense of "Russianness" in the quartets, then, is a cosmopolitan one: the *thèmes russes* are not treated as exotic elements at a remove from the prevailing musical language, but rather as the generating materials of the movements in which they appear. In a larger context, Opus 59 thus belongs to a lineage of works by European composers from Bach's time onward in which the Russian polity is not merely figured as an exotic Other, but is rather inscribed within the system of European powers.[90] As the Russian ambassador to Austria, Razumovsky was expected to uphold precisely this position for Russia, both in his negotiations and in his everyday actions. In his manners, his dress, his language, and his artistic pursuits, Razumovsky was no mujik: he rather exemplified the European Russian. Beethoven's settings reflect his patron's double identity, negotiating as might a diplomat the complex social space between Russia and Europe.

OF RUSSIAN THEMES AND RESCUE FANTASIES: NEW LIGHT ON OPUS 59, NO. 3

In the final part of this chapter, I would like to revisit a question that has lingered over Opus 59 since it was first posed by one of Beethoven's own pupils: "Has it yet

89. John Irving has suggested that the prospect of reliable professional performances facilitated by Razumovsky's financing of the Schuppanzigh quartet may have encouraged Beethoven to invest Opus 59 with "quasi-symphonic character, orchestral breadth of scale and sonority, and expanded technical demands." In this sense, one might also view the learned treatments of the *thèmes russes* as a form of response to the Schuppanzigh quartet's technical proficiency; Irving, "Invention of Tradition," in Jim Samson, ed., *The Cambridge History of Nineteenth-Century Music* (Cambridge: Cambridge University Press, 2001), 178–212, 180.

90. One such piece that Beethoven may have known was Paul Wranitzky's Symphony in D Major, Op. 36, which includes a "Russe" and a "Polonese" (both associated with Russia) as the second and third movements of an otherwise typically Viennese four-movement symphony.

been determined whether the theme of the Romanze in the third Razumovsky Quartet, A Minor, Op. 59, is really Russian or was invented by Beethoven?" So wondered Carl Czerny, inaugurating an unsolved mystery.[91] For while Beethoven included Russian folksongs from the LPC in his first two Opus 59 quartets, marking their appearances "*thème russe*" in the autograph and printed score, no similar marking exists in Opus 59, no. 3. Indeed, the melody of the Andante—with its entrance on the weak part of the measure, prominent augmented second from G-sharp to F-natural and unusually wide compass spanning a minor tenth—has little in common with any of the melodies in Lvov-Pratsch.

For modern commentators, this has been seen as a boon: "Folksongs," writes Kerman, "did not much help the first two quartets, but Rasumovsky's notion came to superb fruition in the third, where Beethoven gave up the idea of incorporating preexisting tunes and instead wrote the haunting A-minor Andante in what he must have conceived to be a Russian idiom."[92] Scholars and critics alike have tended to endorse the idea that the Andante represents Beethoven's abstract impression of Russian music, rather than a third (doomed) setting of a Russian folksong.[93] Czerny's oft-quoted remark that Beethoven "undertook to weave a Russian folk melody into each of the quartets"[94] has thus engendered both confusion and speculation: did Beethoven abandon his plans to weave a Russian melody into the third "Razumovsky" quartet, and if so, why?

It may be possible to shed new light on this mystery. In July 1804, the *Allgemeine musikalische Zeitung*—a publication Beethoven followed with interest—printed a short article on folk music by the philosopher Christian Schreiber featuring an arrangement of the Russian folksong "Ty wospoi, wospoi, mlad Shaworontschek."[95] The strophic eight-bar tune, translated as "Singe, sing' ein Lied," appeared prominently on the issue's front page with one stanza of German text and a simple bass-line accompaniment (see Example 3.7a). The relevant section of the *AmZ* article is included in Appendix 3.2. In its

---

91. Czerny, *On the Proper Performance of All Beethoven's Works for the Piano*, 13.

92. Joseph Kerman et al., "Beethoven, Ludwig van." In *Grove Music Online*, http://www.oxfordmusiconline.com/subscriber/article/grove/music/40026pg15.

93. A number of scholars have heard a Russian (or at least exotic) quality in the Andante, citing its use of the harmonic minor scale (with the augmented second G-sharp—F-natural between the sharp seventh and minor sixth scale degrees), repeated plucked E in the cello, and melancholic quality (viewed by many commentators as characteristically Russian). See, among others, Walter Riezler, *Beethoven*, trans. G. D. H. Pidcock (London: M. C. Forrester, 1938), 172; Kerman, *Beethoven Quartets*, 145; Marion M. Scott, *Beethoven*, rev. Sir Jack Westrup (London: Dent & Sons, 1974), 256–7; Steinberg, "Middle Quartets," 193; and Kinderman, *Beethoven*, 135.

94. Czerny, *On the Proper Performance of All Beethoven's Works for Piano*, 13.

95. C[hristian] Schreiber, "Etwas über Volkslieder," *Allgemeine musikalische Zeitung* 6, no. 43 (July 25, 1804): cols. 713–18. Schreiber would later prepare the German texts for Beethoven's *Four Arias and a Duet*, Op. 82, and the Mass in C, Op. 86, for Breitkopf and Härtel.

EXAMPLE 3.7. Beethoven's Quotation of "Singe, sing'ein Lied" in Op. 59, no. 3, ii.

a. "Singe, sing'ein Lied" (Ty wospoi, wospoi, mlad Shaworontschek), as it appears in the *Allgemeine musikalische Zeitung* (July 25, 1804)

b. "Singe, sing'ein Lied," mm. 1–2, displaced by one beat

c. Beethoven, String Quartet No. 9 in C Major, Op. 59, no. 3, ii, mm. 1–5

key (A minor), meter (6/8), and tempo (Andantino), the folksong arrangement resembles the Andante movement of Opus 59, no. 3.[96]

In light of Beethoven's manipulations of the *thème russe* in the fugato section of Opus 59, no. 1's finale, however, it seems possible to go further. The first two measures of "Singe, sing'ein Lied" may be heard as a gestalt, with the initial melody in the right hand (m. 1) continued or completed by the eighth-note figuration in the left hand (m. 2). Adjusting for register, this concatenated melody ascends in stepwise motion from a^1 to c^2, and then descends, again in stepwise motion, through the A-harmonic-minor scale all the way down to B. The contour is strikingly similar to that of the Andante's opening theme. As mentioned earlier, a distinctive aspect of the Andante's melody is that it begins on the weak part of the measure. Indeed, by displacing the melody of "Singe, sing'ein Lied" one beat, the Andante's opening theme becomes apparent (see Examples 3.7b and 3.7c).

In an unexpected way, Beethoven appears to have included Russian folksongs in all three Opus 59 quartets. But his manner of incorporating a folksong into the Andante of No. 3—if this hypothesis be accepted—sets it apart from his other efforts: rather than quoting and elaborating a preexisting *melody*, here he appears to draw on a preexisting *arrangement* of a Russian folksong, using the concatenated melody from the opening of "Singe, sing'ein Lied" as a kind of musical synecdoche—a part that is meant to represent the whole. By placing the quotation in lockstep with the prevailing metrical pattern, and by treating it as the beginning of a longer phrase, he doubly conceals the allusion. This may help to explain why Beethoven left out the marking "*thème russe*" on the autograph and printed score: the label would have been misleading, since the Russian theme has been abstracted rather than quoted verbatim.

Promoted as "one of the finest" examples of Russian folksong, "Singe, sing'ein Lied" may also have been especially appealing to Beethoven because of its text. The seventeen-stanza poem, printed in German on the page after the arrangement, concerns a young rogue who has been imprisoned for stealing. The rogue writes a letter to his parents in which he pleads for their help,

---

96. The melody is found in both early editions of the LPC. In the 1790 edition ([Lvov] and Pratsch, *Sobraniye narodnikh russkikh pesen s ikh golosami*), it appears as "Ty vospoi, vospoi zhavorono-chek" (A minor, 6/8, Andantino), with a slightly (though significantly for my purposes) different accompaniment. It also appears in the 1806 edition as "Kak na dubchike" (C minor, 3/8, Molto Andante) with an arpeggiated left-hand accompaniment and 3-bar phrases (see Brown, *Collection of Russian Folk Songs*, facs. 193 [21]). I am not the first to suggest a possible candidate for a Russian folksong in the Andante. According to Lini Hübsch, the passage from measures 23 to 28 derives from the "type" of the Russian harvest song, of which she gives two A-minor examples; *Ludwig van Beethoven: Die Rasumowsky-Quartette: Op. 59 Nr. 1 F-dur, Nr. 2 e-moll, Nr. 3 C-dur*, Meisterwerke der Musik 40 (Munich: Wilhelm Fink, 1983) 31–2; also 90–3. My own hypothesis neither supports nor refutes her claim; however, I necessarily disagree with her treatment of the opening theme as (merely) an "anticipated paraphrase of the Russian song [in m. 23]" (91).

attaching his epistle to a lark. His parents, unwilling to shame the family name, refuse to save him. He sends a second letter, again via the lark, to his beloved:

> Und in Briefe schrieb
> Der Gefangene:
> "Liebstes Mädchen, Du!
> Meine Trauteste!
>
> Bist Du, wie vorhin
> Mir noch immer hold?
> O so rette doch
> Deinen Treusten!"
>
> (And in the letter wrote
> The prisoner:
> "Beloved maiden, you!
> My most faithful!
>
> Are you, as before,
> Still ever dear to me?
> O then rescue
> Your most true!")[97]

Moved by his plea, the maiden tells her servants to unlock all the treasure chests, take the money within, and buy back the rogue. The beloved's rescue of the male prisoner recalls the central theme of *Leonore/Fidelio*, a work that was well underway when the *AmZ* article appeared. In fact, one sketchleaf preserves ideas for the Andante alongside drafts for the overture *Leonore No. 1*.[98] Beethoven's opera, and perhaps also his own rescue fantasies, offer a new and intriguing way of thinking about the Andante movement.[99]

Whether Beethoven was drawn to the *AmZ* article because of its touted example of Russian folksong, its author's pithy observations about national character in music and dance (Schreiber was a student of Herder's—see Appendix 3.2), or the *Fidelio*-like narrative of "Singe, sing'ein Lied," it seems plausible that his reading of it helped shape his approach to the Andante of Opus 59, no. 3. Indeed, his concept for the movement may have also been informed by

---

97. Schreiber, "Etwas über Volkslieder," col. 715.

98. Royal College of Music London (MS 2175 = SV 336). See Douglas Johnson, Alan Tyson, and Robert Winter, *The Beethoven Sketchbooks: History, Reconstruction, Inventory*, ed. Douglas Johnson, California Studies in 19th-Century Music 4 (Berkeley: University of California Press, 1985), 524. In this context, it is interesting to note Lockwood's observations about the quartet's first movement, the slow introduction of which "draws . . . closely on some of the same harmonic resources we find in the F-minor introduction to Florestan's dungeon scene, written in 1805–6 just before his main work on these quartets." See Lockwood, *Beethoven: The Music and the Life*, 325.

99. See Nancy November, *Beethoven's Theatrical Quartets: Opp. 59, 74 and 95* (Cambridge: Cambridge University Press, 2013), 136–52.

Schreiber's brief description of the Balalaika, a long-necked lute traditionally used to accompany Russian folk singers. The unusual plucked cello line in the Andante might be heard as a stylized representation of Balalaika playing, designed to accompany a stylized representation of a Russian folksong.[100]

If Beethoven's learned treatments of the Russian themes in Opus 59, nos. 1 and 2 reflect his engagement with a cosmopolitan notion of musical Russianness—one gained from his interactions with Razumovsky—then his stylized rendition of "Singe, sing'ein Lied" takes this notion even further. Czerny's verb "einflechten" (to weave, to interlace) seems particularly apt here, insofar as Beethoven has seemingly woven the *thème russe* into the very fabric of the Andante's opening theme. In so doing, he offers a third and final perspective on Russian folksong as a form- and content-generating element in Opus 59. In all three settings, artifice serves as a mediating force that alternately conceals and reveals the generative significance of the Russian folksongs. Perhaps following Schreiber's delineation of three distinct types of Russian folksong—a "ceremonious Largo, a tranquil Andantino, or a rushing Allegro"—Beethoven completed a coherent and diverse triptych of Russian folksong settings, each in a separate key, tempo, and character.[101] Taken together, these settings not only represent three complementary solutions to the problem of merging folksong with learned style but also posit a transnational musical aesthetic, one that needs to be understood from multiple perspectives.

Indeed, as the quartets' elaborate dedication page makes plain, there was more at stake here than Beethoven's individual compositional achievement.[102] Opus 59 certainly broke new musical ground, but it did so in the service of a cross-cultural collaboration whose political implications were as richly complex as its interpersonal ones.

100. Beethoven's pizzicato bassline suggests the contrabass balalaika, tuned EE AA D; Karl Geiringer, *Instruments in the History of Western Music*, 3rd ed. (New York: Oxford University Press, 1978), 218.

101. Schreiber, "Etwas über Volkslieder," col. 714.

102. In the center of the dedication page is the Razumovsky family crest, emblazoned with the motto (from Virgil's *Aeneid*) "Famam extendere factis" (To extend one's fame by deeds). The text of the dedication reads: "Trois Quatuors / Très humblement Dédiés à / son Excellence Monsieur le / Comte de Rasoumoffsky / Conseiller privé actuel de / Sa Majesté l'Empereur de toutes les Russies / Sénateur, Chevalier des ordres / de Saint André, de Saint Alexandre-Newsky et Grand-Croix / de celui de Saint Wladimir de la prémière Classe. &c. &c. / par / Louis van Beethoven." *Trois Quatuors pour deux Violons, Alto, et Violoncello. Composés par Louis van Beethoven. Oeuvre 59ᵐᵉ* (Vienna: Bureau des Arts et d'Industrie, 1808).

APPENDIX 3.1 RUSSIAN FOLKSONGS FROM THE LVOV-PRATSCH
COLLECTION (LPC) IN WORKS BY BEETHOVEN.

Folksong	Facsim. no. in facsim. ed. of LPC 1806 ed. (ed. Brown)	Work	Year published
Pri doli-nushke kalinushka	273	Twelve Variations for Piano on the Russian Dance from Wranitzky's *Das Waldmädchen*, WoO 71	1797
Akh! talan li moi, talan takoy	177	Three String Quartets, Op. 59, no. 1, iv	1808
Uzh kak slava Tebe Bozhe	297	Three String Quartets, Op. 59, no. 2, iii	1808
Vo lesochke komaroch-kov mnogo urodilos'	219	Twenty-Three Songs of Various Nationalities, WoO 158a, no. 13	1816–18
Akh rechen'ki, rechen'ki	27	Twenty-Three Songs of Various Nationalities, WoO 158a, no. 14	1816–18
Kak poshli nashi podruzkhi	109	Twenty-Three Songs of Various Nationalities, WoO 158a, no. 15	1816–18
Ekhav kozak za Dunai	162	Twenty-Three Songs of Various Nationalities, WoO 158a, no. 16	1816–18
" "	" "	Ten National Airs with Variations for piano, flute or cello, Op. 107, no. 7	1819/1820

APPENDIX 3.2 EXCERPT ON RUSSIAN FOLKSONG FROM "ETWAS
ÜBER VOLKSLIEDER," *Allgemeine musikalische Zeitung* 6, NO. 43
(JULY 25, 1804), COL. 714.

Music and dance attain for almost every people a distinctive character. The
phenomenon is entirely explainable; these arts adapt themselves the most to

the emotion, the enthusiasm, and the universal character of men, and the one who performs them can only give what he himself feels, and what lies closest to his individual temperament. The more individuality a people possesses, the more characteristic is its music. This is especially applicable to so-called folksongs, which, not yet cultivated through higher art and not yet brought nearer to the ideal, usually give a true impression of national character.—Most folksongs have been produced by France, Spain, and especially Russia. [This] because the Russian sings constantly, and even while at work, if it is at all possible. (The songs are typically accompanied by the Wolinka, a bagpipe, or the Balalaika, a type of lute.) A number of these folk melodies were published in a journal not long ago, and at the same time the remark was added that Russian folksongs are nothing like the bouncing, trifling song of the French; instead either a ceremonious Largo, a tranquil Andantino, or a rushing Allegro prevails. Incidentally, they are almost all short and simple, and one would need to hear them sung full-voiced by Russians for them to truly delight the ear. Here is one of the finest ones to try out: ["Ty wospoi, wospoi, mlad Shaworontschek"].

Musik und Tanz gewinnen fast bey jedem Volke einen eigenen Charakter. Die Erscheinung ist sehr erklärbar; denn diese Künste schmiegen sich dem Gefühl, der Begeisterung, und dem universellen Charakter der Menschen am meisten an, und derjenige, der sie ausübt, kann nur geben, was er selbst fühlt, und was seinem individuellen Temperament am nächsten liegt. Je mehr daher ein Volk Eigenthumlichkeit besitzt, desto charakteristischer ist seine Musik. Dies ist besonders auf die sogenannten Volkslieder anwendbar, die, durch höhere Kunst noch nicht gebildet und dem Idealen näher gebracht, gewöhnlich ein treuer Abdruck des Nationalcharakters sind.—Die meisten Volkslieder hat Frankreich, Spanien, und besonders Russland hervorgebracht. Denn der Russe singt beständig, und sogar bey der Arbeit, wenn es irgend zulässig ist. (Der Gesang wird gewöhnlich mit der Wolinka [Sackpfeife] oder der Balalaika [einer Art Laute] begleitet). Mehrere solcher Volksmelodien wurden uns vor einiger Zeit in einem öffentlichen Blatte mitgetheilt, und zugleich die Bemerkung hinzugefügt, dass in den Russischen Volksliedern nie jener hüpfende, tändelnde Gesang der Franzosen, sondern entweder ein feyerliches Largo, ein ruhiges Andantino, oder ein rauschendes Allegro herrsche. Uebrigens wären sie fast alle kurz und einfach, und man müsste sie vollstimmig von Russen singen hören, wenn sie recht viel Anziehendes für das Ohr haben sollten. Hier eins der vorzüglichsten zur Probe: ["Ty wospoi, wospoi, mlad Shaworontschek"].

CHAPTER 4

MUSIC FOR A CULTURE HERO

Opus 60

As early as 1831, a British commentator noted that Beethoven's Fourth Symphony was the "least frequently brought forward" of the first six, though, he hastened to add, it was "not inferior to any."[1] Seven years later, a French critic wrote that in Paris the "sublime symphony in B-flat" had not only been neglected but was also routinely dismissed as "a work of folly, without true beauty and without meaning."[2] While the Fourth Symphony came to occupy a significant place on European concert programs in the later nineteenth century, it remained a seldom-performed work in many American concert halls through much of the twentieth. On the centennial of Beethoven's death in 1927, the British conductor Sir Henry Wood was astonished to find that the Fourth Symphony had never before been heard in Los Angeles: "Think of so attractive a work having been almost entirely neglected. I put in that 'almost,' because it appeared that some conductors had gone as far as rehearsing it. But when the pinch came their courage failed, and down went No. 5 instead!"[3]

Wood's account highlights the discomfort this symphony has often caused for performers, critics, and even audiences. Indeed, the symphony's reception history is a tale of apologias and rescue attempts—as one critic opined, the Fourth Symphony has been subject to "more misrepresentation than any other work by Beethoven."[4] Lacking descriptive titles and other extramusical signifiers, it posed a problem for nineteenth-century critics applying programmatic

---

1. "Music: Philharmonic Society," *London Literary Gazette and Journal of Belles Lettres, Arts, Sciences, etc. for the Year 1831* (London: James Moyes, 1831), 381.

2. "On a regardé long-temps la sublime symphonie en si bémol de Beethoven comme une œuvre de folie, sans beauté véritable et sans signification." T[héophile] Thoré, "Salon de 1838: Dernier Article." *Revue de Paris*, n.s., 53 (1838): 50–9, 52.

3. "Concerning Beethoven's Symphonies: A Talk with Sir Henry Wood," *The Musical Times* 68, no. 1009 (March 1, 1927), 216–19, 218.

4. Burnett James, *Beethoven and Human Destiny* (London: Phoenix House, 1960), 38. On the symphony's reception history, see Mark Ferraguto, "Beethoven's Fourth Symphony: Reception, Aesthetics, Performance History" (PhD diss., Cornell University, 2012), 12–64.

modes of analysis to Beethoven's music, leading Alexandre Oulibicheff, in 1857, to label it the "bête noire" of Beethoven criticism.[5] More recently, its aesthetic has been viewed as incongruent with that of Beethoven's "heroic style," a critical paradigm that has inspired an extraordinary proliferation of scholarship on the mature odd-numbered symphonies and, for more complicated reasons, the *Pastoral*, but has tended to marginalize the others. And yet the Fourth is by no means a neglected work today. According to the League of American Orchestras, the symphony received over two hundred performances by major American orchestras in the first decade of the twenty-first century; in the 2007–8 season (two centuries after its Viennese premiere in 1807), it was among the twenty most frequently programmed orchestral works in the country.[6]

One aspect of the Fourth Symphony that has garnered critical attention is its apparent indebtedness to Haydn and, to a lesser extent, Mozart. Scholars have attributed this indebtedness to a number of musical features: it begins with a "Haydnesque" slow introduction rather than *in medias res*; its codas are short and to the point, not expansive and dramatic; its textures and forms are relatively transparent; it concludes with a light, even comic, finale rather than a transcendent, weighty one; and it requires no additional instruments beyond the standard complement of the late eighteenth century (and only one flute). Donald Francis Tovey has suggested further points of contact: in the first movement, for instance, Beethoven handles rhythm in such a way that "Mozart's own freedom of movement reappears as one of the most striking qualities of the whole."[7] The finale, he argues, likewise conjures up Mozart and Haydn, even to the point of creating a stylistic paradox: it "represents Beethoven's full maturity in that subtlest of all disguises, his discovery of the true inwardness of Mozart and Haydn; a discovery inaccessible to him whenever, as in a few early works (notably the Septet), he seemed or tried to imitate them, but possible as soon as he obtained full freedom in handling his own resources."[8]

But it is the influence of Haydn, not Mozart, that has tended to dominate critical accounts of this symphony—and this particularly with respect to

5. Alexandre Oulibicheff, *Beethoven: Ses critiques et ses glossateurs* (Leipzig and Paris: F.A. Brockhaus & Jules Gavelot, 1857), 187.

6. League of American Orchestras, "2007–2008 Season Orchestra Repertoire Report" (pdf version, http://www.americanorchestras.org/interest_areas/librarians.html), 4. Five of Beethoven's symphonies made the top twenty in 2007–8: the Fourth Symphony ranked 16th, the *Pastoral* Symphony 12th, the Ninth Symphony 4th, the Seventh Symphony 2nd, and the Fifth Symphony 1st. Astonishingly, the *Eroica* did not make the list that season; however, it frequently made the top ten in the century's first decade (3rd in 2001–2, 8th in 2004–5, 7th in 2006–7), whereas the Fourth's 2007–8 ranking is an anomaly, seemingly explained by the bicentennial year. My thanks to Michael Ferraguto for pointing me to this data.

7. Donald Francis Tovey, *Essays in Musical Analysis: Symphonies and Other Orchestral Works* (London: Oxford University Press, 1981; originally published 1935–9), 50.

8. Ibid., 52.

its first movement. The hushed, minor-mode ruminations of the slow introduction, followed by the explosion of major-mode affirmation in the Allegro,
have especially reminded critics of the transition from "chaos" to "order" at the
beginning of Haydn's oratorio *The Creation*. For A. Peter Brown, the opening Adagio of the Fourth is "in the best sense, a 'Chaos' parody, which must
have been apparent to any Viennese connoisseur."[9] Maynard Solomon reaches
a similar conclusion, referring to the introduction as a possible "sibling" of the
"Chaos" movement.[10] Taking a different view, James Webster has noted affinities between this slow introduction and those of Haydn's "London" symphonies, suggesting that Beethoven may in fact have been inspired by the "sublime"
opening Largo of Symphony No. 102; also in the key of B-flat, this introduction
begins with similar alternations between a "long, unfathomably deep unison
tonic" and a higher contrasting idea.[11] Christopher Hatch has also examined
affinities between these two introductions.[12]

While many critics have remarked on the Fourth Symphony's apparent
indebtedness to Haydn, neither the extent of Haydn's influence nor Beethoven's
possible motivations for emulating him has been carefully explored. Was
Beethoven consciously imitating or even modeling Haydn in this work? If so,
why at this moment, in this symphony? In this chapter, I argue that in order
to answer these questions, it is necessary to explore the ways in which Haydn's
legacy was constructed in the first decade of the 1800s. Beethoven's compositional process in the Fourth Symphony was mediated not by Haydn but by
"Haydn," the culture hero who had conquered Paris, London, and Vienna to
become Europe's most celebrated living composer. Not only was Haydn mania
sweeping the theaters and salons that Beethoven frequented, but the principal
firm with which he was negotiating to publish his new symphony—Breitkopf
& Härtel in Leipzig—was aggressively marketing Haydn's music and image,
a fact of which Beethoven was well aware. This chapter begins by reexamining Beethoven's negotiations with the firm—and its promotion of Haydn—in
the period leading up to the composition of the Fourth Symphony. It then
considers the symphony's "Haydnesque" elements in greater detail, ultimately
suggesting a new way of thinking about the nature of Beethoven's relationship
with his celebrated mentor in the first decade of the 1800s.

9. See A. Peter Brown, "The Creation and The Seasons: Some Allusions, Quotations, and
Models from Handel to Mendelssohn," *Current Musicology* 51 (1991): 26–58, 26, and *The Symphonic
Repertoire Volume 2: The First Golden Age of the Viennese Symphony* (Bloomington: Indiana University
Press, 2002), 476.

10. Maynard Solomon, "Some Images of Creation in Music of the Viennese Classical School,"
Musical Quarterly 89, no. 1 (2006): 121–35.

11. James Webster, "*The Creation*, Haydn's Late Vocal Music, and the Musical Sublime," in Elaine
Sisman, ed., *Haydn and His World* (Princeton: Princeton University Press, 1997), 57–102.

12. Christopher Hatch, "Internal and External References in Beethoven's Fourth Symphony,"
College Music Symposium 24, no. 1 (Spring 1984): 107–17.

BEETHOVEN AND HAYDN AFTER *Leonore*

As the revision and restaging of *Leonore* reached its conclusion in the spring of 1806, Beethoven sought out publishers for his new large-scale instrumental works. Breitkopf & Härtel was his first choice, in spite of the fact that negotiations over several earlier works had failed to bear fruit. The firm also published the most important musical journal of the period, the *Allgemeine musikalische Zeitung (AmZ)*; Beethoven kept up with this journal and recognized that it had the potential to influence the commercial success of his music. Hence, it was a disappointment for him to learn of an unflattering report on the Third Symphony that had appeared in the journal's pages in May 1805, shortly before the firm declined to publish the symphony.[13] Here is an excerpt from a July 1806 letter from Beethoven to the firm's head Gottfried Härtel:

> I hear that in the Musikalische Zeitung someone has railed violently against the *symphony* which I sent you last year and which *you* returned to *me*. *I have not read the article.* If you fancy that you can injure *me* by publishing articles of that kind, you are very much mistaken. On the contrary, by so doing you merely bring your journal into disrepute, the more so as I have made *no secret* whatever of the fact that you returned to me *that particular* symphony together with some other compositions.[14]

Not only does Beethoven blame the firm both for refusing to publish his third symphony and for printing the negative report but he also claims that they have done themselves a disservice. The letter demonstrates Beethoven's awareness of what the critics had to say and of how such evaluations might impact his career as a freelance composer.

The letter about the report on the *Eroica* was the last Beethoven sent from Vienna before arriving in Silesia (in modern-day Poland), where he would stay during the summer of 1806. He set out to write his next symphony almost immediately after arriving there and completed it quickly. By September, he was offering the Fourth Symphony to none other than Breitkopf & Härtel. Despite having

---

13. The report was part of a "Nachrichten" column, *Allgemeine musikalische Zeitung* 31 (May 1, 1805): cols. 500–4. For an English translation of the relevant passage, see Wayne M. Senner, Robin Wallace, and William Meredith, eds., *The Critical Reception of Beethoven's Compositions by his German Contemporaries* 2 (Lincoln and London: University of Nebraska Press, 2001), 17–18. Breitkopf & Härtel indicated their intention to return the manuscript of the Third Symphony and other works to Beethoven in June 1805; see Theodore Albrecht, trans. and ed., *Letters to Beethoven and Other Correspondence* 1 (Lincoln and London: University of Nebraska Press, 1996), No. 104 (June 21, 1805), 164–6.

14. Anderson, vol. 1, no. 132, pp. 150–1 (July 5, 1806). "[I]ch höre, daß <sie> Man in der Musikal. Zeitung so über die *sinfonie*, die ich ihnen voriges Jahr geschikt, und die *sie mir* wieder zurückgeschikt, so loßgezogen hat, *gelesen habe ich's nicht*, Wenn sie glauben, daß sie *mir* damit schaden, so irren sie sich, vielmehr bringen sie ihre Zeitung durch so etwas in Mißkredit—um so mehr, da ich auch gar *kein Geheimniß* draus gemacht habe, daß sie mir *diese* Sinfonie mit andern Kompositionen zurük geschikt hätten." *Briefwechsel*, vol. 1, no. 254, pp. 286–8.

declined to publish the *Eroica*, the firm remained the most prestigious of its kind, and Beethoven hoped that by publishing with them he could enhance his international reputation. Whether or to what extent the Fourth Symphony was shaped by criticisms of the *Eroica* is difficult to gauge. What seems clear, however, is that the genesis of this new symphony coincided with Beethoven's desire to reengage with the instrumental music of both Haydn and Mozart. At the end of the letter cited above, Beethoven adds that he would like to receive the firm's "*printed* scores of Haydn and Mozart" should their present negotiations bear fruit.[15]

This request for printed scores likely refers to the latest in a series of projects initiated by Gottfried Härtel with the intent of memorializing the two great composers. Officially announced in the *AmZ*'s pages just ten days prior to Beethoven's letter, the new project proposed to offer inexpensive editions of "all truly masterful symphonies, selected but for the present only from the choicest of Haydn and Mozart, in full printed score; specifically, that each such score, including the grandest and longest symphonies, will cost sixteen Groschen at most—several even less, but certainly none more!"[16] Printing a symphony in score was lavish and impractical for playing purposes, but it allowed connoisseurs to study the music in a way that was otherwise very difficult. Beethoven had earlier expressed enthusiasm for scores of Haydn's symphonies that had been published in Paris, asking Breitkopf & Härtel to print the *Eroica* the same way (which they declined to do). That Haydn's and Mozart's symphonies were becoming increasingly available in this format testifies to their widespread popularity. At the same time, the Leipzig firm's promotion of these "masterful" symphonies demonstrated its conviction that these works would outlast others of their kind, a fact that surely was not lost on Beethoven as he prepared to compose his next work in this genre.

The new collection, of which No. 1 was Haydn's "Drumroll" Symphony, furthered a sustained effort on Härtel's part to promote Haydn's music and image. Such promotion had an economic motivation, but it was also tied in with a newfound reverence for Haydn's genius and an incipient sense of German nationalism. In the *AmZ*, this heady brew found expression in engravings, designs for monuments, laudatory verses, poetic encomiums, and more. A telling example is the well-known "Sun of German Composers" (Figure 4.1) that was reprinted in one of the journal's earliest issues. Featuring the names of thirty-two composers arranged hierarchically in two rows, each circumscribing a central triangle of four names, the design helps to explain Haydn's special status in the early 1800s. Haydn is the only living composer to be included in the central triangle; he is placed on a par with Handel and Graun, both of whom had died in 1759 and represent (like J. S. Bach, whose name occupies the center) an earlier generation.

15. Anderson, vol. 1, no. 132, p. 151.

16. "Merkwürdige Novität," *Allgemeine musikalische Zeitung* 39 (June 25, 1806), cols. 616–22, col. 619.

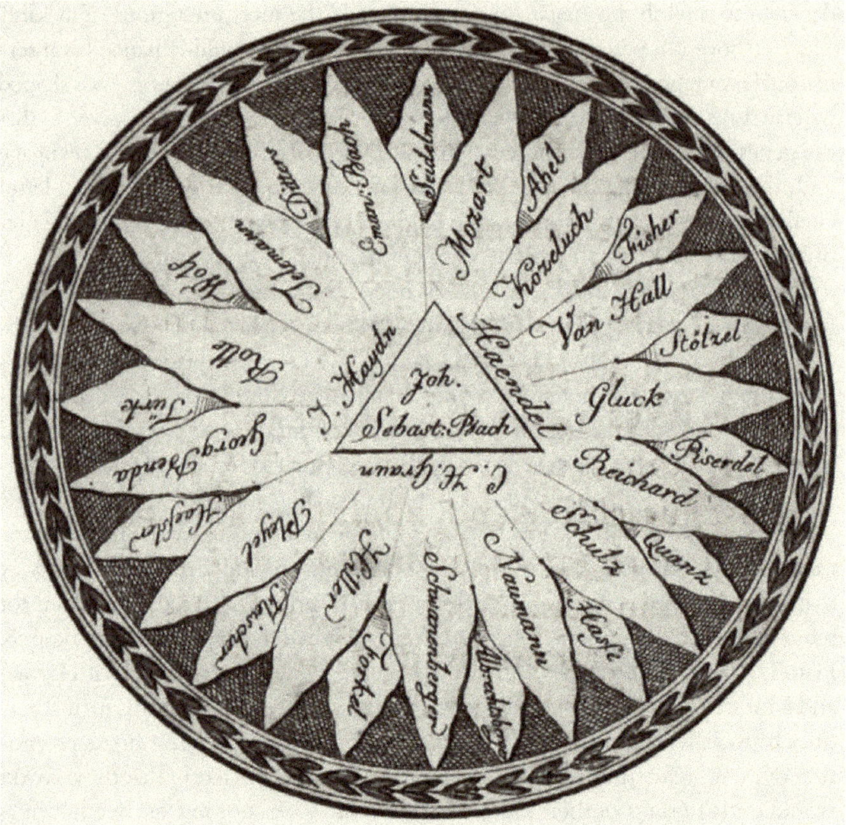

FIGURE 4.1. "Sun of German Composers." Engraving by A. F. C. Kollmann. Reprinted in "Anekdote," *Allgemeine musikalische Zeitung* 2, no. 5 (October 30, 1799), cols. 102–4, 104.

Haydn was also the first living composer to be honored in a title vignette on the cover of the *AmZ* (Figure 4.2a). Mozart, already deceased for a decade and a half, would not be honored until a year later (Figure 4.2b), and Beethoven not until 1817.[17] In effect, Haydn was already seen as standing outside of history well before his death in 1809. Indeed, his early monumentalization took on a comical aspect in 1805, when premature rumors of his death spread throughout Europe. Haydn, hearing of a funeral mass in his honor, joked that if he had only known sooner he would have conducted the requiem himself.

As Thomas Tolley has amply documented, Haydn played an active role in the process of his monumentalization.[18] He was apparently eager to place himself in

17. Vol. 19. However, Breitkopf & Härtel had earlier included a portrait of Beethoven as a supplement to vol. 6, no. 20 (February 15, 1804). My thanks to Robin Wallace for bringing this to my attention.

18. Thomas Tolley, *Painting the Cannon's Roar: Music, the Visual Arts and the Rise of an Attentive Public in the Age of Haydn, c. 1750 to c. 1810* (Aldershot: Ashgate, 2001).

a lineage of great German composers, even if prematurely. According to Johann Nikolaus Forkel, he reportedly approved of the "Sun of German Composers," saying that he was "not at all ashamed to be adjacent to Handel and Graun, much less has he found it wrong that Joh. Seb. Bach is the center of the sun, and thus the man from which all true musical wisdom emanates."[19] As James Webster has observed, there are reasons to be skeptical of Forkel's claim—most notably, a lack of general evidence regarding Haydn's reception of Bach's music.[20] Even so, the idea that German genius flowed from Bach to Haydn was made explicit in the final portrait for which the latter composer sat, painted in 1806 by Isidor Neugass, in which a statue of Apollo and a bust of Bach look over the composer's shoulder (Figure 4.3). Beethoven would doubtless have known about this imposing, seven-by-six-foot portrait (commissioned by the Esterházys), since he too sat for a portrait in Neugass's studio at around this time (Figure 4.4). Neugass's elegant Beethoven portrait, of which Prince Lichnowsky and the Brunsvik family commissioned the two known versions, is devoid of the striking symbolism found in Neugass's Haydn depiction. Measuring roughly 2 by 2.5 feet, it is in all respects less ostentatious than Neugass's Haydn.

Hence, while Beethoven struggled to make ends meet, Haydn, though frail and increasingly unable to compose, was enjoying the fruits of a remarkable career. More than this, Haydn was helping to shape his own legacy, through publications, iconography, performances, celebrations, biographical interviews, and the like. It is in this double context, I would suggest—that of Beethoven's frustrated attempts to market his large-scale instrumental works, on the one hand, and of Haydn's extraordinary success in this arena, on the other hand—that Beethoven's renewed interest in Haydn's symphonies should be viewed.

Nonetheless, it seems unlikely that Beethoven would have been able to procure Breitkopf & Härtel's new printed edition of the "Drumroll" Symphony before he left for Silesia. In any case, while Härtel's new project seems to have piqued his interest, earlier letters indicate that Beethoven was already acquainted with scores of Haydn's symphonies published in Paris. It is clear from Carl van Beethoven's description of these scores as being in "small format" that they were in fact Pleyel's editions of Symphonies Nos. 99, 102, 103, and 104 published as part of his *Bibliothèque musicale* around 1803. These were, according to some modern scholars, the first ever miniature orchestral scores; measuring roughly 20 cm high, they are similar in proportion to today's Dover miniature

---

19. "Anekdoten," *Allgemeine musikalische Zeitung* 2, no. 5 (October 30, 1799): cols. 102–4, 104.

20. A. F. C. Kollmann originally published the "Sun" on an engraved sheet in London. It was reprinted in 1799 in the *AmZ*, along with commentary by Forkel. But Forkel's claim about Haydn's approval of the design is explicitly described as hearsay, and the chronology, in Webster's view, makes this claim unlikely. See James Webster, "The Century of Handel and Haydn," in Sean Gallagher and Thomas Forrest Kelly, eds., *The Century of Bach and Mozart: Perspectives on Historiography, Composition, Theory, and Performance*, Isham Library Papers 7, Harvard Publications in Music 22 (Cambridge: Harvard University Press, 2008), 297–315, 308.

(a)

A L L G E·M E I N E
MUSIKALISCHE ZEITUNG.

SIEBENTER JAHRGANG
vom 3. Oktober 1804 bis 25. September 1805.

Joseph Haydn.

L e i p z i g,
bey Breitkopf und Härtel

FIGURE 4.2. Cover pages with title vignettes showing Haydn and Mozart, *Allgemeine musikalische Zeitung* 7 (1804–5) and 8 (1805–6).

scores. Precisely when Beethoven gained access to these scores is unclear, but the catalogue of printed materials in his *Nachlass* shows that at some point he acquired all fourteen volumes of Pleyel's Haydn series (including the four symphony volumes and ten volumes of quartets, all in score). Beethoven met Pleyel and his son in Vienna in 1805 and could well have acquired some or all of these volumes at this time (hence, prior to composing the Fourth Symphony). In matters of design, these symphonies relate strongly to the Fourth, and it seems plausible that Beethoven had access to them at the time of composition.

(b)

ALLGEMEINE
MUSIKALISCHE ZEITUNG.

ACHTER JAHRGANG
vom 2. Oktober 1805 bis 24. September 1806.

Leipzig,
bey Breitkopf und Härtel.

FIGURE 4.2. Continued

Reconsidering Beethoven's relationship with Haydn through the medium of these symphonies opens up new ways of thinking about the Fourth Symphony.

"HAYDNESQUE" ELEMENTS IN THE FOURTH SYMPHONY

I will focus my discussion here on three elements of this symphony as it relates to the "London" Symphonies (especially No. 102 in B-flat and No. 99 in E-flat, two of the four published under Pleyel's auspices in 1803): orchestration and key choice, thematic design and structural articulations, and cyclic integration.

FIGURE 4.3. *Joseph Haydn* (1806). Portrait by Isidor Neugass (c. 1780–a. 1847). Photo: Gerhard Wasserbauer, Vienna. Used by permission of the Esterhazy Privatstiftung, Eisenstadt Palace.

FIGURE 4.4. *Ludwig van Beethoven* (1806). Portrait by Isidor Neugass (c. 1780–a. 1847). Fassung Lichnowsky. Used by permission of the Beethoven-Haus Bonn.

TABLE 4.1 Haydn's use of trumpets and timpani in B-flat, 1792–1802.

Date	Title	Movements
1792	Sinfonia Concertante	i, iii
1792	Symphony No. 98	i, iii, iv
1794	Symphony No. 102	i, iii, iv
1796	Missa Sancti Bernardi von Officia ("Heiligmesse")	i–vi
1796–8	Die Schöpfung	11b: Vivace, 14b: Andante
1799	"Theresienmesse"	i–vi
1799–1801	Die Jahreszeiten	5b: Maestoso (incl. fugue)
1801	"Schöpfungsmesse"	i–vi
1802	"Harmoniemesse"	i–vi

Orchestration and Key Choice

The Fourth Symphony is the only one of Beethoven's nine symphonies to call for a single flute instead of the typical pair, a scoring also indicated in two of Haydn's "London" symphonies.[21] More unusual, however, is Beethoven's choice of key. The concept of a symphony in B-flat with trumpets and timpani—usually reserved for C and D—was a novelty in Vienna in the 1790s. Haydn's Symphonies No. 98 (1792) and No. 102 (1794) were among the first symphonies in B-flat to feature trumpets and drums.[22] Though these symphonies were composed for London orchestras, they quickly became part of the Viennese repertoire. Moreover, the success of these works encouraged Haydn to further explore this new orchestral sonority: four of his late masses, as well as some of the most important movements in *The Creation* and *The Seasons*, exploit this new sound (Table 4.1). As Haydn developed this idiom, other composers followed suit.

By expanding his orchestra in this way, Haydn blended the tempered quality of B-flat major with the festive character that trumpets and drums connoted. This effect drew praise from Friedrich Rochlitz in an 1802 review of Haydn's *Missa Sancti Bernardi von Officia*:

> [T]he composer, through a great deal of reflection and long experience, has under-
> stood how to give even the most shining effects their nobility and pious attributes, by
> means of many devices that are far from apparent at first glance—of which we would
> draw attention only to one feature, namely that in those movements of the Mass in

21. Nos. 95 in C Minor (1791) and 98 in B-flat Major (1792). No. 100 in G Major (1794) is unusual in that it calls for two flutes but includes no divisi writing. Prior to the "London" Symphonies, a single flute (or no flute at all) was the rule for Haydn; only Symphonies Nos. 7 and 9 (both in C Major, 1761), and No. 54 in G Major (1774, in a version probably revised for performance in London) require the pair.

22. Michael Haydn had used trumpets and drums in this key in a 1788 symphony, and earlier in his sacred vocal music. H. C. Robbins Landon, *Haydn: Chronicle and Works*, 5 vols. (London: Thames & Hudson, 1977), vol. 4, 139.

B-flat, the trumpets and drums (not used exactly sparingly) are, *because of their low pitch*, of the greatest strength, dignity and gravity.[23]

It was precisely the effect of "strength, dignity, and gravity" that Beethoven sought in composing a B-flat symphony with trumpets and drums. That he may have particularly looked to Symphony No. 102 for inspiration is suggested by a number of similarities in the scoring. In the first movement, for example, both Beethoven and Haydn use the timpani as a means of augmenting the dramatic impact of the retransition (Example 4.1). Symphony No. 102 is the only one of . Haydn's "London" Symphonies in which a drumroll ushers in the return of the main theme in the tonic after the development section. Beethoven follows suit but expands this gesture to mammoth proportions. Haydn's drumroll on the dominant lasts four bars; Beethoven's, on the tonic, lasts twenty-five.[24]

Beethoven's choice of B-flat major for his Fourth Symphony has further implications when considered in light of his larger instrumental output. Almost exclusively, he turned for his slow movements in these works to triple-meter *Adagios* in the key of E-flat: examples include the *Adagio con espressione* (3/4) of the piano trio Op. 11 (1797[–8?]); the *Adagio* (3/4) of the Second Piano Concerto (c. 1788–1801); the *Adagio con molta espressione* (9/8) of the piano sonata Op. 22 (1800); and, of course, the *Adagio* (3/4) of the Fourth Symphony.[25] The *Adagio ma non troppo* of the string quartet Op. 18, no. 6 (c. 1800) is also in E-flat, but in 2/4 meter. The association persisted for Beethoven's whole career: the Cavatina of the late string quartet Op. 130

---

23. *Allgemeine musikalische Zeitung* 4, no. 44 (July 28, 1802), cols. 705–18, 707. My translation is a slightly emended version of the one given in Landon, *Haydn: Chronicle and Works*, vol. 4, 158–61, 158 (emphasis in original). The "Heiligmesse" was published in Vienna in May 1802.

24. Such a technique might be understood as an example of the monumentalization of classical syntax associated with the "heroic" style. Burnham suggests that Beethoven is able to "overrun the superficial boundaries of the [sonata] style, in order to mark the underlying boundaries more emphatically. When he marks these boundaries with his own incomparable drama (as in the case of the *Eroica* horn call, or the famous parallel harmonies at the outset of the coda to that movement) he is in effect narrating them, for such moments rise above the musical texture and assert the presence of Beethoven's unique and unmistakable voice, now heard to speak across the present moment, telling of things like imminent return, or glorious consummation." *Beethoven Hero*, 143. Haydn's "Drumroll" Symphony, No. 103, also resonates with the Fourth Symphony in its deployment of orchestral resources. In No. 103's opening gesture (as well as in the coda), the kettledrums are detached from the orchestra, performing their own part independently of the trumpets. In the development section of the Fourth Symphony's first movement, similarly, Beethoven detaches the kettledrums from the ensemble and places the drumroll in dialogue with the strings. In this striking passage, the dominant chords from the introduction (where trumpets and timpani first entered, together) are transformed: on F-sharp (= G-flat) instead of F, in the strings alone instead of tutti, marked *ppp* instead of *ff*. The double function of the kettledrums' B-flat—as the third of V^7 on G-flat and as the root of the tonic triad—allows the drumroll to provide a sense of continuity to this unusual development section, in which harmonic events unfold at an uncharacteristically slow pace.

25. The "Archduke" Piano Trio, Op. 97 (1811), has an *Andante cantabile ma peró con moto* in D major, and the "Hammerklavier" Sonata in B-flat, Op. 106 (1818), has an *Adagio sostenuto* in F-sharp minor.

EXAMPLE 4.1. Comparison of first-movement retransition sections.

a. Haydn, Symphony No. 102 in B-flat Major, Hob. I:102 (Paris: Ignaz Pleyel, 1803)

b. Beethoven, Symphony No. 4 in B-flat Major, Op. 60 (Bonn: N. Simrock, 1823)

EXAMPLE 4.1. (CONT.)

EXAMPLE 4.1. (CONT.)

(b)

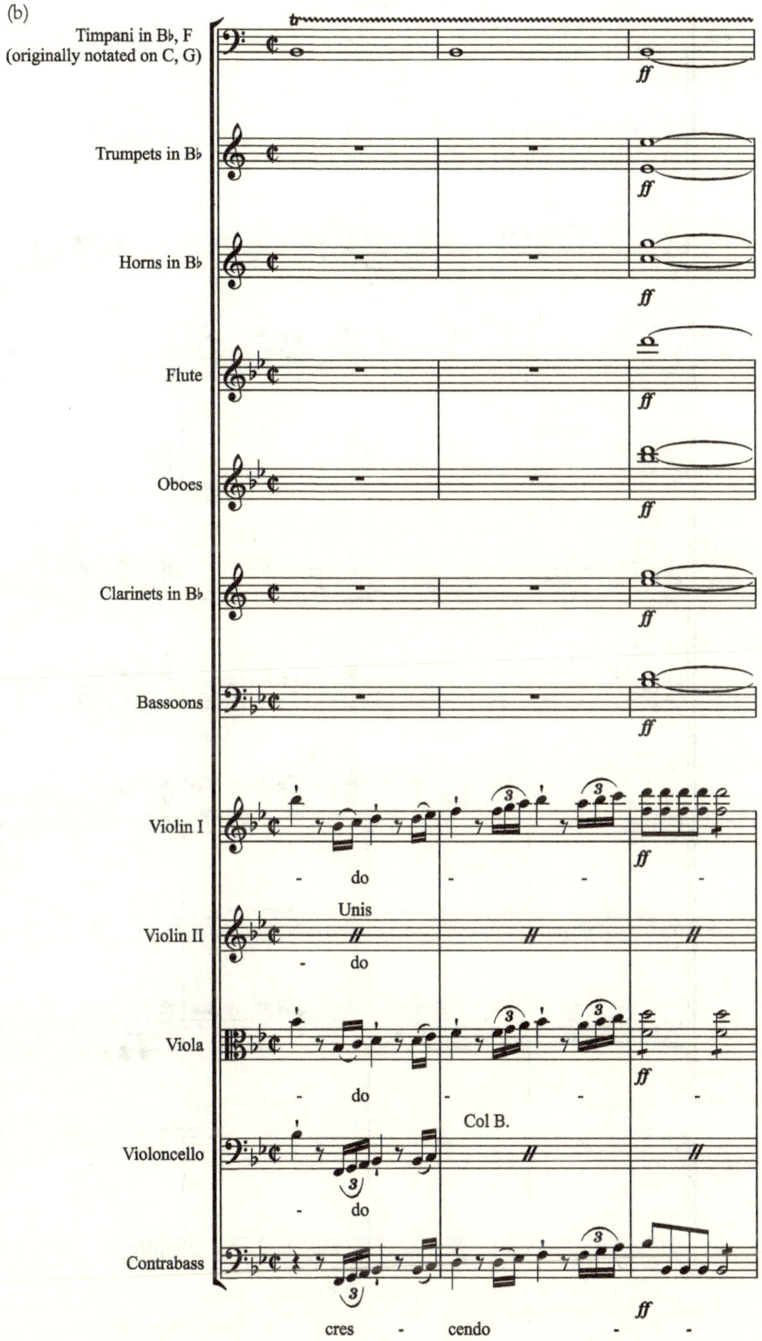

EXAMPLE 4.1. (CONT.)

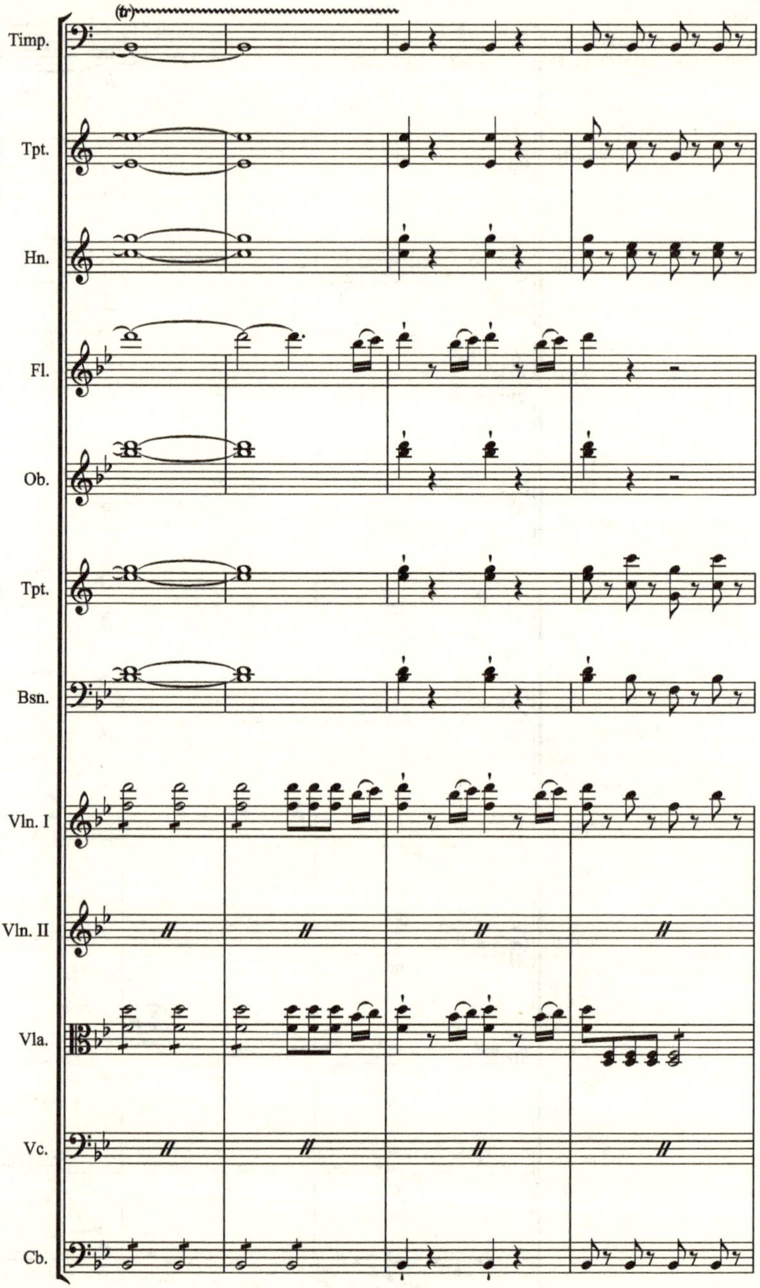

(1825–6) is a 3/4 *Adagio molto espressivo* in E-flat. In this sense, B-flat seems to have generated a particular progression of moods for Beethoven, one that further suggests the influence of both Haydn and Mozart. Mozart relied on this tonal and affective pairing frequently in his B-flat works, though he sometimes preferred for his slow movements the lighter character of the *Andante* or *Larghetto*.[26] Haydn also turned to E-flat major within a B-flat major context frequently, but tended toward the more expressive type of E-flat slow movement that Beethoven favored.[27] Key associations were then, as now, a matter of subjective perception, but there is no question that elements such as affect, topics, temperament, the design and limitation of instruments, and vocal tessitura strongly influenced a composer's choice of key. By choosing B-flat major for his newest symphony, Beethoven was engaging with a tradition of works whose character was mediated by this key and its associations.[28]

Thematic Design and Structural Articulations

The relationship between Haydn's Symphony No. 102 and Beethoven's Fourth Symphony becomes more apparent in a comparison of their themes. As mentioned earlier, the slow introductions of these two symphonies have much in common, in large part due to their similar opening ideas (Example 4.2). No. 102 begins *piano* on a unison B-flat in octaves. Strings, winds, brass, and rolling timpani (interestingly, minus the flutes, oboes, and bassoons in Pleyel's edition) crescendo to an apex and then decrescendo back to *piano*. The opening of the Fourth Symphony recalls this memorable gesture in its long-held unison B-flat (mm. 1–5) and dramatic hairpin crescendo (m. 5). In both introductions, the opening unison B-flat returns after several bars of contrasting material (Haydn: m. 6, Beethoven: m. 13).

---

26. Mozart's B-flat works with E-flat, triple-meter slow movements include Violin Concerto No. 1, K. 207 (1773), *Adagio*, 3/4; Piano Concerto No. 6, K. 238 (1776), *Andante un poco Adagio*, 3/4; and Piano Concerto No. 15, K. 450 (1784), *Andante*, 3/8. His B-flat works with E-flat, duple-meter slow movements include the unnumbered symphony K. Anh. 214 (1768); Symphonies Nos. 24, K. 182 (1773) and 33, K. 319 (1779); String Quartets K. 159 (1773), K. 172 (1773), K. 458 (1784), and K. 589 (1790); the String Quintet K. 174 (1773); and Piano Concerto No. 27, K. 595 (1791).

27. Examples include the *Adagios* of String Quartets Op. 50, no. 1 (1787); Op. 55, no. 3 (1788); Op. 64, no. 3 (1790); Op. 76, no. 4 (1797); and the *Largo* of Op. 33, no. 4 (1781), among others. Although the two "London" Symphonies in B-flat (Nos. 98 and 102) include slow movements in F major, Symphony No. 85 in B-flat, "La Reine" (c. 1785) features an E-flat-major *Romance* as its second movement.

28. There is a growing literature on the significance of key characteristics in this period. The classic text is Rita Steblin, *A History of Key Characteristics in the Eighteenth and Early Nineteenth Centuries* (Rochester: University of Rochester Press, 1983, rev. ed. 2002). See also Paul Ellison, *The Key to Beethoven: Connecting Tonality and Meaning in His Music* (Hillsdale, NY: Pendragon Press, 2014); Jessica Waldoff, "Does Haydn Have a C-minor Mood?," in Mary Hunter and Richard Will, eds., *Engaging Haydn: Culture, Context, and Criticism* (Cambridge: Cambridge University Press, 2012), 158–86; and John David Wilson, "Of Hunting, Horns, and Heroes: A Brief History of E♭ Major before the *Eroica*," *Journal of Musicological Research* 32, nos. 2–3 (2013): 163–82.

EXAMPLE 4.2. Comparison of opening themes.

a. Haydn, Symphony No. 102 in B-flat Major, Hob. I:102 (Paris: Ignaz Pleyel, 1803)

b. Beethoven, Symphony No. 4 in B-flat Major, Op. 60 (Bonn: N. Simrock, 1823)

EXAMPLE 4.2. (CONT.)

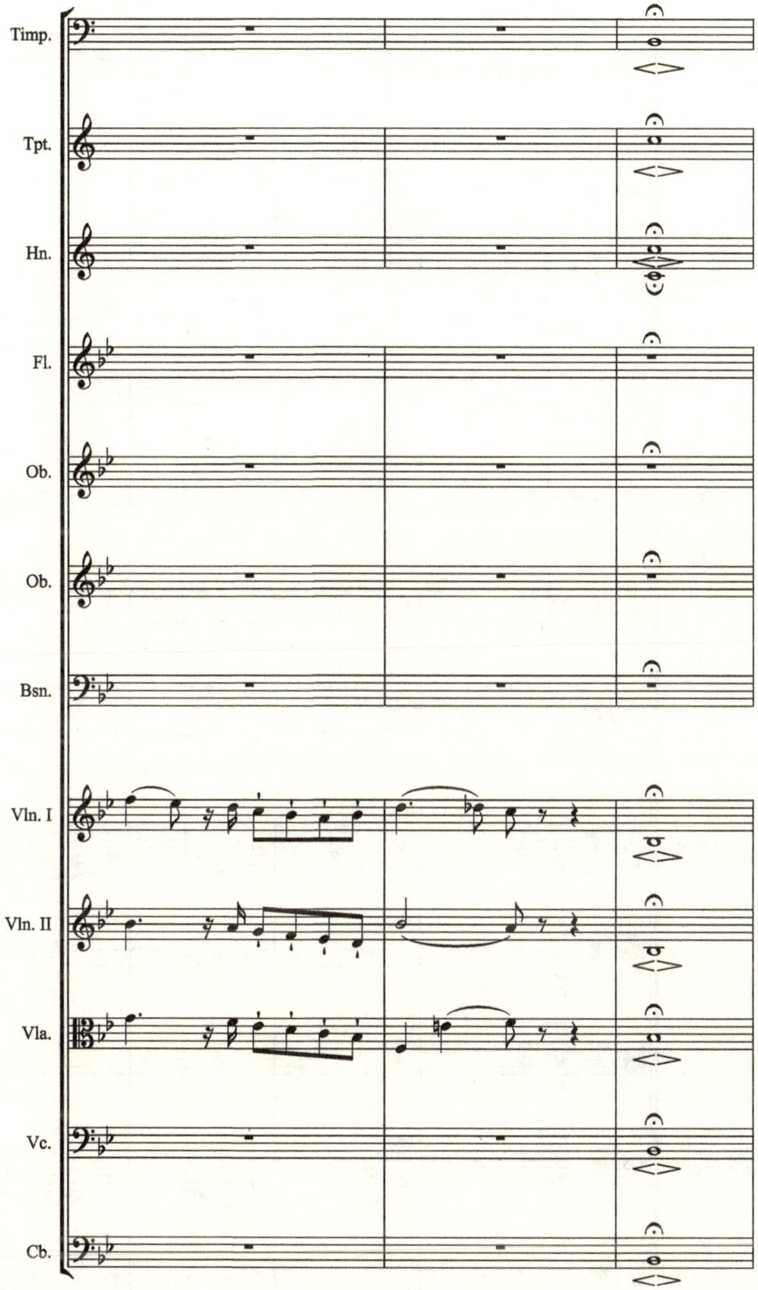

EXAMPLE 4.2. (CONT.)

(b)

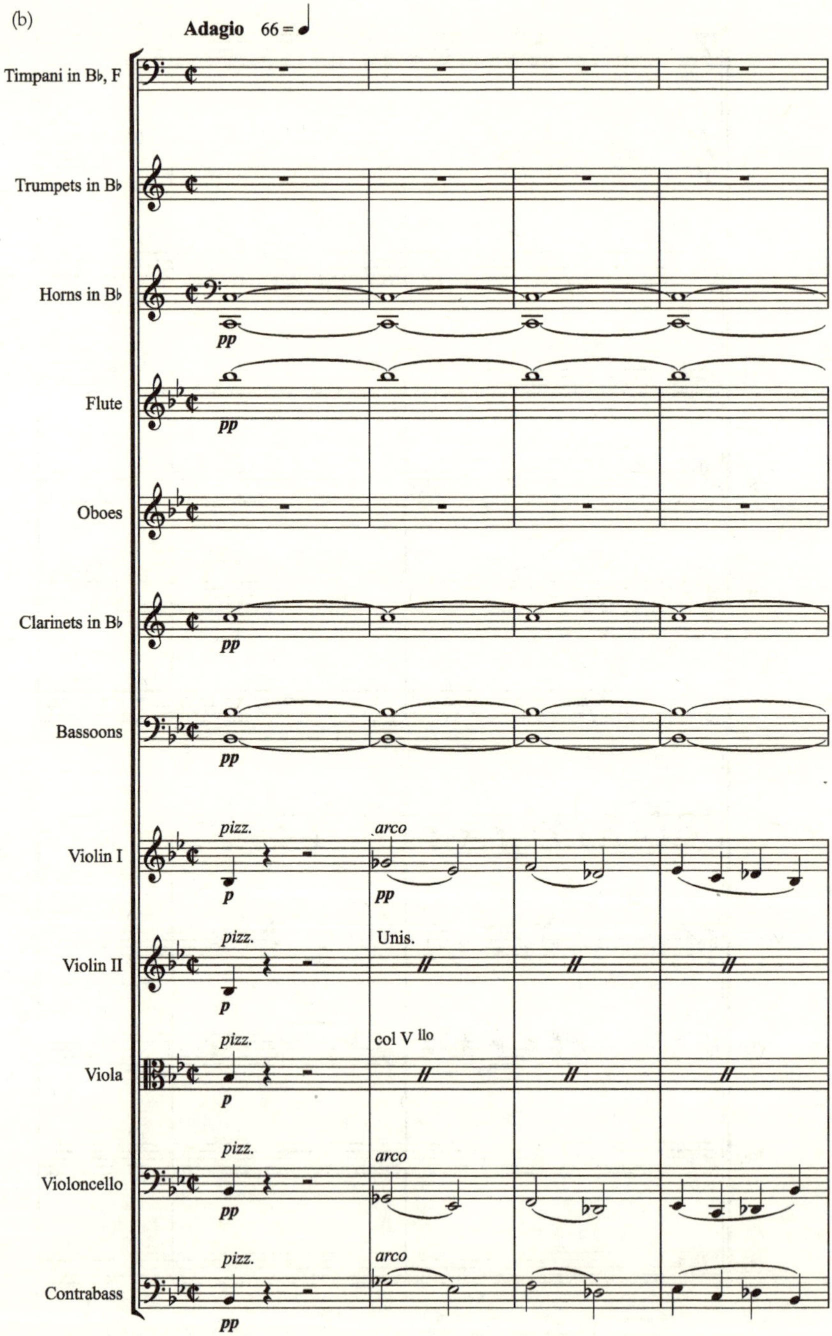

EXAMPLE 4.2. (CONT.)

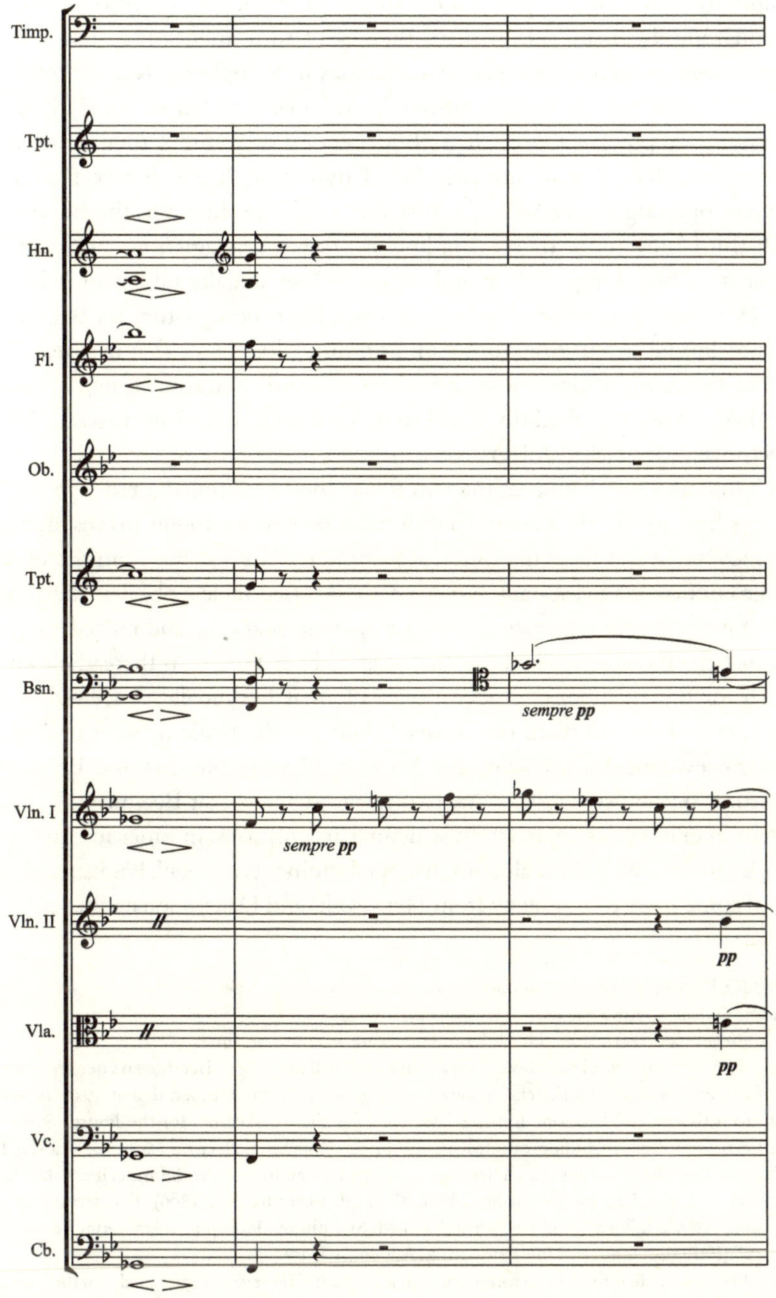

But this is not the only striking thematic resemblance between these two symphonies. As Karl Nef pointed out in a 1912 article on Beethoven's so-called Haydn reminiscences, the primary themes of movements 1, 2, and 3 in the Fourth seem to echo their analogous themes in Symphony No. 102 (see Table 4.2a).[29] Briefly put: both first movement themes share an unusually high tessitura and emphasize the pitch d^3; both second movement themes are slow-moving and lyrical with similarly florid figuration (note that Nef compares Haydn's opening theme with the first variant of the theme in the Beethoven); both third movement themes outline ascending arpeggiations of the B-flat-major triad beginning with an upbeat on f^1. Nef actually undermines his own case by introducing errors into his examples: the time signature for Beethoven's Allegro should be cut time (not common time), like Haydn's movement,[30] and that of the Adagio movement should be 3/4 (not common time), again, like Haydn's movement. Additionally, Haydn's minuet should be marked Allegro (Beethoven's is marked Allegro vivace).

Comparing the themes of the two finales, however, posed a problem for Nef, leading him to the unlikely suggestion that Beethoven found his inspiration in this movement not from the finale of Symphony No. 102 but from the opening Allegro of Haydn's Symphony No. 9 in C Major (see Table 4.2b). The theme itself, as Nef notes, has an Italianate, somewhat operatic character, and indeed, given the fact that Beethoven sketched this theme as early as 1804 (it is the earliest known sketch for the symphony), it seems plausible that he initially conceived of it in conjunction with his work on *Leonore*.[31] And yet, the finale presents perhaps the strongest evidence of a relationship between Haydn's No. 102 and Beethoven's Fourth. A side-by-side look at the two finales suggests that Beethoven looked to Haydn in crafting his approach to structural articulations. In order to explore this idea, let me examine six analogous structural moments in detail. For clarity, I make use of some basic terminology from Hepokoski and Darcy's sonata theory.[32]

---

29. Karl Nef, "Haydn-Reminiszenzen bei Beethoven." *Sammelbände der Internationalen Musikgesellschaft* 13, no. 2 (January–March 1912): 336–48.

30. Pleyel incorrectly gives Haydn's time signature as common time.

31. The orchestral works of 1806–7 are among the small number in Beethoven's oeuvre after circa 1798 for which few (or no) sketches survive. It has generally been assumed that at least one sketchbook from this period has gone missing. Even so, a handful of sketches for the Fourth Symphony have been identified, including one leaf in the H. C. Bodmer collection at the Beethoven-Haus in Bonn (the earliest known sketch, from c. 1804) and several leaves in the miscellany sketchbook *Landsberg 12*, housed in the Berlin Staatsbibliothek (all likely from c. 1806). For details and transcriptions, see Mark Ferraguto, "Beethoven's Fourth Symphony: Reception, Aesthetics, Performance History" (PhD diss. Cornell University, 2012), Appendix I, 176–90.

32. Haydn's finale is in a sonata rondo form that characterizes several of the finales of the "London" Symphonies. Hepokoski and Darcy describe it as a "Type 4" finale with a quasi-symmetrical recapitulation in which the latter is thoroughly recomposed but still provides the sense of balance necessary to create the impression of sonata form. Because this movement has strong sonata-like tendencies, it does not seem farfetched that Beethoven could have looked to it as a model for his own finale, more clearly a "textbook" variety sonata form with an unmistakable tripartite division and strong thematic differentiation (Hepokoski and Darcy's Type 3).

TABLE 4.2A Comparison of themes in Haydn's Symphony No. 102 and Beethoven's Symphony No. 4. Karl Nef, "Haydn-Reminiszenzen bei Beethoven" (1912; N.B. includes errors).

TABLE 4.2B Comparison of themes in Haydn's Symphony No. 9 (i) and Beethoven's Symphony No. 4 (iv). Nef, "Haydn-Reminiszenzen."

[Haydn, Symphony No. 9, *Allegro molto*]

Example 4.3 shows the onset of the transition from I to V immediately following the main theme. The example begins with the cadence into the transition, in both cases a rapidly descending series of four sixteenth notes culminating in a two eighth-note leap up to F. The transition proper begins in bar 2: both passages are grounded by a reattacked B-flat pedal point. Meanwhile,

EXAMPLE 4.3. Onset of transition.

Reductions based on Joseph Haydn, *Simphonie* [No. 102 in B-flat Major, Hob. I:102], vol. 3 of *Oeuvres de Haydn en Partitions*, ed. Ignaz Pleyel (Paris, 1803); and Ludwig van Beethoven, *Symphony No. 4 in B-flat Major, Op. 60*, ed. Jonathan Del Mar (Kassel: Bärenreiter, 2001).

a. Haydn, Symphony No. 102, iv, mm. 37–45

b. Beethoven, Symphony No. 4, iv, mm. 24–32 (cf. 192–210)

the melody begins on b-flat but rockets up two octaves over the span of the next two measures. High tessitura and jagged arpeggiations characterize both melodies. Harmonically, both transitions include (starting in measure 2) two bars of tonic followed by two bars of dominant (with emphasis on the seventh) and then a return to the tonic. Haydn continues in the same vein, while Beethoven diverges and begins to move toward V/V. Both passages divide evenly into two subphrases of four bars each.

Example 4.4 shows an auxiliary idea that appears shortly after the secondary theme in the dominant key of F major. After the presentation of the S-theme—in Haydn's case, a variant of the rondo idea, in Beethoven's a new lyrical idea—this new quasi-thematic material—what I have called an "Auxiliary Idea in

EXAMPLE 4.4. Auxiliary idea in S-Space.

> Reductions based on Joseph Haydn, *Simphonie* [No. 102 in B-flat Major, Hob. I:102],
> vol. 3 of *Oeuvres de Haydn en Partitions*, ed. Ignaz Pleyel (Paris, 1803); and Ludwig
> van Beethoven, *Symphony No. 4 in B-flat Major, Op. 60*, ed. Jonathan Del Mar (Kassel:
> Bärenreiter, 2001).

a. Haydn, Symphony No. 102, iv, mm. 78–85 (cf. 234–41)

b. Beethoven, Symphony No. 4, iv, mm. 42–9 (cf. 230–9)

S-Space"—occurs over a dominant C pedal, again reattacked in both instances. Although Beethoven's melody, unlike Haydn's, is divided antiphonally between woodwinds and strings, they share a similar contour. Adjusting for register, both melodies ascend chromatically and descend diatonically, staying confined within a relatively tight ambitus and hovering around the seventh of the chord, B-flat. The passages again divide into two subphrases of four bars each.

Both Haydn and Beethoven again deploy a reattacked pedal point after the structural cadence (Hepokoski and Darcy's "essential expositional closure," or EEC), as the grounding for a closing idea in F major, as shown in Example 4.5. The excerpts share a similar texture, with a perpetual-motion sixteenth-note figuration exchanged between violins 1 and 2. In Haydn, this exchange occurs after four bars, in Beethoven it happens every two bars. Both passages again divide evenly into four-bar subgroupings. Note also that both melodies emphasize scale degree five, reaching the apex of c^3—Beethoven throughout and Haydn the second time through.

As shown in Example 4.6, both finales include four places where striking *sforzando* or *rinforzando* accents occur in regular four-measure patterns. These moments forcefully interrupt the prevailing discourse and serve as a point of crisis in the developmental sections of both finales. Haydn here enacts an enharmonic shift while Beethoven instead harps on the dominant with its minor ninth sounding.

EXAMPLE 4.5. Closing (postcadential) idea.

> Reductions based on Joseph Haydn, *Simphonie* [No. 102 in B-flat Major, Hob. I:102], vol. 3 of *Oeuvres de Haydn en Partitions*, ed. Ignaz Pleyel (Paris, 1803); and Ludwig van Beethoven, *Symphony No. 4 in B-flat Major, Op. 60*, ed. Jonathan Del Mar (Kassel: Bärenreiter, 2001).

a. Haydn, Symphony No. 102, iv, mm. 110–17 (cf. 298–305)

b. Beethoven, Symphony No. 4, iv, mm. 88–95 (cf. 266–73)

Haydn and Beethoven also handle the retransition analogously, as shown in Example 4.7. Shortly after the crisis moments, both movements decrescendo. The movement's *Hauptmotiv*, detached from the theme, is divided among the string parts, creating a chain of motives. The effect is of gliding effortlessly into the recapitulation. Beethoven thoroughly absorbed this technique and used it elsewhere, for example in the finale of the second "Razumovsky" Quartet, in a moment Joseph Kerman labeled a "travesty of a Haydn retransition."[33] In Beethoven as in Haydn, the rapid motivic exchanges serve as a clever segue

---

33. Joseph Kerman, *The Beethoven Quartets* (New York: Norton, 1979), 132.

EXAMPLE 4.6. "Crisis" in developmental space.

Reductions based on Joseph Haydn, *Simphonie* [No. 102 in B-flat Major, Hob. I:102], vol. 3 of *Oeuvres de Haydn en Partitions*, ed. Ignaz Pleyel (Paris, 1803); and Ludwig van Beethoven, *Symphony No. 4 in B-flat Major, Op. 60*, ed. Jonathan Del Mar (Kassel: Bärenreiter, 2001).

a. Haydn, Symphony No. 102, iv, mm. 165–74 (cf. 86–9, 242–5, 286–9)

b. Beethoven, Symphony No. 4, iv, mm. 169–76 (cf. 64–77, 242–8, 290–4)

into the main thematic materials. Beethoven here preempts the recapitulation proper with a notoriously difficult bassoon solo.

Finally, in the coda spaces of both movements (Example 4.8) both composers insert halting versions of the main theme punctuated by silence. These are followed by forceful gestures of completion that reorient the movement to bring it to its eventual close.

Cyclic Design

In terms of the Fourth Symphony's cyclic design, it is instructive to turn to another of Haydn's "London" Symphonies, No. 99 in E-flat. Completed in

EXAMPLE 4.7. Retransition.

> Reductions based on Joseph Haydn, *Simphonie* [No. 102 in B-flat Major, Hob. I:102], vol. 3 of *Oeuvres de Haydn en Partitions*, ed. Ignaz Pleyel (Paris, 1803); and Ludwig van Beethoven, *Symphony No. 4 in B-flat Major, Op. 60*, ed. Jonathan Del Mar (Kassel: Bärenreiter, 2001).

a. Haydn, Symphony No. 102, iv, mm. 208–17 (cf. 181–8)

b. Beethoven, Symphony No. 4, iv, mm. 181–9 (cf. 290–9)

1793, Symphony No. 99 represents a particularly innovative approach to cyclic design. Unlike some of Haydn's more overtly cyclic works, No. 99 does not contain run-on movement pairs or overt reminiscences. Rather, as Webster observes, it "employs remote keys and sonorities so pervasively that they become the primary source of cyclic integration."[34] The symphony's modus operandi is established in the slow introduction, which passes from the tonic

---

34. Webster, *Haydn's "Farewell" Symphony and the Idea of Classical Style* (Cambridge: Cambridge University Press, 1991), 320.

EXAMPLE 4.8. "Joke" in coda space.

> Reductions based on Joseph Haydn, *Simphonie* [No. 102 in B-flat Major, Hob. I:102], vol. 3 of *Oeuvres de Haydn en Partitions*, ed. Ignaz Pleyel (Paris, 1803); and Ludwig van Beethoven, *Symphony No. 4 in B-flat Major, Op. 60*, ed. Jonathan Del Mar (Kassel: Bärenreiter, 2001).

a. Haydn, Symphony No. 102, iv, mm. 272–85

b. Beethoven, Symphony No. 4, iv, mm. 345–55

E-flat, through E minor (the enharmonic Neapolitan), to the dominant of C minor. The latter harmony connects via an unprepared B-flat dominant seventh to the tonic E-flat and the start of the exposition.[35] This tonal progression and the means by which it is implemented strongly influence the design of the first movement, as well as the larger conception.

Haydn worked on Symphony No. 99 during the year he interacted with Beethoven most closely,[36] and Webster has noted affinities between this

---

35. The slow introduction of Symphony No. 103 also moves to the dominant of C minor, but without the intervening harmony.

36. Haydn was probably at work on the first three symphonies of the second "London" group (Nos. 99, 100, 101) during the period he was tutoring Beethoven. The autographs of these three

TABLE 4.3 Shared signposts in the Adagio introductions of Haydn, Symphony No. 99 and Beethoven, Symphony No. 4.

Signpost	Haydn No. 99, i	Beethoven No. 4, i
(a) stable section in I or i	mm. 1–8	mm. 1–16
(b) emphasis of scale degree flat-six ($\flat\hat{6}$)	mm. 9–10	mm. 17–18
(c) reinterpretation of $\flat\hat{6}$ as $\hat{5}/\flat\text{II}$	m. 11	m. 18 [mm. 18–24 = mm. 6–12 transposed to $\flat$II]
(d) modulation	mm. 11–14	mm. 25–32
(e) arrival on V/minor key	mm. 14–17	mm. 32–5
(f) arrival on V^7	mm. 18	mm. 36–42

symphony and two of Beethoven's early compositions in E-flat, the piano sonata Op. 7 and the piano trio Op. 1, no. 1.[37] There are also striking parallels between this symphony and the Fourth Symphony, particularly with respect to the persistent use of scale degree $\flat\hat{6}$ as a destabilizing element. In addition, the relationship between the slow introduction and development section in No. 99's first movement—including Haydn's use of enharmonic notation and remote tonal juxtapositions—anticipates Beethoven's strategy of tonal planning in the Fourth.

To be sure, the opening Adagio of No. 99 has a different expressive character from that of the Fourth Symphony's Adagio: it is in the major mode; its opening is characterized by bold gestures and call-and-response textures; and it contains pervasive dotted rhythms, a characteristic of the French overture style. In harmonic terms, however, the two introductions run a similar course. One might identify their principal harmonic "signposts" as follows: (a) a stable section in the tonic key, (b) an unexpected emphasis of scale degree $\flat\hat{6}$, (c) a reinterpretation of $\flat\hat{6}$ as the fifth scale degree of the Neapolitan (flat-II), (d) a modulatory passage, (e) a culminatory arrival on the dominant of a minor key, (f) an unprepared dominant seventh of the tonic key. Table 4.3 shows where these six harmonic signposts are located in the two introductions. Table 4.4 compares the relevant passages from both introductions side-by-side. The comparison helps illustrate how Beethoven has reimagined this unusual tonal framework to suit the aesthetic of his slow introduction.

symphonies are partly or wholly on the Italian papers used in Vienna at this time. See Douglas Johnson, "1794–1795: Decisive Years in Beethoven's Early Development," in Alan Tyson, ed., *Beethoven Studies 3* (Cambridge: Cambridge University Press, 1982), 1–28, 17. Of the earlier group (Nos. 93–98), several also appear to have had their Viennese premieres during this period; however, Nos. 95 and 96 more likely premiered in 1791. See *Joseph Haydn Werke*, I/15, viii, n. 14.

37. Webster, Haydn's "Farewell" Symphony, 323.

TABLE 4.4 Selected passages from the slow introductions of Haydn, Symphony No. 99 (Paris: Ignaz Pleyel, 1803) and Beethoven, Symphony No. 4 (Kassel: Bärenreiter, 2001).

Emphasis and respelling of flat-six:

Symphony No. 99, mm. 10–11

Symphony No. 4, mm. 17–18

Culmination on off-tonic V and appearance of unprepared home V⁷:

Symphony No. 99, mm. 16–18

Symphony No. 4, mm. 34–37

The main difference between these two introductions is scale. What Haydn does in eighteen bars Beethoven expands to thirty-eight. First, Beethoven's initial tonic expansion (mm. 1–16) takes twice as long as Haydn's move from tonic to dominant (mm. 1–8). Second, since he repeats much of the music from his tonic expansion a semitone higher after emphasizing ♭6̂, his evocation of the Neapolitan lasts considerably longer (mm. 18–24). (Significantly, he never actually confirms the Neapolitan as a tonic, lingering instead on its dominant.) Beethoven's modulatory section (mm. 25–31) is also longer by four bars. Most notably, what for Haydn was a poignant one-measure-long dominant seventh chord (m. 18) is for Beethoven the most overtly theatrical gesture of his introduction: the massive tutti dominant seventh chords that elide with the Allegro vivace (mm. 36ff.).

The rhetorical stance of the two introductions also differs. Beethoven's emphatic ♭6̂ (G-flat, mm. 17–18) occurs within a *pianissimo* context, and makes sense only in reference to the first six bars, in which G-flat resolves to F. In measure 17, this resolution is withheld as the strings refuse to relinquish G-flat, gently propelling the music into the Neapolitan. By contrast, Haydn's C-flat (mm. 9–10) emerges *fortissimo* as an upper neighbor, intruding with considerable force on E-flat major. Likewise, Haydn's standing on the dominant of C minor (mm. 14–17) is marked *forte* and carries through the fierce dotted rhythms from earlier in the introduction; the unprepared B-flat dominant seventh that follows provides a marked contrast, played by winds alone in high register and marked *piano*. In Beethoven's introduction, the sense of contrast is equally striking, but the dynamic levels are reversed: the standing on the dominant of D minor (mm. 32–5) reaches a hushed *pianissimo*, and the surprise F dominant seventh bursts out at full volume and with the full orchestra (including trumpets and drums for the first time). Hence, while Beethoven's introduction follows roughly the same plan as Haydn's, it uses a different expressive palette.

Beethoven also articulates the cyclic design of the Fourth Symphony in ways that recall Haydn's procedure in Symphony No. 99. In both symphonies, scale degree ♭6̂—and its alter-ego, 5̂ of ♭II—decisively shapes the mostly diatonic discourse, often appearing at major structural junctures. In both first movements, ♭6̂ colors the transitional passages that follow the double presentation of the main theme in the tonic. Both passages create the impression of a push and pull between the forward momentum of the Allegro and the destabilizing elements of the slow introduction. In the Haydn transition (mm. 34ff.), the strings begin with a cascade downward from a high b-flat² , *sforzando*; the winds respond promptly with a cascade from c-flat³ (♭6̂), *sforzando* (while the strings provide a militaristic accompaniment). As if to cancel out the errant C-flat, the strings start their next cascade on C-natural. However, the effect is short-lived, as the next two cascades invert the problem, ending on B-natural (C-flat's alter-ego).

After several upward flourishes reaching to high B-flat, C, and D, winds and strings ruminate in unison on the interval of a semitone, with pointed *sforzandi* on G-flat, ♭6̂ of the now-tonicized dominant. In the Beethoven transition (mm. 65ff.), the sense of push and pull derives from the increasingly tense semitone banter between the first and second violins. What at first sounds like an operatic idiom—reminiscent of Mozart's overture to *The Marriage of Figaro*—quickly becomes a reminder of the symphony's slow introduction, as the second violins and violas color the first violins' scalar ascent with diminished sonorities. At the moment of climax (m. 77), the insistent semitone figure sounds in the second violins on g-flat² (♭6̂). Here, the reminder of the slow introduction becomes explicit, with the semitone figure G-flat—F expressively augmented over four bars.[38]

There are also similar harmonic relationships between the slow introduction and development section in the first movements of these two symphonies. Haydn's development section opens on a surprising G-major chord (mm. 90–3), which functions as dominant of C minor (V/vi). This relates to V/vi as the goal of the slow introduction, heard immediately before the unprepared B-flat dominant chord. Moreover, since the resolution of V/vi was preempted in the introduction, its return in the development seems inevitable. Haydn thus implies that the development section will answer some of the questions posed by the introduction—not least the whereabouts of the missing C-minor resolution. Of course, the fifth bar of the introduction would be too soon. Rather, he surprises in another way by turning to C major (VI♮) and to the "closing" theme.

Beethoven elides his exposition and development section as he had done with the slow introduction and exposition. This leads him to treat the development section's first eighteen bars as a broad expansion of V, acting like a codetta to the exposition. Hence, the first real harmonic activity does not occur until bar 203. At this point, the final cadence of the expansion is subverted by a startling, hushed A major (V/iii, in first inversion)—a moment of "suspended time" in Adorno's formulation. This harmony, of course, recalls the unresolved V/iii from the slow introduction. Beethoven, like Haydn, frames the reappearance as an important event: where Haydn surrounds his G major with fermatas, Beethoven prolongs his A major for a remarkable fourteen bars. At the end of the prolongation, again like Haydn, Beethoven avoids moving to the expected minor tonic, turning instead to D major (III♯) in measure 217. In both works,

---

38. On Beethoven's use of the semitone motive as a means of cyclic integration across all four movements, see Ferraguto, "Beethoven's Fourth Symphony," 92–103. For other aspects of cyclic integration, see Ludwig Misch, *Die Faktoren der Einheit in der Mehrsätzigkeit der Werke Beethovens* (Munich and Duisberg: G. Henle, 1958), 54–72, and "Ein unbemerkter thematischer Zusammenhang in Beethovens IV. Symphonie," in *Neue Beethoven-Studien und andere Themen* (Bonn: Beethoven-Haus, 1967), 56–8.

the turn to the parallel major is crucial: it prevents the seemingly inevitable "working-out" from taking place, delaying it until later in the form and creating the impression of goal-orientedness.

COMMEMORATING HAYDN

As the most celebrated composer of the 1790s and early 1800s, Haydn was an obvious model for other composers to admire and emulate. As Emily H. Green has noted, more musical works were dedicated to him than to any other composer of the eighteenth and early nineteenth centuries, "effectively elevating him to the status of a pseudo patron of the arts."[39] These dedications, she notes, functioned as self-promotional tools as much as gracious acknowledgments, and the epigraph *"élève de Haydn"* appended to a composer's name could be a branding strategy in its own right. Among the many instrumental works dedicated to Haydn, Mozart's six "Haydn" string quartets (published in 1785) have stood out as particularly noteworthy, both because of the florid language of the dedication itself and because they seem to suggest an intimate musical as well as personal relationship between the two masters. Many scholars have interpreted Mozart's quartets as *homages* or musical tributes to Haydn, despite the fact that Mozart does not present the works in these terms.

Beethoven, who studied with Haydn from November 1792 through December 1793 or January 1794, dedicated his first set of three piano sonatas (Op. 2, published 1796) to his mentor. While this dedication was a significant public attestation of Beethoven's relationship with Haydn, the former's apparent refusal to style himself as an *"élève de Haydn"* on his early title pages has often been interpreted as evidence that their relationship was strained. Since the nineteenth century, critics have sought to distance Beethoven from "Papa Haydn," characterizing their relationship as one of mutual distrust, jealousy, and anxiety. But as Webster has observed, this tradition is largely based on apocryphal accounts, and the evidence does not particularly support the idea of a "falling-out" between the two men.[40] In any case, scholars have placed so much emphasis on the personal rapport between Haydn and Beethoven that they have missed the larger picture. Haydn's legacy was, in the first decade of the 1800s, a far more important influence in Beethoven's life than Haydn himself. By 1806, Haydn the man had already been eclipsed by Haydn the phenomenon, and

---

39. Emily H. Green, "A Patron among Peers: Dedications to Haydn and the Economy of Celebrity," *Eighteenth-Century Music* 8, no. 2: 215–37, 215–16.

40. See James Webster, "The Falling-Out between Haydn and Beethoven: The Evidence of the Sources," in Lewis Lockwood and Phyllis Benjamin, eds., *Beethoven Essays: Studies in Honor of Elliot Forbes* (Cambridge, MA: Harvard University Press, 1984), 3–45.

Beethoven—whatever his personal feelings—was too shrewd to overlook the fact that emulating Haydn's approach could be a successful commercial strategy.

Did Beethoven model his Fourth Symphony on either or both of the late Haydn symphonies discussed earlier? This question proves vexing to answer, in no small part due to the absence of sketches documenting Beethoven's creative process during this period (a sketchbook from 1806 appears to have gone missing).[41] Outright modeling was by no means unusual for Beethoven: a notable example is the string quartet Op. 18, no. 5, which Beethoven closely modeled on one of Mozart's "Haydn" quartets, K. 464.[42] Nearer to the period of the Fourth Symphony, Beethoven made extensive studies of operatic ensembles by Mozart and Cherubini in preparation for the composition of *Leonore*. Such a practice is also possible here, although there is no evidence in this regard.

That said, the Fourth Symphony is so distinct from its Haydnesque forebears in certain respects that a claim of outright modeling seems overstated. Beethoven's operatic studies from this period show that he often paid close attention to certain musical elements while ignoring others, for example, copying out intricate vocal passages from Mozart's ensembles but leaving out the orchestration (and not always bothering to write out the entire ensemble). One might similarly hypothesize that Beethoven looked to Haydn's symphonies when assembling the "bones" of his new B-flat symphony—main themes, structural joints, pivotal transitions, elements of scoring—but that the working-out of material represents a freer approach. This more oblique method of modeling would not only have provided a sure footing for Beethoven as he renewed his relationship with the symphony in the wake of criticisms of the *Eroica* but also have enabled him to capitalize on Haydn's success without "seeming or trying to imitate" him, to borrow Tovey's formulation. Indeed, what sets the Fourth apart from mere imitations of Haydn is the way it seems to refract Haydnesque gestures, ideas, and topics through the prism of Beethoven's personal style. As a symphony in dialogue with Haydn's music, the Fourth also functions as a kind of commemoration, articulating his living legacy in much the same way as icons, portraits, poems, and dedications. The fact that this commemoration was motivated at least in part by economic concerns makes it all the more fitting a tribute to a figure who understood the business of composing better than perhaps anyone else in his day.

---

41. See note 31.

42. Bathia Churgin has noted thirteen examples from Mozart's music that Beethoven copied into his own manuscripts throughout his life. See her "Beethoven and Mozart's Requiem: A New Connection," *Journal of Musicology* 5 (1987): 457–77; the thirteen items are tabulated in an appendix. Beethoven seems to have copied fewer works of Haydn's, but there are exceptions: in 1793 or 1794, during his lessons with Haydn, he copied out the entire String Quartet in E-flat, Op. 20, no. 1. See Elaine Sisman, "'The Spirit of Mozart from Haydn's Hands': Beethoven's Musical Inheritance," in Glenn Stanley, ed., *The Cambridge Companion to Beethoven* (Cambridge: Cambridge University Press, 2000), 45–63, 52–3. For a recent discussion of K. 464's influence on Beethoven, see Stephen Rumph, "What Beethoven Learned from K. 464," *Eighteenth-Century Music* 11, no. 1 (March 2014): 55–77.

CHAPTER 5

MUSIC FOR A FRENCH PIANO

WoO 80

In late 1803, Beethoven acquired a new grand piano from the French firm of Sébastien Erard. This piano differed in important respects from the one built by Anton Walter that he owned in the late 1790s, most notably in its heavier construction, English-style action rather than the lighter Viennese action, triple stringing, four pedal stops (lute, dampers, buff, *una corda*), and five-and-a-half octave range from FF to c^4. By 1805, Beethoven had already twice asked a builder to lighten up the instrument's stiff action, bringing it closer to the Viennese action to which he was accustomed. By 1810, he was complaining to piano maker Johann Andreas Streicher that his French piano was beyond repair and useless to him.

Now housed in the Linz Schlossmuseum, Beethoven's Erard remains in unplayable condition.[1] Apart from visible damage to the keyboard, case, and action, the instrument suffered from both "neglect and casual repair," this presumably under Beethoven's ownership.[2] Tilman Skowroneck estimates that Beethoven broke up to 78 percent of the instrument's strings during the period he was using it regularly; many of the replacement strings have a diameter that is inappropriate to their pitch.[3] Clearly, the instrument was put under various kinds of stress, perhaps in part resulting from Beethoven's own manner of playing. As early as 1816, Peter Josef Simrock noted that it was "Completely worn

---

1. Beethoven gave the instrument to his brother Johann, an apothecary who established a shop in Linz, in 1824. From Johann it passed to Linz's Oberösterreichisches Landesmuseum. See Alfons Huber, "Beethovens 'Erard'-Flügel: Überlegungen zu seiner Restaurierung," *Restauro* 3 (1990): 181–8, 181. My thanks to curator Stefan Gschwendtner for discussing the piano with me in person.

2. Tilman Skowroneck, *Beethoven the Pianist*, Musical Performance and Reception (Cambridge: Cambridge University Press, 2010), 102. Skowroneck's chapter on Beethoven's Erard, to which I refer several times, is based on his earlier article, "Beethoven's Erard Piano: Its Influence on His Compositions and on Viennese Fortepiano Building," *Early Music* 30, no. 4 (November 2002): 522–38. I cite the more recent version here.

3. Skowroneck, *Beethoven the Pianist*, 102.

out, out of tune; several strings were in fact missing."[4] By that time, Beethoven could scarcely hear how bad things had gotten and evidently tortured his houseguests with out-of-tune performances.

In light of Beethoven's own dismissals of the Erard, it was long supposed that the piano was of little value to him. More recently, Skowroneck and others have opened up the possibility that this piano, an instrument with which Beethoven was at least initially "enchanted,"[5] in fact served as an important compositional resource for him in the early 1800s.[6] This notion has been bolstered by Maria Rose van Epenhuysen's discovery that the Erard was not a gift from the Parisian firm but was rather ordered by Beethoven, perhaps as part of his ongoing effort to develop his reputation in France.[7] The instrument's imprint on Beethoven's piano music is most evident in his increased use of the five-and-a-half octave range. Beethoven had previously used this range in his Third Piano Concerto, a work he performed publicly on an unknown instrument (he included *ossia* passages in the published version to allow for performance on five-octave instruments). Beginning around 1803, the five-and-a-half octave compass became a more common feature of his published piano music. Not only this, but certain scores from this period incorporate elements of touch, sonority, and pedaling that seem to relate directly to his experience with the Erard.

How might an appreciation of the Erard's unique qualities allow us to better understand the piano music that Beethoven composed during this period? In what ways can such an appreciation help shape modern-day performances of this music? Given the current state of the Erard (and given the fact that it was modified during Beethoven's lifetime), any response to these questions necessarily involves speculation.[8] Nonetheless, there is value in the

4. Friedrich Kerst, *Die Erinnerungen an Beethoven*, 2 vols. (Stuttgart: Julius Hoffmann, 1913), vol. 1, 204, quoted and translated in Skowroneck, *Beethoven the Pianist*, 102.

5. On the Erard as compositional resource, see Skowroneck, *Beethoven the Pianist*, 103–15, and Andrea Botticelli, "'Creating Tone': The Relationship between Beethoven's Piano Sonority and Evolving Instrument Designs, 1800–1810" (DMA thesis, University of Toronto, 2014), 35–83.

6. In a letter to publisher Breitkopf & Härtel dated December 14, 1803, Georg August Griesinger reported that Beethoven was so enchanted by his new piano that he now regarded the local Viennese instruments as "rubbish" (*Quark*). Otto Biba, ed., *"Eben komme ich von Haydn . . .": Georg August Griesingers Korrespondenz mit Joseph Haydns Verleger Breitkopf & Härtel 1799–1819* (Zurich: Atlantis Musikbuch-Verlag, 1987), 216.

7. According to a sales book in the Erard archives, Beethoven owed the firm 1,500 francs for his *"piano en forme de clavecin"* (serial no. 133). It remains unknown whether he ever paid the bill. Griesinger incorrectly reported that the piano was a "gift" from the firm (Erard had gifted Haydn a similar piano in 1801), a notion that was erroneously reconfirmed by the firm itself in the late nineteenth century. See Maria Rose van Epenhuysen, "Beethoven and His 'French Piano': Proof of Purchase," *Musique–Images–Instruments* 7 (2005): 110–22.

8. Another form of evidence comes from copies of Erard pianos from the period, of which there are now several fine examples. One is Christopher Clarke's facsimile of an 1802 Erard held in the Musée de la musique in Paris (E.986.8.1). Another is Alain Moysan's facsimile of an 1803 Erard, which may be heard on the recording *Beethoven et le pianoforte Érard: Variation & Pièces diverses à 2 et 4 mains, 1803–1806*, Pierre Bouyer and Sophie Liger, Diligence, DIL6, 2007, compact disc. More

asking, insofar as thinking about these issues allows us to revisit our relationship with the musical text and to look at even the most elemental aspects of musical notation from another perspective. Fundamental to this perspective is the idea that, for Beethoven, the piano was not merely the implement for which he destined his piano music; rather, it helped determine, to a greater or lesser degree, the very process of composition. Put differently, following Latour, the piano was a mediator, "transform[ing], translat[ing], distort[ing], and modify[ing]" musical ideas, even as those ideas were further refined through sketching, reflection, and written-out elaboration.[9] Thinking about Beethoven's pianos as mediators allows us to read his scores less as prescriptive "recipes" for performance and more as descriptive "records" of a creative process that reflects the capacities and limitations of specific instruments. Reading the score in this way, in turn, opens up new interpretive pathways through well-traveled musical territory.

My approach in this chapter is to look closely at one work composed during the Erard period, the Thirty-Two Variations on an Original Theme (WoO 80). Written in 1806 and published the following year, WoO 80 makes use of the entire five-and-a-half octave range. It is unique among Beethoven's piano works in its adoption of the passacaglia as a governing structural principle. Beethoven appears to have become interested in passacaglias and chaconnes through his study of Handel, whose Chaconne in G Major (HWV 442) bears striking affinities to WoO 80.[10] While Handel served as an important model, however, WoO 80 may also be understood as a deliberate and even somewhat systematic exploration of piano techniques, for which the straightforward passacaglia form served as an ideal vehicle. More specifically, here Beethoven updates and reimagines the passacaglia form by placing it in dialogue with modern English and French pianistic approaches. I will begin by examining the work's larger structure from this vantage point, after which I will explore in depth the ways in which the Erard's extended keyboard compass served as an aesthetic resource. Considering WoO 80 in light of the Erard's capacities and limitations offers new ways of conceptualizing and shaping interpretation in this work.

recently, a team of researchers at the Orpheus Instituut in Belgium, led by Tom Beghin, Chris Maene, and Tilman Skowroneck, has created a facsimile of Beethoven's Erard.

9. Bruno Latour, *Reassembling the Social: An Introduction to Actor-Network Theory* (Oxford and New York: Oxford University Press, 2005), 39.

10. Martin Staehelin, "'auf eine wirklich ganz *alte* Manier'? Händel-Anlehnung und Eigenständigkeit in Beethovens Klavier-Variationen c-Moll WoO 80," in Nicole Ristow, Wolfgang Sandberger, and Dorothea Schröder, eds., *"Critica musica": Studien zum 17. und 18. Jahrhundert: Festschrift Hans Joachim Marx zum 65. Geburtstag* (Stuttgart: J. B. Metzler, 2001), 281–97.

Variazioni quasi una passacaglia

In a letter dated October 18, 1802, Beethoven announced to the publisher Breitkopf & Härtel that he wished to have two new sets of keyboard variations engraved. These, he claimed, were composed "in a really entirely *new manner*" (*auf eine wircklich ganz* neue Manier).[11] Scholars have made much, occasionally too much, of Beethoven's assertion; language emphasizing novelty was, after all, boilerplate when it came to courting publishers. But there is no doubt that these variation sets—eventually Opp. 34 and 35—were highly innovative, and for different reasons. They also helped to set the stage for Beethoven's approach in WoO 80.

In the Six Variations on an Original Theme, Op. 34, Beethoven sought a new method of large-scale tonal organization. Rather than adopting the relatively stable harmonic plan typical of the theme and variations form—in which most variations are set in the same key as the theme, with perhaps one or two variations in contrasting keys (usually the parallel major or minor)—here, he is more systematic. After the theme is presented in F major, Variation 1 begins, unexpectedly, in the remote key of D major. Following suit, each of the next four variations sounds a major or minor third lower than the previous, resulting in a descending sequence of third-related tonal juxtapositions: F major, D major, B-flat major, G major, E-flat major, C minor. Variation 5 ends on the dominant seventh of F major, preparing the return of the home key for the final variation and coda (and hence motivating for the first and only time a fifth-related tonal juxtaposition).

What is remarkable about Op. 34 is not so much the use of third-related juxtapositions between sections, but rather the way that these juxtapositions are systematically deployed and hence elevated to a kind of structural or aesthetic principle. By contrast, the Fifteen Variations and Fugue on an Original Theme, Op. 35 (better known as the "Eroica" Variations because of Beethoven's appropriation of its materials in the finale of the *Eroica* Symphony), is entirely conventional from a tonal point of view. But it, too, represents a novel way of structuring the theme and variations form. The set begins with an "Introduzione" in which a bass line is stated in unison octaves and then varied with increasing contrapuntal complexity (first in two voices, then in three, then in four). At length, the "theme"—a contredanse tune from Beethoven's ballet *The Creatures of Prometheus*—enters, and in counterpoint with the original bass line, no less. The fifteen variations that ensue are pianistically the most impressive and challenging Beethoven had yet written. But even these are arguably outdone by the massive fugue that follows. Hearkening back to the introduction, the fugue

---

11. Anderson, vol. 1, no. 62, pp. 76–7, 77 (*Briefwechsel*, vol. 1, no. 108, pp. 126–7, 126). Translation emended.

cements the work's marriage of variation technique with learned-style counterpoint and ushers in a triumphant coda.

At first blush, it would seem that Beethoven did not hold WoO 80 in such high esteem as these two pathbreaking variation sets. He did not assign it an opus number, a designation he reserved for what he considered his most important compositions. And if we are to believe an oft-quoted anecdote, he even disparaged it:

> Beethoven once found Streicher's daughter practicing these Variations. After he had listened for a while he asked her: "By whom is that?" "By you." "Such nonsense by me? Oh Beethoven, what an ass you were!"[12]

Of course, it is easy to place too much stock in this anecdote, which, if true, probably reflects the ironic and self-effacing attitude of a seasoned composer more than actual derision. In any case, *pace* Beethoven, WoO 80 has passed the test of time. And although it is perhaps less overtly radical than either Op. 34 or Op. 35, it is no less distinctive.

Rather than infusing the theme and variations form with baroque contrapuntal techniques as he had done in Op. 35, here Beethoven turned to the baroque form of the passacaglia and infused it with modern pianistic techniques. An early reviewer for the *Allgemeine musikalische Zeitung* (*AmZ*) noted this mixture of old and new elements:

> B[eethoven] follows in this little work the oldest, especially the old German, manner of writing variations more than [the manner that is] customary today. And particularly, Handel worked out variations in this genre, only with far less freely and lightly flowing (but also less fluttering around) fantasy. Through this procedure, Beethoven knew how to give even this small product an attractive allure of the unusual.[13]

More recently, Martin Staehelin has convincingly argued that Beethoven modeled WoO 80 on Handel's Chaconne in G Major (HWV 442), a work Beethoven may have first encountered through his friend and fellow Bonn native Nikolaus Simrock, who published it with a dedication to Beethoven in 1808.[14] Both works are relatively long variation sets built on eight-bar themes,

---

12. Thayer/Forbes, vol. 1, 410. The anecdote was first noted down by Otto Jahn.

13. "B. folgt in diesem Werkchen der ältesten, besonders der altdeutschen Weise, Variationen zu schreiben, mehr, als der jetzt gebräuchlichen; und namentlich hat Händel Variat. in dieser Gattung, nur allerdings mit weit weniger frey und leicht bewegter, aber auch weniger hin- und herflatternder Phantasie, ausgearbeitet. Durch diese Prozedur hat B. auch diesem kleinen Produkte einen anziehenden Reiz des Ungewöhnlichen zu geben gewusst." "Trente deux variations p. le pianoforte comp. par Louis v. Beethoven," *Allgemeine musikalische Zeitung* 10, no. 6 (November 4, 1807): cols. 94–6, 94.

14. Simrock had also published the first edition of Bach's sonatas and partitas for solo violin (BWV 1001–1006) in 1802. This set included the famous chaconne in D minor, another potential impetus for Beethoven's variations. My thanks to Elaine Sisman for calling this to my attention.

and each theme is built on a ground bass that begins with a descending tetra-chord (Handel's diatonic, Beethoven's chromatic). Certain figurations in WoO 80 seem to be directly imported from Handel. Most strikingly, the Chaconne seems to have inspired Beethoven's atypical use of three-variation chains in which a particular figuration is played first by one hand, then by the other, and finally by both hands together.[15]

Emulating Handel's chaconne seems to have provided Beethoven with yet another solution to the problem of structural monotony inherent in the theme and variations form. By adopting an eight-bar phrase model with no internal repeats, he created a fast-paced variation set in which the main expressive contrasts result neither from tonal juxtapositions (as in Op. 34) nor from stylistic oppositions (as in Op. 35) but rather from rapid shifts of technique, figuration, and sonority. The Handelian form, in short, was an ideal vehicle through which he could probe the expressive possibilities of the piano.

WoO 80 consists of an eight-measure theme, thirty-two eight-measure variations, and a forty-three-measure coda (eliding with the last measure of Variation 32). Christa Jost has proposed that these sections may be grouped into a larger five-part structure: (1) Theme through Variation 11, (2) Variations 12 through 16 (corresponding to the *maggiore* variations), (3) Variations 17 through 22, (4) Variations 23 through 30, and (5) Variation 31 through the Coda.[16] Against the backdrop of this larger structure, however, is an alternation among standalone variations, Handelian variation chains, and variations linked by other means (such as the varied repetition of a motif).[17] As such, the resulting conception sounds less like a large multipart structure as it unfolds and more like a series of vignettes, some of which are more obviously grouped together than others. The above-mentioned reviewer for the *AmZ* perhaps put it best, stating that the variations are arranged "as a long series of images, like those laid out by ancient oriental poets, whereby all of these depict the same subject but from different and mutually opposing sides."[18] The strong internal contrasts among

15. See the musical examples in Staehelin, "'auf eine wirklich ganz *alte* Manier'?" 289–92.

16. Christa Jost, "*32 Variationen c-Moll für Klavier WoO 80*," in Albrecht Riethmüller, Carl Dahlhaus, and Alexander L. Ringer, eds., *Beethoven: Interpretationen seiner Werke*, 2 vols. (Laaber: Laaber-Verlag, 1994–6), vol. 2, 481–5, 483.

17. As William Kinderman notes (*Beethoven*, 2nd ed. [Oxford and New York: Oxford University Press, 2009], 145), the variation groupings "by no means exhaust the many relationships between individual variations, which are based on general rhythmic and textural features and on modal contrast [. . .]." To give just one example of a relationship that cuts across variations, consider the way in which cross-rhythms are progressively complexified, from 2 against 3 (Variation 9) to 3 against 4 (Variation 16), to 7 against 8, 7 against 10, and 8 against 10 (Variation 32).

18. "[. . .] wie eine lange Reihe Bilder, dergleichen alte orientalische Dichter aufstellen, und wovon alle denselben Gegenstand, aber von verschiedenen und einander entgegenstehenden Seiten, darstellen." "Trente deux variations," col. 95.

variations (and groups of variations) result in large part from the work's kaleidoscope of pianistic techniques, as shown in Table 5.1.

While WoO 80's outward design was influenced by Handel, its pianistic character reflects contemporary developments in English and French pianism and piano construction. Here, it is worth noting that English and French pianos were part of the same tradition, but that there were also differences in their design. Compared to Broadwoods, Erards had considerably thinner soundboards in the treble register, more efficient damping mechanisms, and differently shaped hammers with more substantial wood cores, and hence thinner hammer leathers.[19] Nonetheless, from a mechanical point of view English and French pianos were alike and contrasted significantly with the Viennese pianos with which Beethoven was most familiar. Put briefly, English and French instruments were typically heavier, louder, more resonant, and less efficient at damping than their Viennese counterparts. While English and French instruments were designed for large halls, Viennese pianos, with their lightning-quick action and responsive touch, were better suited to the salon. Beethoven had already begun to explore an "Anglophile" manner in some of his sonatas, including the Sonata in C Major, Op. 53 ("Waldstein"), probably the first he composed with the Erard in mind.[20] The extent to which he derived his Anglophile textures and sonorities through experimentation, versus through engagement with the English and French repertories, is difficult to discern.[21] Nevertheless, WoO 80 contains several hallmarks of the English manner, including the use of grand, two-handed chords reminiscent of orchestral scoring (Variations 6, 18, 26), the use of long slurs to create a singing legato (Variations 7, 15, 28), and the use of wide gaps between the hands to highlight the English-style piano's stronger balance between bass and treble (Variations 3, 29, 32).[22]

Beethoven may have been directly inspired in WoO 80 by two sets of etudes, both written by German composers who were deeply familiar with English (and, in the case of the latter composer, also French) pianism and pianos. These were Johann Baptist Cramer's *Étude pour le piano forte en quarante deux exercises dans les différents tons* (1804) and Daniel Steibelt's *Etude pour le pianoforte contenant 50 exercices de différents genres* (1805). Beethoven is known to have valued Cramer's etudes tremendously; indeed, a copy survives with annotations by

19. See Christopher Clarke, "Erard and Broadwood in the Classical Era: Two Schools of Piano Making," *Musique–Images–Instruments* 11 (2009): 98–125, 109–16. See also Thierry Maniguet, "Le piano en forme de clavecin Érard," *Musique–Images–Instruments* 11 (2009): 82–98.

20. See Skowroneck, *Beethoven the Pianist*, 103–15, and Rose-van Epenhuysen, 120–2.

21. On Beethoven and the English repertoire, see Alexander L. Ringer, "Beethoven and the London Pianoforte School," *The Musical Quarterly* 56, no. 4 (October 1970): 742–58, and Bart van Oort, *The English Classical Piano Style and Its Influence on Haydn and Beethoven* (DMA thesis, Cornell University, 1993), 166–73.

22. A summary of distinctively English pianistic elements is given in Bart van Oort, "Haydn and the English Classical Piano Style," *Early Music* 28, no. 1 (February 2000): 73–89.

Section	Key	Techniques emphasized	Dynamics	Expression
Tema	C minor	Tirades	*f–sf–p*	
V1		Arpeggios, repeated notes (RH)	*p–sf–p*	*leggiermente*
V2		Arpeggios, repeated notes (LH)	*p–f–p*	*leggiermente*
V3		Arpeggios (contrary motion), repeated notes (BH)		
V4		RH plays 2 real parts	*p–sfp*	
V5		Slurred parallel octaves, leaps (RH), repeated notes (LH), hand crossing	*cresc–sf*	
V6		Jagged arpeggios (BH)	*ff*	*sempre staccato e forzato*
V7		Slurred parallel octaves (RH), leaps (LH)	*p–sf–>–p*	
V8		Jagged arpeggios alternating between octaves and thirds (RH), leaps (LH)		
V9		RH plays 2 real parts, 2 vs. 3 rhythm	*sf–p*	*espressione*
V10		Rapid scales (LH), octaves (RH)	*sempre f–sf–>*	
V11		Rapid scales (RH), octaves (LH)	*sempre f*	
V12	C major	Legato, cantabile melody (RH)	*p–sf–sf–p*	
V13		Legato, cantabile melody (LH)	*p*	
V14		Legato, cantabile melody (LH), staccato parallel thirds (RH)	*sf*	*sempre staccato*
V15		Syncopated slurred parallel octaves (RH), slurred leaps (LH)	*cresc*	*dolce–risoluto*
V16		Parallel octaves (RH), slurred leaps (LH), 4 vs. 3 rhythm	*cresc–rinf–dim*	

(continued)

TABLE 5.1 Continued

Section	Key	Techniques emphasized	Dynamics	Expression
V17	C minor	RH (then LH) plays 2 real parts, leaps (LH)	cresc–sf–sf–p	dolce
V18		Rapid long scales (RH)	f–f–f–sf–sf–sf–sf–sf	
V19		Rapid triplet arpeggios (RH)	f–p–f–p–f–p–f–p–f–p–cresc–f	
V20		Rapid triplet turns (LH)	sempre f–sf–sf	
V21		Rapid triplet turns (RH)	sempre f	
V22		Octaves, canonic imitation (BH)	f–sf ten–sf ten–ten–ten–sf–sf	
V23		Repeated notes (BH)	pp–sf–pp	
V24		Staccato triplets with grace notes (RH), repeated notes (BH)	sempre pp–sf–sf–sf–sf–sf–sf–sf	staccato
V25		Continuous sixteenth-note motion with grace notes	p–sfp	leggiermente
V26		Leaps, parallel thirds (BH)	f	
V27		Rapid parallel thirds, imitation	f–f	
V28		Long slurred melody (RH), leaps (LH)	p	semplice
V29		Rapid arpeggios in contrary motion (BH), octave leaps (LH)	ff–f–ff	
V30		Portato	pp–cresc –>–dim–pp	
V31		Rapid slurred arpeggios (LH), parallel octaves, tirades (RH)	sempre pp–pp–cresc	
V32		Rapid slurred arpeggios (LH); scales (RH); 7 vs. 8, 7 vs. 10, and 8 vs. 10 rhythms	più cresc–ff	
Coda (mm. 264–306)		Rapid scales and arpeggios, rapid slurred sixteenth-note pairs, RH plays two real parts, repeated notes, leaps, parallel octaves (incl. slurred, portato, marcato)	ff–sf–sf–pp–sf–pp–p–cresc–ff–p–sf–sf–<>–sf–<>–sf–cresc–ff–p	

Beethoven, although the authenticity of these has been debated.[23] In a more general sense, etudes would have been useful models for the variations in WoO 80, since they tend to focus on the rigorous exploitation of a single figure or technical problem, without lapsing into the more prosaic realm of the exercise.

Beethoven's Variation No. 8, for instance, recalls Cramer's Etude No. 18 (see Examples 5.1a and 5.1b). Both make use of a relatively straightforward left-hand accompaniment (chordal or quasi-broken) and a right-hand figure that jaggedly arpeggiates upward and downward, wave-like, over two-bar periods. Beethoven's right-hand figuration, which alternates between octaves and thirds or fourths, is more complex than Cramer's. The technique was probably one of Beethoven's specialties; a similar example appears in the "Eroica" Variations (Variation 12).

If Beethoven's Variation No. 8 is an elaborated version of Cramer's Etude No. 18, then his Variation No. 20 is a simplified version of Cramer's Etude No. 19 (see Examples 5.2a and 5.2b). Both are built on a left-hand scalar ascent with interpolated lower neighbor notes in triplet rhythm. Cramer's figuration, with its persistent parallel thirds, is considerably more challenging to execute.

One of the most unusual variations in WoO 80, No. 22, may also have its roots in the English-style etude. This variation, a kind of free canon between the hands with each voice in octaves, is reminiscent of Steibelt's Etude No. 22, also in the key of C minor (see Examples 5.3a and 5.3b). This unusual texture (right hand/left hand imitation in octaves) seems to have appealed to Beethoven and is especially prominent in the first movement of another Erard-period work, the Sonata in F Major, Op. 54. Beethoven and Steibelt may well have discovered the texture independently of each other; what is significant is that in both cases it seems to have been linked to English-style pianos, perhaps because their stronger treble register (relative to the Viennese piano) allowed for greater balance between the voices.

While many of the figurations in WoO 80 seem calculated to bring out the resonant bass, penetrating treble, and generally "orchestral" sound of the Erard, there are exceptions. In the coda, for instance, Beethoven adopts a conspicuously "Viennese" articulation during what amounts to an unlabeled thirty-third variation of the theme (see Example 5.4). Here, sixteenth notes in the right hand are slurred in pairs against the beat, such that their accent pattern conflicts with that of the left hand. This intricate phrasing is much better suited to the "speaking" quality of the Viennese piano than to the "singing" quality of the English-style piano and may have been difficult to execute clearly on the Erard. A similar issue arises with the use of rapid repeated notes (as, for example, in the first three variations). While these would have been relatively easy to execute

---

23. See William S. Newman, "Yet Another Major Beethoven Forgery by Schindler?," *Journal of Musicology* 3 (1984): 397–422.

EXAMPLE 5.1A. Johann Baptist Cramer, *Étude pour le piano forte en quarante deux exercises dans les differents tons* (Paris: Erard, 1804), No. 18.

using the precise Viennese action, the English-style single escapement action of the Erard could be unreliable. Sébastien Erard acknowledged this defect himself in 1796 and went on to patent two new and improved actions thereafter, a single escapement action with stirrups in 1809 and the revolutionary double escapement action in 1822.[24] Beethoven's modifications to the Erard, undertaken prior to the composition of WoO 80, may have been intended to ameliorate these issues, though how successful they were is unknown.[25]

PLAYING WITH LIMITS

One of the Erard's most obvious benefits was its extended keyboard compass of five-and-a-half octaves. However, as is well known, Beethoven did not immediately or consistently exploit the new high notes f-sharp^3 through c^4 (see Table 5.2). This led scholars to speculate that certain piano works that could plausibly be associated with the Erard were in fact written with smaller-compass

24. Robert Adelson, Alain Roudier, Jenny Nex, Laure Barthel, and Michel Foussard, eds., *The History of the Erard Piano and Harp in Letters and Documents, 1785–1959*, 2 vols. (Cambridge: Cambridge University Press, 2015), vol. 1, 19–20.

25. See also Skowroneck, *Beethoven the Pianist*, 91–3.

EXAMPLE 5.1B. Beethoven, Thirty-Two Variations on an Original Theme, WoO 80
(Vienna: Bureau des Arts et d'Industrie, 1807), No. 8.

EXAMPLE 5.2A. Johann Baptist Cramer, *Étude pour le piano forte en quarante deux exercises dans
les différents tons* (Paris: Erard, 1804), No. 19.

instruments in mind. But Beethoven was under no obligation to use the new
high register fully or at all, and in the somewhat controversial case of Op. 53—a
work whose range Beethoven extended during the compositional process, but
only up to a³—he may have had specific reasons to avoid the Erard's uppermost notes.[26] More importantly, this was a time of rapid transition in piano

26. Ibid., 104–11. See also Barry Cooper, "The Evolution of the First Movement of Beethoven's
'Waldstein' Sonata," *Music and Letters* 58, no. 2 (April 1977): 170–91, 184–5.

EXAMPLE 5.2B. Beethoven, Thirty-Two Variations on an Original Theme, WoO 80 (Vienna: Bureau des Arts et d'Industrie, 1807), No. 20.

EXAMPLE 5.3A. Daniel Steibelt, *Étude pour le pianoforte contenant 50 exercices de différents genres* (Leipzig: Breitkopf & Härtel, 1805), No. 22.

making during which the question of keyboard compass hinged on a complex economic equation that involved composers, players, publishers, and builders. To put it simply, however much a composer may have wanted to exploit the new five-and-a-half- and six-octave compasses, he or she was restricted both by what consumers could play and by what publishers would agree to print.[27] Steibelt's piano method provides a good illustration of this point: published

27. See Tilman Skowroneck and Andrew Pinnock, "Grand and Grander: Economic Sidelights on Piano Design and Piano Salesmanship in Early Nineteenth-Century Vienna," in Andrew Woolley and

EXAMPLE 5.3B. Beethoven, Thirty-Two Variations on an Original Theme, WoO 80 (Vienna: Bureau des Arts et d'Industrie, 1807), No. 22.

bilingually in French and German around 1809, it refers to the five-octave instrument as the *"piano ordinaire"* (*"gewöhnlich Forte Piano"*) but includes scales for the "augmented" keyboard of five-and-a-half octaves, with *ossia* reworkings for the "ordinary" five-octave keyboard as needed.[28] This contradiction in terms suggests that while Steibelt and his German publisher sought to acknowledge an emerging new standard, they also felt compelled to account for the many consumers for whom five-octave instruments were still the norm.

John Kitchen, eds., *Interpreting Historical Keyboard Music: Sources, Contexts and Performance* (Farnham, UK, and Burlington, VT: Ashgate, 2013), 221–32.

28. Daniel Steibelt, *Méthode de piano ou l'art d'enseigner cet instrument/Pianoforte-schule* (Leipzig: Breitkopf and Härtel, [1809]), 7, 20ff.

EXAMPLE 5.4. Beethoven, Thirty-Two Variations on an Original Theme, WoO 80
(Vienna: Bureau des Arts et d'Industrie, 1807), Coda (mm. 275–80).

While it is not necessarily possible to "match" Beethoven's piano works with specific instruments, it is notable that most of the works he composed between 1803 and 1810 (when he complained that the Erard was now "useless" to him) can be played on a five-and-a-half octave keyboard. Exceptions include two large-scale works intended for public performance in Vienna, perhaps on borrowed or house instruments (the Choral Fantasy, Op. 80, and the Fifth Piano Concerto, Op. 73), and one work, the Piano Trio in E-flat Major, Op. 70, no. 2, for which the explanation remains less clear.[29] The *Lebewohl* Sonata in E-flat Major, Op. 81a, may reflect a transition: while its first two movements, composed in 1809, fit the compass of the Erard, the finale (composed on Archduke Rudolph's return in 1810) requires the six-octave keyboard. Beginning around this time, Beethoven began to exploit the six-octave keyboard with greater frequency; although the Erard remained in his possession until 1824, he now

29. It is worth noting that one work, Beethoven's transcription of his Violin Concerto, Op. 61a, was expressly commissioned by Clementi to be playable on larger pianos ("ce dernier concert arrangé pour le piano avec des notes additionnelles"). Anderson, vol. 3, pp. 1419–20, 1419.

TABLE 5.2 Beethoven's piano works, c. 1803–10.

No.	Title	Composition	Publication	Top note
WoO 74	Six Variations on Beethoven's "Ich denke dein" for four hands in D Major	1799, 1803	Vienna, 1805	e^3
WoO 78	Seven Variations on "God Save the King" in C Major	1802/3	Vienna, 1804	f^3
WoO 79	Five Variations on "Rule Britannia" in D Major	1803	Vienna, 1804	e^3
WoO 55	Prelude in F Minor	c. 1803	Vienna, 1805	c^3
WoO 57	Andante in F Major ("Andante favori")—original slow mvt. of Op. 53	1803	Vienna, 1805	f^3
WoO 82	Minuet in E Major	c. 1803	Vienna, 1805	f^3
Op. 45	Three Marches for four hands in C Major, E Major, D Major	1803	Vienna, 1804	f^3
Op. 53	Piano Sonata in C Major ("Waldstein")	1803–4	Vienna, 1805	a^3★
Op. 54	Piano Sonata in F Major	1804–5	Vienna, 1807	f^3
Op. 57	Piano Sonata in F Minor ("Appassionata")	1804–5	Vienna, 1807	c^4★
Op. 58	Piano Concerto No. 4 in G Major	1804–6/7	Vienna, 1808	c^4★
Op. 56	Concerto for Piano, Violin, and Violoncello in C Major ("Triple")	1804–7	Vienna, 1807	c^4★
WoO 80	Thirty-Two Variations on an Original Theme in C Minor	1806	Vienna, 1807	c^4★
Op. 61	Violin Concerto in D Major, arr. for piano	1807	Vienna, 1808; London, 1810	c^4★
Op. 69	Cello Sonata in A Major	1807–8	Leipzig, 1809	b^3★
Op. 70/1	Piano Trio in D Major ("Ghost")	1808	Leipzig, 1809	c^4★
Op. 70/2	Piano Trio in E-flat Major	1808	Leipzig, 1809	f^4†
Op. 80	Fantasia for Piano, Chorus, and Orchestra in C Minor	1808, rev. 1809	London, 1810; Leipzig 1811	f^4†
Op. 76	Six Variations on an Original Theme in D Major	1809	Leipzig and London, 1810	g^3★
Op. 77	Fantasia for Piano in G Minor/B Major	1809	Leipzig and London, 1810	a^3★
Op. 78	Piano Sonata in F-sharp Major	1809	Leipzig and London, 1810	a-sharp^3★
Op. 79	Piano Sonata in G Major	1809	Leipzig and London, 1810	a^3★
Op. 73	Piano Concerto in E-flat Major ("Emperor")	1809	London, 1810; Leipzig, 1811	f^4†
Op. 81a	Piano Sonata in E-flat Major (Lebewohl)	1809–10	Leipzig and London, 1811	f^4†
WoO 59	Bagatelle in A Minor ("Für Elise")	1808/10	L. Nohl: Neue Briefe Beethovens (Stuttgart, 1867)	e^4†

★ Exceeds the traditional five-octave range (FF–f^3).

† Exceeds the five-and-a-half-octave range of the Erard (FF–c^4).

may have relied more steadily on loaned pianos until he received the gift of a six-octave Broadwood (CC–c⁴) in 1818.[30]

Within the limited repertory of works that were presumably composed with the Erard in mind, several stand out for the particular manner in which Beethoven treats the instrument's highest register (f-sharp³ through c⁴); namely, as an essential compositional parameter rather than simply a useful extension. Indeed, in three early Erard-period works—Op. 57, Op. 58, and WoO 80—Beethoven strategically deploys the highest register of the five-and-a-half octave piano in moments of heightened lyricism and expressive climax. In what follows, I will briefly consider the most striking of these moments before turning to the relationship between register and interpretation in WoO 80.

Sonata in F Minor, Op. 57 ("Appassionata")

Grandiose chords, orchestral tremolos, long slurred phrases, and unison octaves are just some of the elements that seem to mark the "Appassionata" Sonata, Op. 57, as an Erard-influenced work. That the Erard's expanded five-and-a-half octave compass also plays a significant aesthetic role in the sonata is suggested early on: by measure 2, Beethoven has already sounded his lowest available note (FF), and by measure 15, he has surpassed the highest note of the traditional five-octave range (f³) in a broken chord figuration that reaches up to b-flat³. This predilection for registral extremes, moreover, is central to the sonata's thematic design. As Robert L. Marshall has noted in reference to the opening theme, the "essence of the thematic idea" lies "in the extraordinary registration (the range, the spacing, the doubling), not in the contour or the particular pitches."[31] One might go so far as to say that "extraordinary registration" serves as a thematic element in its own right.

This idea is most forcefully dramatized in the third movement's breakneck coda, a section charged with concluding both the breathless finale and the entire three-movement sonata. The coda, beginning in measure 308, feels like a peroration: the tempo ratchets up to *Presto* and a new theme is introduced, one that contrasts sharply with the perpetual motion sixteenth-note figuration that has dominated since measure 1 of the finale. The new eight-measure

30. Beethoven did not exclusively adopt the six-octave compass after Op. 81a; the Piano Sonata in E Minor, Op. 90 (1814), for instance, uses the earlier compass. See J. H. van der Meer, "Beethoven et le pianoforte," in *L'interprétation de la musique classique de Haydn à Schubert. Colloque International, Evry, 13–15 octobre 1977* (Paris: Minkoff, 1980), 67–85, 73, and Skowroneck, *Beethoven the Pianist,* 107n.89.

31. Robert L. Marshall, "Sonority and Structure: Observations on Beethoven's Early and Middle-Period Piano Compositions," in Robert Curry, David Gable, and Robert L. Marshall, eds., *Variations on the Canon: Essays on Music from Bach to Boulez in Honor of Charles Rosen on His Eightieth Birthday* (Rochester: University of Rochester Press, 2008), 100–29, 116.

theme comprises two half-note-length chords marked ff and sf, followed by a series of *staccato* eighth-note-length chords marked p and a final quarter-note-length arrival in unison octaves. Its appearance also heralds a new internal phrase structure made up of repeating sections of eight and ten bars each, with the harmonic plan | |: i–V:| |: III–i:| |. The voicing is tight and low throughout, with thick left-hand chords that frequently include the low FF.

The second ending (measure 325) marks the close of this bizarre and perhaps overdetermined attempt at a conclusion and returns again to the movement's opening theme, now to be played faster than ever before (see Example 5.5). As the texture opens up, so too does the register: the theme in the right hand, sounding in eight-measure phrases, begins first on f^1, then an octave higher on f^2, and then an octave higher than that on f^3. This last iteration quickly dissolves into a series of two-measure cadential figures that reach all the way to the extreme c^4. In the next (and final) phrase, these cadential figures are compressed into one-measure units, further intensifying the need for closure. The left hand, which had itself been steadily ascending along with the right, now rapidly descends three octaves from f^1 to f to F to FF. Here, for the first time in the sonata, the lowest and highest available notes on the five-and-a-half-octave keyboard sound simultaneously.[32] The cadential figures are further compressed into half-measure units, finally resolving into a climactic F-minor arpeggiation in both hands, marked ff (m. 353). This shattering climax, again juxtaposing the low FF in the left hand against the high c^4 in the right hand, spills over into a rapid descending arpeggiation in the right hand accompanied by an unwavering upward arpeggiation in the left. Three grand F-minor chords bring these pyrotechnics (and the sonata) to an end. As this carefully calculated coda illustrates, the Erard's keyboard did much more than stimulate this sonata's unique voicings and textures—it also helped to shape its form.

Piano Concerto No. 4 in G Major, Op. 58

That the Erard was equally vital to the conception of the Fourth Piano Concerto is most apparent in its second movement, which calls for a pedal crescendo from *una corda* to *due corde* to *tre corde*, an effect possible neither on Viennese pianos of the day nor on modern pianos. Beethoven expressed great interest in this new pedal technology, and it was doubtless one of the most compelling reasons for him to commission a piano with such a pedal from the Erard firm. While his pedal indications (and lack thereof) have received much

---

32. This is the most extreme example of Beethoven's tendency during this period to place the right and left hands at opposite ends of the keyboard, leaving the middle register empty. For other examples, see Botticelli, "'Creating Tone,'" 52–7.

EXAMPLE 5.5. Beethoven, Sonata No. 23 in F Minor, Op. 57 ("Appassionata")
(Vienna: Bureau des Arts et d'Industrie, 1807), iii, Coda (mm. 325–61).

EXAMPLE 5.5. (CONT.)

attention, however, less has been said about register in the concerto.[33] And yet, Beethoven's manipulation of registral extremes is no less striking here than in Op. 57, albeit for entirely different aesthetic reasons.

As in the sonata, Beethoven strategically deploys the piano's highest register in moments of expressive significance. But here, registral extremes are linked not to climactic outbursts but rather to lyrical utterances of the kind that strongly characterize this concerto. The concerto's propensity toward introspective lyricism (discussed in chapter 2) is already apparent in the opening measures, in which the piano's serene opening phrase in G major gives way to a response by the strings in the wondrously remote key of B major. This propensity emerges perhaps most distinctly, however, in those moments where the soloist interrupts, suspends, or prolongs processes that would ordinarily lead to a specific harmonic or formal goal. Such moments are calculated to surprise and have the effect of a sudden drawing down of virtuoso brilliance in lieu of the more pensive, quasi-cantabile style first articulated in the concerto's opening phrase.

Two moments in the first movement deserve mention in this context: mm. 105–11 and 275–81 (see Example 5.6). In both passages, marked *pianissimo* and *espressivo*, a *cantabile*-style melody in the right hand of the piano emerges against an arpeggiated accompaniment in the left hand. Along with a sudden change of texture and topic, there is a shift of harmony, from G major to the remote keys of B-flat major (in the exposition) and E-flat major (in the recapitulation). Michael Steinberg calls these striking passages "dream episodes"; Leon Plantinga, "tiny island[s] of relaxation, far on the flat side . . . at which the piano pauses for rest and reflection."[34] But whether we are dreaming or sunbathing, both passages interrupt the foregoing musical discourse; the soloist effectively changes the topic of discussion here, temporarily derailing the formal process.

One of the most interesting aspects of these passages is their registration. In the first passage, the hands are placed at a considerable distance from each other, starting four-and-a-half octaves apart. By measure 106, the distance has increased to five octaves and a second, with the right hand leaping by a third—in a poignant appoggiatura on the extreme c^4 that marks the phrase's highpoint—before falling down again in stepwise motion. When this idea returns in the recapitulation, it is transformed: the melodic line begins by descending rather than ascending, the rhythms are altered, and the accompaniment has rapid sixteenth-note sextuplets in place of eighth-note triplets. Yet in spite of all this,

33. On pedals and pedaling, see, among others, David Breitman, *The Damper Pedal and the Beethoven Piano Sonatas: A Historical Perspective* (DMA thesis, Cornell University, 1993), and David Rowland, "Beethoven's Pianoforte Pedaling," in Robin Stowell, ed., *Performing Beethoven* (Cambridge: Cambridge University Press, 1994), 46–69.

34. Michael Steinberg, *The Concerto: A Listener's Guide* (New York: Oxford University Press, 1998), 68; Leon Plantinga, *Beethoven's Concertos: History, Style, Performance* (New York and London: W. W. Norton & Co., 1999), 203.

EXAMPLE 5.6A. Beethoven, Piano Concerto No. 4 in G Major, Op. 58 (Vienna: Bureau des Arts et d'Industrie, 1808), i, mm. 104–7.

EXAMPLE 5.6B. Beethoven, Piano Concerto No. 4 in G Major, Op. 58 (Vienna: Bureau des Arts et d'Industrie, 1808), i, mm. 275–9.

Beethoven manages to exploit the very same registral gap between the hands—five octaves and a second—in another rhapsodic flight up to c^4 (measure 278). In short, here we have a musical idea in which the keyboard's physical disposition is seemingly crucial to the utterance itself.

Thirty-Two Variations on an Original Theme, WoO 80

The eight-measure theme of WoO 80 occupies a relatively limited ambitus in the keyboard's middle range. The idea of registral ascent and descent, however, is embodied in the theme itself: the right-hand melody and left-hand bass, beginning on c^2 and c, respectively, move away from each other in contrary stepwise motion on each successive downbeat. This deliberate progression is suddenly accelerated by the surprising "early" arrival of F minor, marked *sf*, on beat 2 of measure 6, after which the hands join together in a unison cadential motif, marked *p*. See Example 5.7.

The descent of the passacaglia bass to F in measure 6 opens up the possibility of strategically exploiting the low FF in later variations, which Beethoven does on a number of occasions. Variation 3, notable for its symmetrical sixteenth-note arpeggiations and repeated notes, provides a good example (see Example 5.8). Here, the theme is reharmonized (with, among other things, the striking substitution of ♭II/IV for the theme's more "vanilla" applied dominant chord) and the original bass sounds an octave lower as part of the left-hand figuration. In measure 6, the harmony changes on beat 2 as it did in the theme (albeit here to a diminished chord), but rather than disrupting the figuration with a *sf* outburst and sudden arrival on FF in the bass, Beethoven places a legato slur

EXAMPLE 5.7. Beethoven, Thirty-Two Variations on an Original Theme, WoO 80 (Vienna: Bureau des Arts et d'Industrie, 1807), Theme.

EXAMPLE 5.8. Beethoven, Thirty-Two Variations on an Original Theme, WoO 80
(Vienna: Bureau des Arts et d'Industrie, 1807), No. 3.

over the entire measure and forces the phrase's climax onto the downbeat of the
next measure. The left hand now arpeggiates downward to FF while the right
hand arpeggiates upward to a-flat³, reaching a new "axis of reflection" precisely
on the downbeat. At this moment, the distance between the hands is also wider
than ever before, encompassing five octaves and a minor third.

While Beethoven exploits the expressive potential of the low FF numerous
times in WoO 80, he strategically avoids the high c⁴, reserving it instead for a
single moment of dramatic import. This comes in the work's fifth and final section, a throughcomposed unit comprising Variations 31 and 32 and the coda.
Beginning in Variation 31, the tension mounts with a repeating ostinato accompaniment in the left hand comprising rapid four- and five-note slurred upward

arpeggios built on C. While this obsessive accompaniment mostly follows the harmonic outline of the theme, the original passacaglia bass is absent (or rather subsumed into the texture), replaced by the reattacked C as pedal point. In the right hand appears the most explicit statement of the theme since the work's opening measures—a clear indication that the end is nigh. In the final measure of Variation 31, this recall of the theme dissolves into a series of slurred downward and upward scales in rapid septuplet rhythm. This figuration dominates the right hand in Variation 32, even as the left hand continues its ostinato from the previous variation. The result is a wash-like texture replete with complex cross-rhythms: 7 against 8, 7 against 10, and 8 against 10 (see Example 5.9).

Along with this rhythmic intensification come a long, progressive crescendo (from *pp* in Variations 30 and 31 to *ff* at the end of Variation 32) and a steady registral ascent in the right hand. In Variation 30, the right-hand melody begins on c^1; in Variation 31, on c^2; in Variation 32, on c^3. The ascent continues in Variation 32 as the right-hand figuration outlines the theme's contour on each successive downbeat, but here in the piano's highest available register (c^3, d^3, e-natural^3, etc.). Upon reaching an apex on a-flat^3, however, Beethoven departs from the theme's contour; rather than cadencing downward to c^3, he uses the scalar figuration to launch *upward* to c^4.

This climactic arrival on c^4 in the right hand (against a low, thickly voiced C-minor chord in the left), marked *ff*, is a significant event for multiple reasons: it signals the apex of the long crescendo and registral ascent that began in Variation 30; it initiates the first change in texture and topic since the beginning of Variation 31 (including the cessation of the C pedal point); it marks the end of Variation 32 and the variation set proper, as well as the start of the coda; and it represents the first and only time in WoO 80 that the top note of the five-and-a-half-octave keyboard is sounded. In other words, Beethoven has carefully planned for the aesthetic highpoint of WoO 80 to coincide with the hard-won attainment of the keyboard's uppermost limit. As in the coda of Op. 57, the keyboard itself mediates the compositional drama.

LATOUR'S SPEED BUMPS, BEETHOVEN'S LIMITS

What implications does all this have for interpretation? Here, a brief detour—through a school zone—is helpful. In his discussion of the agency of objects, Latour makes the point that a motorist driving through a school zone will respond differently to a yellow sign marked 30 MPH than to a concrete speed bump.[35] The sign, he maintains, merely poses a moral dilemma whereas the speed bump poses both a moral dilemma and a physical threat (to the vehicle's

---

35. Latour, *Reassembling the Social*, 77–8.

EXAMPLE 5.9. Beethoven, Thirty-Two Variations on an Original Theme, WoO 80
(Vienna: Bureau des Arts et d'Industrie, 1807), End of No. 31 through Start of Coda (mm.
256–67).

EXAMPLE 5.9. (CONT.)

[Coda]

suspension). While both objects are designed to provoke the same response ("slow down"), the physicality of the speed bump mediates the driver's actions in ways that need to be taken into account.

Similarly, in Beethoven's Erard-period works, the high c^4 represents more than an abstract compositional limit (a "yellow sign")—it also represents a physical one (a "speed bump"). Not only does c^4 mark the end of the five-and-a-half-octave keyboard, but it is also the note with the shortest string length (and hence the weakest sustaining power) in the instrument. In both WoO 80 and Op. 57, Beethoven reaches spectacularly for this note only when it seems he has exhausted all his other possibilities—it represents both threshold and summa. When played on a five-and-a-half-octave instrument, these moments demand something impossible, or nearly so, from the performer: achieve greater tone and volume than ever before, but do so with fewer, rather than more, resources.

In his brief discussion of WoO 80, Beethoven's pupil Carl Czerny offers one strategy for interpreting the work's climax: "In the 31st and 32nd Variation the *crescendo* leading to *ff* must especially be well observed, and aided by all the means of performance, particularly by the pedal."[36] Without a carefully controlled build-up, he suggests, this climactic arrival will not have the desired impact. Following Czerny's lead, one might go so far as to say that the *ff* in measure 264 is qualitatively different from earlier *ff*'s in the piece. Ultimately, it is not an increase in volume that matters here; rather, it is the impression that this moment marks the culmination of an expressive intensification that began back in Variation 31. One needs to harness "all the means of performance" to achieve the right effect.

In a broader sense, Beethoven's use of registral extremes in WoO 80 and other Erard-period works exemplifies his tendency to push the boundaries of pianos and pianism. Some scholars have regarded this tendency as evidence that he was dissatisfied with the instruments of his day and longed for something akin to the larger and more resonant pianos of the later nineteenth and twentieth centuries. But when we undervalue Beethoven's relationship with the instruments at his disposal, we risk ignoring the ways in which their designs mediated (and can continue to mediate) the horizon of possible interpretations. Put differently, the constraints of Beethoven's pianos need not be ignored or accommodated in performance—they should rather be embraced. Moreover, meaning and expression are lost when these constraints are no longer present. In WoO 80, as in Op. 57, the piano's limits—even more than the notes themselves—are the "subject matter," to paraphrase Malcolm

---

36. Carl Czerny, *On the Proper Performance of All Beethoven's Works for the Piano: Czerny's Reminiscences of Beethoven and Chapters II and III from Volume IV of the* Complete Theoretical and Practical Piano Forte School, *Op. 500,* ed. Paul Badura-Skoda (Vienna: Universal Edition, 1970), 60.

Bilson (paraphrasing C. P. E. Bach).[37] Few pianists today have access to any kind of period piano, let alone a five-and-a-half-octave Erard. But even if modern pianos preclude playing Beethoven's piano music "with limits" in the strict sense, engaging critically with the instruments of his day can help us to recognize and appreciate where those limits were once drawn, inviting richer and more nuanced interpretations.

37. Bilson draws attention to the opening gesture of Op. 111, a descending diminished seventh leap in octaves. Beethoven notates the leap for the left hand alone, but many pianists prefer to split the octaves between the hands (and some later editions even notate it this way). For Bilson, this accommodation misses the point: "It is a very dangerous leap. . . . I say go out on the stage and be plenty nervous because it's dangerous. And because that's what Beethoven wrote . . . and that's part of the excitement. Beethoven doesn't write a thing like that for a string quartet; he writes it for a piano, because in the piano it's difficult. To me, the leap is the subject matter, as Philipp Emanuel Bach would say. The notes are almost secondary." Malcolm Bilson, *Knowing the Score* (Ithaca: Cornell University Press, 2005).

CHAPTER 6

MUSIC FOR A PLAYWRIGHT

Opus 62

On September 1, 1813, a new monument was unveiled in Vienna's baroque Karlskirche. Designed by Heinrich Füger, director of the city's Imperial Gallery, it was a model of Empire-style restraint, an elegant counterpoint to the church's opulent décor. At the foot of the monument's central panel, a high relief frieze depicts two male figures, each seated on an oak trunk and looking away from the other. The Genius of Poetry, seated on the left side, holds in his left hand a laurel branch, with which he touches one of seven scrolls, and in his right hand an ouroboros, symbolizing the scrolls' immortality. The Genius of Death, seated on the right side, brushes the scrolls with a dead cypress branch, holding in his left hand the torch of death. Above the scrolls sits a winged lyre with golden strings. And above the frieze, the following inscription:

DEM. VATERLAENDISCHEN. DICHTER

HEINRICH. COLLIN

MDCCCXIII.

Heinrich Joseph von Collin, Beethoven's junior by one year, had had a remarkable rise to fame. Emerging from relative obscurity with the premiere of his five-act tragedy *Regulus* in 1801, Collin quickly established himself as the greatest Austrian dramatist of his generation. Hailed in Vienna as a German Corneille, he distinguished himself primarily through his tragedies on classical themes, of which six—*Regulus* (1801), *Coriolan* (1802), *Polyxena* (1803), *Balboa* (1805), *Bianca della Porta* (1807), and *Mäon* (1807)—premiered in the city during his lifetime.[1] But it was in many ways his shorter wartime works—not least the *Lieder Österreichischer Wehrmänner* (1809), from which Beethoven sketched the song "Österreich über alles"—that earned him his reputation as "the Poet of

---

1. A seventh tragedy, *Die Horatier und Curatier*, was first performed in Vienna on January 20, 1817.

the Fatherland."[2] Ironically, this moniker could hardly have been applied to any poet prior to Collin—the concept of a distinctly Austrian fatherland had come into being largely in response to the French occupations of Vienna in 1805 and 1809. Indeed, through his writings, which ranged from the solemn to the jingoistic, Collin had helped to invent the very fatherland that now honored his memory.

The unveiling of Collin's *Denkmal* in 1813 represented the culmination of a fundraising campaign that had begun shortly after his death in 1811. The monument's cost, about 10,000 florins, was subsidized by an impressive roster of 251 subscribers, including Emperor Francis II and nine other members of the imperial family, as well as a who's who of artistic patrons in and around Vienna (among them Prince Lichnowsky, Prince Lobkowitz, Count Razumovsky, Prince Kinsky, Count Fries, and Baron Würth). The proceeds from three memorial concerts (two in Vienna and one in Lemberg) as well as a staging of Collin's final tragedy *Die Horatier und Curiatier* in Prague also went toward the monument's construction. Salieri voluntarily directed a performance of Mozart's *Requiem* during the unveiling ceremony, which Moritz von Dietrichstein, who spearheaded the project, described as "in the truest sense a moving and uplifting celebration of the memory of the departed."[3] Füger's monument, which also features a likeness of the poet after a portrait by Joseph Lange—the actor who created the role of Coriolan—still stands in the Karlskirche's Agnes chapel today (see Figure 6.1).

With Collin's passing, Vienna lost not only its most significant poet but also an eager musical collaborator. Eagerness particularly characterized Collin's relationship with Beethoven; results, however, far less so (see Table 6.1). The two met as early as December 1805, when, as Röckel reports, Beethoven's friends and colleagues gathered at Prince Lichnowsky's palace to discuss revisions to *Leonore*. Probably they had already been introduced at the salons of Dietrichstein, at which both were regular attendees.[4] In the next several years, at least three collaborations began to take shape, only to dissipate one after the other: an oratorio, *Die Befreyung von Jerusalem* (Beethoven considered but ultimately rejected the libretto, which was later set by Stadler); an opera, *Bradamante* (Beethoven vacillated over the libretto, which Collin finally offered to Reichardt, to Beethoven's regret), and a second opera, *Macbeth* (Beethoven began sketching the overture but abandoned the project, and Collin never completed the

---

2. On the sketch, see Leon Plantinga, "Beethoven, Napoleon, and Political Romanticism," in Jane F. Fulcher, ed., *The Oxford Handbook of the New Cultural History of Music* (Oxford and New York: Oxford University Press, 2011), 484–500.

3. Moritz von Dietrichstein, *Ueber das Denkmahl des k. k. Hofrathes und Ritters des Leopold-Ordens, Heinrich Joseph Edlen von Collin* (Vienna: Anton Strauß, 1813), 7.

4. See Franz Carl Weldmann, *Moritz, Graf von Dietrichstein: Sein Leben und Wirken* (Vienna: Wilhelm Braumüller, 1867), 41–2.

FIGURE 6.1. Design for Heinrich von Collin's funeral monument by Heinrich Friedrich Füger. Frontispiece to Moritz von Dietrichstein, *Ueber das Denkmahl des k. k. Hofrathes und Ritters des Leopold-Ordens, Heinrich Joseph Edlen von Collin* (Vienna: Anton Strauß, 1813). Bayerische Staatsbibliothek München, 4 Don.Lud. XV, 20, p. 4, urn:nbn:de:bvb:12-bsb10678278-2. Used by permission.

libretto). In spite of many attempts, only one completed work attests to the relationship between composer and playwright: Beethoven's "Ouverture / de CORIOLAN / Tragédie de Mr. de Collin," published in 1808 along with a dedication to Collin. And yet, its claim to being an actual collaboration is tenuous at best: there is no evidence that Collin commissioned or otherwise influenced the composition of the overture, and it was only ever performed once as an introduction to the tragedy (for reasons that remain unknown), on April 24, 1807, in the Burgtheater.[5]

5. There is also confusion regarding the title. A reviewer for the *Allgemeine musikalische Zeitung* wrote in December 1807, "A *new* overture by this composer . . . is full of fire and power; according to the inscription, it was intended for Collin's *Coriolan*." Likewise, the first edition, published in January 1808, includes the reference to Collin's tragedy. However, on the autograph manuscript, located in the Beethovenhaus, the words "zum Trauerspiel" have been crossed out. Thayer/Forbes, vol. 1, 416–17, esp. note 6.

TABLE 6.1 Collin and Beethoven, 1801–13.

Year	Event(s)	Other
1801	*Regulus* premieres in Vienna (October 3)	
1802	*Coriolan* premieres in Vienna with entr'actes from Mozart's *Idomeneo*, arr. by Stadler (November 24); it is repeated four more times this year	Vertot's "*Révolutions romaines*" published in Vienna
1803	Collin is named Court Secretary and is ennobled (May); *Coriolan* is performed six times in Vienna and twice in Berlin (August 3–4); *Polyxena* premieres in Vienna (October 15)	Füger makes sketches for a painting on *Coriolan*
1804	*Coriolan* is published in Berlin and is performed four times in Vienna	
1805	*Coriolan* is performed once in Vienna (March 5) and once in Gratz (July 13), with Lange in the title role; *Balboa* premieres in Vienna (March 16); Beethoven's *Leonore* premieres in Vienna and is repeated twice (November 20–22); Beethoven and Collin meet at Prince Lichnowsky's to discuss revisions to *Leonore* (December)	Füger paints *Veturia fordert Coriolan auf, die Stadt zu verschonen*
1806	Rumors begin to circulate that a "Gesellschaft der Cavaliere" will assume the theater management in Vienna (January); *Coriolan* is performed in Vienna (February 20, 1806); Beethoven's revised *Leonore* is performed at least twice (March 29 and April 10); Collin reprints a review of Lange's Gratz performances (including *Coriolan*) in the *Wiener Hoftheater Almanach*; Collin proposes reforms to the Viennese stage (May); *Der Freymüthige* reports that Collin will supervise and direct the Hoftheater stages (July 4); Lange writes to Collin that audiences in Gratz wish to see *Coriolan* again (July 12); Beethoven considers but ultimately rejects Collin's libretto for *Die Befreyung von Jerusalem* (b. October 30)	
1807	Gesellschaft der Cavaliere takes control of theater direction; Collin's *Bianca della Porta* premieres in the Burgtheater and Gluck's *Iphigenia in Tauris* at the Kärntnerthortheater as the first pieces under the new theater direction (January 1); Beethoven composes his *Coriolan* overture, which premieres at Prince Lobkowitz's (March) and is repeated at Prince Lichnowsky's (b. April 8); Beethoven's overture is performed with Collin's play for the first and only time (April 24); Collin publishes "Brief über das gesungene Drama" (May 21); Collin offers Beethoven the libretto to *Bradamante*; Beethoven petitions the theater directorship for position as opera composer (December); *Coriolan* overture is performed at the Liebhaber-Konzerte (December 13); *Mäon* premieres in Vienna (December 29)	Kininger begins engraving Füger's *Coriolan* (October 19)

TABLE 6.1 Continued

Year	Event(s)	Other
1808	*Coriolan* overture is performed at the Liebhaber-Konzerte (February 2); the overture is published with dedication to Collin; Beethoven discusses opera subjects with Collin and begins sketching *Macbeth*, but Collin does not finish the libretto; Beethoven hesitates over Collin's *Bradamante* libretto; Collin honors Haydn with a poem, "Du hast die Welt in deiner Brust getragen," at a gala performance of the *Creation* in honor of Haydn's 76th birthday (March 27, 1808)—he later publishes "Haydns Jubelfeyer," a memento of the event in which Beethoven is also mentioned; Collin offers the libretto of *Bradamante* to Reichardt (November); Beethoven holds his benefit concert at the Theater an der Wien (December 22)	
1809	Reichardt completes his music to *Bradamante* (February) and an unstaged performance takes place at Prince Lobkowitz's, with Beethoven present (March 3); Collin becomes Court Councilor, publishes *Lieder österreichischer Wehrmänner*; Beethoven sketches a melody for the first stanza of "Österreich über alles," one of the *Wehrmannslieder*	Kininger completes his engraving of Füger's *Coriolan* (October 2)
1811	Collin dies in Vienna (July 28); a memorial concert is held in the University Hall, with music directed by Mosel (December 15)	
1812	Further memorial concerts for Collin are held in the Burgtheater (April 3) and in Lemberg (April 11); *Horatier und Curiatier* is staged in Prague (June 20)	
1813	Stadler's *Die Befreyung von Jerusalem* premieres in the University Hall (May); a monument to Collin, designed by Füger, is unveiled in the Karlskirche and a requiem mass is held, at which Mozart's *Requiem* is performed under the direction of Salieri (September 1)	

The uncertainty surrounding the origin of Beethoven's overture has allowed for a great deal of speculation, and many have argued (despite the overt connection to Collin) that Beethoven's inspiration may not have come from Collin's tragedy at all, but rather from Shakespeare's *Coriolanus*. This notion has had a decisive influence on the overture's reception history, in part because it has seemed to account for a perceived stylistic gap between Beethoven's music and Collin's poetry. "By juxtaposing terse, dramatic, agitated music to a dilatory, pathetic, ruminative play," Lawrence Kramer writes, "Beethoven posed a hermeneutic problem that has largely determined the course of the music's critical reception. . . . The solution, for the authors of that reception, has been obvious. . . .

Beethoven's true orientation was Shakespearean."[6] E. T. A. Hoffmann was the first to suggest that Beethoven's overture was too great for Collin's "predominantly reflective poetry," a notion that has since been echoed by such critics as Richard Wagner, Donald Francis Tovey, and Kramer himself.[7] But from a historical point of view, this idea is problematic: leaving aside the question of whether Beethoven knew Shakespeare's *Coriolanus* at the time (of which there is no evidence), he had compelling reasons to engage with Collin's play. Not only was Collin the foremost poet in Vienna, but he was also a civil servant with significant connections. Appointed Court Secretary in 1803, Collin played a role in the reorganization of theatrical life that occurred in January 1807, when a "Gesellschaft der Cavaliere" consisting of Prince Lobkowitz and other aristocrats assumed control of the two court theaters and the Theater an der Wien. The Gesellschaft invited Collin to write a plan to reform the Viennese stage, which he submitted in May 1806; the first play to premiere under the new management was his *Bianca della Porta*. Composing an overture based on one of Collin's plays, then, not only offered Beethoven the prospect of influencing the theater management but also provided fresh evidence of his talents for composing dramatic music—precisely when he was seeking a salaried position as court opera composer. At the same time, as Steven M. Whiting has noted, the overture was a good faith gesture toward Collin after Beethoven's decision not to set *Die Befreyung von Jerusalem* to music, demonstrating what could come out of a collaboration between the two artists if they were to agree on a subject.[8]

There is good cause, then, to share Whiting's conviction that Beethoven composed his overture "nach Collin." While Whiting uses this notion as the springboard for a detailed programmatic analysis of the overture, however, my aim in this chapter is different. In composing his overture for Collin, Beethoven also composed it for a larger sphere. Collin (or Shakespeare for that matter) was hardly the first to engage with the Coriolanus story, and multiple versions of it—across several different media—were familiar in Vienna during the first decade of the 1800s. This chapter aims to illuminate the mediating influence of this wider context on both the composition and early reception of Beethoven's overture. I will begin by reconsidering the overture's design and

6. Lawrence Kramer, "The Strange Case of Beethoven's *Coriolan*: Romantic Aesthetics, Modern Subjectivity, and the Cult of Shakespeare," *Musical Quarterly* 79, no. 2 (Summer 1995): 256–80, 271.

7. Jonathan Kregor, who reads the overture in light of Collin's play, similarly concludes that the overture "distills Collin's material to such a degree that it arguably makes the ensuing play redundant, if not superfluous." Jonathan Kregor, "Expression, Musical Painting, and the Concert Overture," in *Program Music*, Cambridge Introductions to Music (Cambridge: Cambridge University Press, 2015), 39–68, 45.

8. Steven M. Whiting, "Beethovens *Coriolan*-Ouvertüre (nach Collin)," in Oliver Korte and Albrecht Riethmüller, eds., *Das Beethoven-Handbuch*, 6 vols., vol. 1: *Beethovens Orchestermusik und Konzerte* (Laaber: Laaber-Verlag, 2013), 449–61, 452.

reception history, with a focus on the ways in which critics have tended to suppress the overture's connection with Collin's drama in their efforts to link it to Shakespeare. I will then attempt to resituate the overture in its day by placing it alongside other versions of the Coriolanus story known among Beethoven's contemporaries (and specifically within Collin's social circle). This context not only opens up a new perspective on the overture's many possible meanings for its early listeners but also allows us to reflect on the nature of its programmatic design.

Coriolan THEN AND NOW

Against the backdrop of the orchestral works of 1806, Beethoven's overture to Collin's *Coriolan*—composed in early 1807—stands out for its return to an overtly "heroic" musical idiom (or perhaps for its turn toward a new iteration of it). Whether or not one subscribes to the idea of the heroic style, the "heart-stopping pauses," "crashes," and "startling harmonies" that Scott Burnham has described as its signature traits are apparent from the introductory bars of the overture, and it is equally clear from the opening's massive orchestral sound (the piece begins on a unison C) and *fortissimo* dynamic marking that the piece is of the monumental scope typical of such compositions.[9] In addition, the overture is one of only four large-scale orchestral pieces Beethoven had written, or would write, in the key of C minor (the others are the Third Piano Concerto [1803], the Fifth Symphony [1808], and the Choral Fantasy [1808]). Whether or not this key had the special significance for Beethoven that later commentators have often imputed to it, many of his compositions in this key seem to represent a particular aesthetic, perhaps even a "C-minor mood."[10] In any event, the choice of C minor resonates with several other characteristic or quasi-programmatic works in Beethoven's oeuvre, such as the *Grande Sonate pathétique* (1801) and the "Marcia funébre" of the *Eroica* Symphony (1804), as well as his first major vocal work, the *Cantata on the Death of Emperor Joseph II* (1790). Beethoven would later use C minor to reflect the absence of Archduke Rudolph in the "Abwesenheit" movement of the *Lebewohl* Sonata (1809). Death, lament, mourning, absence, but also grandeur, and heroism—all of these characteristics are arguably reflected in Beethoven's choice of key for this overture.

But it is the unique way in which Beethoven uses his musical vocabulary that has suggested to commentators that the overture depicts the character or exploits of Coriolanus. The piece opens with a series of three eight-beat unison

---

9. Scott Burnham, *Beethoven Hero* (Princeton: Princeton University Press, 1995), 29.

10. See Michael Tusa, "Beethoven's 'C-Minor Mood': Some Thoughts on the Structural Implications of Key Choice," *Beethoven Forum 2* (Lincoln: University of Nebraska Press, 1993): 1–27.

Cs in the strings, each of which is followed by a harmonically jarring response including the winds and horns. The effect is striking—the repetition of these forceful chords coupled with the use of silence not only contributes to a sense of abruptness and *in medias res*, but also evokes a sense of conflict that seems to resonate with Coriolanus's persona. The unusual sonorities that follow each of these opening unison blasts (iv, vii°7, vii°7/V) contribute to the sense of conflict by suggesting that C is in fact not the tonic, but rather the dominant of F minor, setting up a harmonic "conflict" between the two sonorities that gains significance as the piece unfolds. The first theme is characterized by an unusual use of rhythmic displacement and syncopation, culminating in a crescendo that reaches its first peak not on C minor, but on iv⁶ (m. 34), again bringing the problem of F minor versus C minor to the fore. The second theme, separated by a bridge of only two measures, falls into periodic four-measure phrases, offering a striking contrast to the choppy, asymmetrical phrases of the main theme, and giving precedence to melody over the escalation of rhythmic and harmonic tension. The striking contrast in mood, texture, orchestration, and key between the first and second themes has encouraged many commentators to seek an extramusical explanation for the piece's design.

In terms of form, there are two particularly unusual problems that have further contributed to the sense that this piece is based, at least in part, on a program. First, the material of the closing group (mm. 102–17) is not only in the "wrong" key (G minor), but also expands into the development section, creating an obsessively monothematic passage that links the closing section of the exposition with the moment of recapitulation (m. 152). This causes the usual pressure points of the sonata form to be underarticulated and culminates in a second problem at the moment of recapitulation, which occurs not on the tonic C, but on the subdominant F. The apparent failure of the so-called double return problematizes the recapitulation and seemingly necessitates the presence of a coda, in which the theme is recapitulated with the proper harmony. (It was by no means unheard of to recapitulate a movement's opening materials in the subdominant rather than the tonic, particularly in overtures; the overture to Gluck's *Alceste* offers one famous example. However, this technique was arguably out of fashion by the time of *Coriolan*, and Beethoven uses it here in a particularly dramatic way).[11] The end of the piece (mm. 276–314) has received much attention; here, the powerful declamatory gestures of the opening are broken down into fragments and the main motif is augmented, bringing the piece to a close that suggests that the music has exhausted itself.

---

11. For more on Beethoven's use of the subdominant in recapitulations, see Charles Rosen, *The Classical Style: Haydn, Mozart, Beethoven*, rev. ed. (New York: Norton, 1997), 460–6.

In a 1991 article, Clifford D. Alper identified three critical stances toward this overture, which he called "structuralist,""expressive," and "narrative" views.[12] These categories—adapted from an article on program music by Ralph P. Locke[13]— remain generally useful in thinking about the overture's reception history; however, it is necessary to expand and update Alper's framework. In the "structuralist" view, the overture's title and associations remain detached from the context of the work itself and wield no meaningful influences on the overture's musical content. The overture is essentially absolute music, no matter what Beethoven (or anybody else) has said about it. Such a hardline position has in fact less often been taken with this overture than with other programmatic pieces by Beethoven—perhaps the paradigmatic example with respect to the overtures is Ernst Oster's analysis of Beethoven's *Egmont* overture, in which he disavows the work's dramatic function and employs Schenkerian and motivic analysis to emphasize the significance of certain musical connections.[14] In the "expressive" view, the focus is on the music's generalized "emotional qualities." Alper offers descriptions by Tovey (1944, not 1936) and Bekker as examples of the expressive view, highlighting the fact that these descriptions focus more on abstract emotional forces ("struggle and conflict," "defeat and submission") than on a chronological illustration of the drama. The "narrative" view, by contrast, denotes explicitly programmatic interpretations. Critics who espouse Alper's "structuralist" and "narrative" views, I would add, may be considered roughly equivalent to Dahlhaus's "formalists" and "content aestheticians," with the "expressivists" falling somewhere in between.[15]

Of course, it is more complicated than this. But one can understand the overture's reception history largely as fluctuating between the "expressive" and "narrative" positions. E. T. A. Hoffmann provides an early example of the expressive view in his 1812 review of the overture published in the *Allgemeine musikalische Zeitung*. For Hoffmann, "the composition serves very well to suggest the intended idea, namely that a great and tragic event is to form the content of the ensuing play. Even without having read the playbill nobody can expect anything else. This overture cannot be followed by domestic tragedy but only by high tragedy,

---

12. Clifford D. Alper, "Beethoven's *Coriolan* Overture, Opus 62, Three Points of View," *The Beethoven Newsletter* 6, no. 2 (Summer 1991): 43–9.

13. Ralph P. Locke, "Program Music," in Don Michael Randel, ed., *The New Harvard Dictionary of Music* (Cambridge, MA: Harvard University Press, 1986), 656–9.

14. Ernst Oster, "The Dramatic Character of the *Egmont* Overture," in David W. Beach, ed., *Aspects of Schenkerian Theory* (New Haven: Yale University Press, 1983), 209–22; originally published in *Musicology* 2, no. 3 (1949): 269–85. Lauri Suurpää has attempted to reconcile the perspectives of literary theory and Schenkerian analysis in his study of the overtures to *Leonore, Coriolan, Egmont*, and *Fidelio*, arguing that extramusical allusions in the foreground interact with tonal tensions at a more remote level to create the works' programmatic quality. Lauri Suurpää, *Music and Drama in Six Beethoven Overtures: Interaction between Programmatic Tensions and Tonal Structure*, Studia musica (Helsinki: Hakapaino Oy for the Sibelius Academy, 1997).

15. See Introduction.

in which heroes appear and perish."[16] He goes so far as to suggest that the overture might introduce any number of great tragedies, mentioning *Hamlet, Macbeth*, and the tragedies of Calderón. This view not only seems to respond more to the overture's musical character than to the specific elements of the Coriolanus story but also implies that the overture lacks the degree of specificity its title denotes. (Hanslick would articulate a similar perspective in a discussion of the *Egmont* overture in which he argued, "The poetic theme is contingent upon the title. . . . That is why it would be conceivable that Beethoven's *Egmont* could be titled 'William Tell' or 'Jeanne d'Arc.'")[17] Carl Czerny, too, may be considered a proponent of the expressive view. Far from offering a programmatic explanation of the overture, his remarks about the piece leave most of it up to the imagination of the listener: "The legend that Coriolanus was stoned by the Volsci surely gave Beethoven the first idea of his Coriolanus overture. This accounts for the characteristic conclusion of the piece too."[18] Czerny's "first idea" might be thought to mean "inspiration," but it seems more likely that he is referring to the first musical idea of the piece, or the opening theme. If this is indeed the case, Czerny draws a parallel between the introduction and the work's "characteristic conclusion," the moment in the coda when the introductory material returns (finally in the right key) and then becomes fragmented. According to this perspective, the musical materials for the piece were generated by an extramusical idea (notably, one that has nothing to do with Collin's play), but this does not necessarily mean that the entire piece is governed by a particular sequence of events.

A more recent iteration of the expressive view comes in Lawrence Kramer's 1995 essay on the overture and its Shakespearean reception. While Kramer critiques the tradition of associating the overture with Shakespeare and not Collin, his reading of the overture aligns him within that same tradition. Like Wagner and Tovey (1936 now, not 1944), Kramer relates Beethoven's overture to Shakespeare's Act V, scene 3—the climactic scene in which Volumnia dissuades her son from attacking Rome. Kramer suggests that Beethoven, like Shakespeare, "[transforms] the external conflict between a man and a woman into an internal conflict between masculine and feminine principles, or more precisely between the masculine and feminine elements of a prototypically masculine subjectivity."[19] However, he hears the overture not as a direct representation of the

16. E. T. A. Hoffmann, "Review of Beethoven's Overture to *Coriolan*," in David Charlton, ed., and Martyn Clarke, trans., *E. T. A. Hoffmann's Musical Writings* (Cambridge: Cambridge University Press, 1989), 286–93, 287. Originally published in the *Allgemeine musikalische Zeitung* 14, no. 5 (August 1812): cols. 519–26.

17. Eduard Hanslick, *On the Musically Beautiful: A Contribution towards the Revision of the Aesthetics of Music*, trans. Geoffrey Payzant (Indianapolis: Hackett Publishing Company, 1986), 75.

18. Carl Czerny, *On the Proper Performance of All Beethoven's Works for the Piano*, ed. Paul Badura-Skoda (Vienna: Universal Edition, 1970), 13.

19. Kramer, "Strange Case," 272.

scene, but rather as something like its "negative image"; Beethoven "[reverses] Shakespeare's emphasis," resulting in a "constructively problematical" relationship between the structure of the scene and the sonata form design of the overture.[20] This leads to the expressivist perspective that the overture is best understood as "a representation . . . of Coriolanus's tumultuous state of mind as he decides whether or not to heed his mother's appeal. . . . [W]hat the overture produces is *not a Coriolanus narrative but a Coriolanean subject-position*, the fatality, but also perhaps the redemption, of which lies in its deep identification with 'woman's tenderness.'"[21]

Others have chosen to understand the *Coriolan* overture as a detailed piece of program music (the "narrative" view). Wagner seems to have set the precedent for this exercise in a program note written in February 1852. Associating the overture with the legend's "most decisive" scene (again, the confrontation between Coriolanus and his mother and wife), Wagner suggests, "The whole tone-piece might well be taken for the musical accompaniment of a pantomimic show."[22] Interestingly, however, there is no indication in the essay itself that Wagner had Shakespeare in mind, and the conclusion of his program—in which Coriolan plunges a sword into his heart at the foot of his mother—more nearly relates to Collin's ending than Shakespeare's (Collin is not mentioned either). But in a letter to Hans von Bülow dated January 30, 1852, Wagner overtly compares Beethoven's overture and Shakespeare's tragedy:

> I was delighted to observe that this entire piece of music is no more and no less than the accompaniment to a graphic [*plastisch*]—almost mimic—scene between C. and his mother and wife in the camp outside Rome. . . . [A]bsolute music can express only feelings, passions, and moods in their antitheses and degrees of intensity, but not relationships of a social or political nature. Beethoven has a splendid instinct for this: I almost prefer *his* poem of Coriolanus to Shakespeare's in its graphic unity and succinctness, which almost allows the subject-matter to achieve the sensuality of myth.[23]

For Wagner, discovering the poetic content of the overture was crucial to understanding it. At the same time, Beethoven is said to have better captured in his musical poetry the essence of the story, crystallizing it into something that transcended language.

Tovey, who regarded Wagner's essay as "one of his finest and most attractive prose works," was the first to realize its analytical implications.[24] Including in his 1936

20. Ibid., 273.

21. Ibid., 273–4 (emphasis mine).

22. Richard Wagner, *Richard Wagner's Prose Works*, trans. William Ashton Ellis, 8 vols. (London: Kegan Paul, Trench, Trübner and Co., 1892–9), vol. 3, 225–8, 226.

23. Quoted in Klaus Kropfinger, *Wagner and Beethoven: Richard Wagner's Reception of Beethoven*, trans. Peter Palmer (Cambridge: Cambridge University Press, 1991), 125.

24. Donald Francis Tovey, *Essays in Musical Analysis: Symphonies and Other Orchestral Works* (London: Oxford University Press, 1981; originally published 1935–9), 143.

commentary on the overture an abridged version of Act V, scene 3 of Shakespeare's play, which he coyly presents as "Shakespeare's analysis of Beethoven's *Coriolanus*," Tovey here seems to upend the view he expresses elsewhere—including in his own 1944 article on program music for *Encyclopedia Britannica*—that Beethoven's music can only be understood in absolute musical terms.[25] Tovey's desire to link Beethoven with Shakespeare (and, one might argue, claim Beethoven for Britain during the Nazi period) also leads him to sidestep Collin. He argues, "It does not greatly matter that the *Coriolanus* for which this overture was written is not Shakespeare's . . . even Collin, as well as Beethoven, had read Shakespeare, who breaks through like Nature in Beethoven's music," although he does attempt to concede that "From Collin's play, Beethoven derives the vacillating development and the abrupt final collapse of this overture."[26] In fact, the claim that Collin had read Shakespeare's *Coriolanus* is erroneous, at least according to the poet's brother Matthäus von Collin.[27] Tovey's commentary nonetheless stands as the most explicit attempt to connect Beethoven's overture to Shakespeare's play, though his analysis, like Wagner's, implies that Beethoven compressed the action significantly rather than hewing closely to the scene's structure.

At least two commentators, Paul Mies (1969, originally published 1938) and Steven M. Whiting (2013), have offered elaborate programs that attempt to link the overture with the drama to which it was originally attached, Collin's *Coriolan*.[28] Collin's play was certainly an important stimulus for the overture, but these programs presuppose a level of congruence between the drama and the music that goes beyond what was typical during the period (and, as I suggest in what follows, for Beethoven in particular). In a broader sense, the tendency to view this overture as a response to either Collin or Shakespeare neglects the fact that the Coriolanus story was part of a richer network of visual, literary, and political associations. The remainder of this chapter explores this wider array of associations as well as the particular aesthetic climate that gave rise to Beethoven's overture.

READING, SEEING, AND HEARING *Coriolanus* IN BEETHOVEN'S VIENNA

The story of Coriolanus was probably best known to Beethoven's contemporaries neither through Shakespeare, nor through Collin, but through accounts by Livy (64 or 59 BC–AD 12 or 17) and Plutarch (c. AD 46–AD 120). Plutarch's account may

25. Ibid., 144. See, for example, his analysis of the *Pastoral* Symphony, in which he attempts to deny the significance of that symphony's authentic program. Ibid., 60–1.

26. Ibid., 143.

27. Heinrich Joseph von Collin, *Sämmtliche Werke*, ed. Matthäus von Collin, 6 vols. (Vienna: Strauß, 1812–14), vol. 6, 366.

28. Paul Mies, "Zur Coriolan-Ouvertüre op. 62," *Beethoven-Jahrbuch* 6 (1969): 260–8 (originally published 1938 in *Zeitschrift für Musik*), and Whiting, "Beethovens *Coriolan*-Ouvertüre," esp. 454–7.

be summarized as follows: Caius Martius, orphaned by his father and raised by his widow mother, Volumnia, quickly ascends the ranks of the Roman army to return a hero from his first campaign at the age of sixteen. A second successful campaign against the Volsican capital of Corioles earns him the nickname "Coriolanus." As a hero in battle, Coriolanus is unmatched, his presence such that the mere "sound of his voice and grimness of his countenance" strike fear into the hearts of his enemies.[29] His valor, however, is accompanied by an excessive vanity: "for lack of education, he was so choleric and impatient that he would yield to no living creature; which made him churlish, uncivil, and altogether unfit for any man's conversation."[30] The achievements of Coriolanus nevertheless lead him to be nominated for the position of Consul in the Roman Senate. On the day of election, however, he unexpectedly loses the support of the plebs and is driven out of the city by the Roman authorities. Plotting revenge, he sides with the Volscians, Rome's enemies, and plans to attack the capital. In response, Rome sends three consecutive embassies to attempt to dissuade him peacefully. The first two embassies fail, but the third and final embassy, comprising his mother, wife, and child, affects him deeply. Volumnia breaks her son's fierce resolve, and at last he relents. Rome is spared, and the Volscian commander Tullus Aufidius, considering Coriolanus a traitor, has him murdered.

Collin and Beethoven may well have been familiar with Plutarch's *Life of Martius Coriolanus* as it appeared in an eight-volume German translation of the *Parallel Lives*, first published in Berlin and Leipzig from 1777 to 1780 and reprinted in Vienna and Prague in 1796.[31] Collin's play, however, differs from this source in several respects. First, as in several other sources (including Livy and Dionysius), Collin calls Coriolan's mother Veturia rather than Volumnia. Second, he opens the play relatively late in the action, after the election tribunal, compressing the drama and limiting the roster of characters. Third, and most importantly, he focuses his characterization of Coriolan on an internal conflict between his loyalty to Rome and his unbreakable oath to the Volscians, Rome's enemies. Collin's Coriolan faces a kind of psychological turmoil that is present neither in the early sources nor even in Shakespeare. Because he has sworn

29. Plutarch, "The Life of Martius Coriolanus," trans. Sir Thomas North, in *Shakespeare's Plutarch*, ed. T. J. B. Spencer (Baltimore: Penguin Books, 1964), 296–362, 307.

30. Ibid., 297.

31. Gottlob Benedict von Schirach, ed. and trans., *Biographien des Plutarchs. Mit Anmerkungen von Gottlob Benedict von Schirach*, 8 vols. (Vienna and Prague: Franz Haas, 1796), vol. 2, 282–335. The Viennese edition was based on an earlier edition published in Berlin and Leipzig by George Jacob Decker from 1777 to 1780. It was subsequently reprinted in Vienna and Prague, again by Franz Haas, in 1805, with commentary by J. F. S. Kaltwasser. Volume 2 of the 1796 and 1805 versions includes a frontispiece depicting the scene between Coriolan and his mother. There were also contemporary German translations of Livy, including *Des Titus Livius aus Padua Römische Geschichte, aus dem Lateinschen ins Deutsche übersetz von Johann Franz Wagner* (Lemgo, 1776); see vol. 2, par. 40, 197–9.

an oath to the Volscians unto death, he is ultimately forced into an insoluble double bind—either betray his family and fatherland by attacking Rome or break his oath by sparing the city. In an attempt to preserve his honor on both of these fronts, Coriolan calls off the attack and then falls on his own sword.[32]

In addition to German translations of Plutarch and Livy, the Coriolanus story was disseminated in Vienna through modern political histories of Rome. One such history, René-Aubert Vertot's "*Révolutions romaines*," was published in a new German translation by the Viennese firm J. B. Degen in 1802, the year of *Coriolan*'s premiere.[33] This highly popular work, originally published in France in 1719, went through at least fifteen editions during the eighteenth century; at least one German translation (Zürich, 1750–53) preceded the Viennese edition. Vertot viewed the Roman Republic not as a stable regime but as one that was undergoing constant "revolutions" that threatened to lead to its collapse. A reviewer of the 1802 edition praised the work as "unpartisan" in contrast to revolutionary histories written by those who had witnessed the French Revolution, but in recent times, it has been critiqued as a thinly veiled defense of absolute monarchy.[34] To be sure, Vertot is critical of Rome's aristocratic culture (especially the patricians' love of luxury, effeminacy, and idleness), but he is even more disparaging toward the plebeians' fickleness and passion for liberty, the causes, in his view, of the endless conflicts that provoked the Republic's collapse. As Martin Breaugh has observed, from Vertot's perspective, only monarchy could resolve such conflicts, and the Roman Republic suffered from a "monarchic deficiency."[35]

Vertot portrays Coriolanus as the arch-patrician, "wise, frugal, disinterested, forthright, and an inviolable adherent to the law . . . too haughty for

Subsequent eighteenth-century German editions of Livy were printed in Hamburg and Frankfurt am Main.

32. As Whiting points out, there are at least three different endings to the legend. In Livy, Plutarch, Dionysius, and Shakespeare, Coriolanus is killed by the Volscians; in a version attributed to Cicero and in Collin, he takes his own life; in Fabius, he lives out an embittered life among the Volscians. Whiting, "Beethovens *Coriolan*-Ouvertüre," 452.

33. René-Aubert Vertot, *Revolutions-Geschichte des alten Roms*, trans. Anton Kreil, 2 vols. (Vienna: J. V. Degen, 1802); also published under the title *Geschichte der römischen Staatsveränderungen*. The original French edition is René-Aubert Vertot, *Histoire des révolutions arrivées dans le gouvernement de la République romaine*, 3 vols. (Paris: F. Barois, 1719).

34. "Vertot beurtheilt nämlich in seinem Zeitalter das Revolutionswesen *unparteyisch*, was der Fall bey den Geschichtsschreibern, welche Zeugen der französischen Revolution waren, nicht der Fall ist, deren Resultat immer, mehr oder weniger einseitig ausfallen muß." "Allgemeine Weltgeschichte und alte Geschichte," *Neue Allgemeine Deutsche Bibliothek* 85, part 2, no. 7 (1803), 420.

35. Martin Breaugh, *The Plebeian Experience: A Discontinuous History of Political Freedom*, trans. Lazer Lederhendler (New York: Columbia University Press, 2013; originally published 2007 by Editions Payot & Rivages), 58–60.

a Republic."[36] Eager to restore the senate to its ancient powers, Coriolanus abhors the plebeian tribunes and disdains sharing "the government and dignities of the state with a vile rabble." He is hence antipopulist and antidemocratic, behind the times politically but nonetheless respected for his military prowess, upstanding moral character, and fidelity to the law. His demise is presented less as a condemnation of personal vanity or patrician arrogance than as an illustration of the flaws inherent to the republican system. Coriolanus's diatribe against the tribunes (the result of a dispute over the pricing of grain after a famine) makes him a cause célèbre for those who advocate, on the one hand, for the advent of a purely aristocratic government, and on the other hand, for the preservation of democracy. The conflict, expressed in the opposite speeches of Decius (a senator) and Appius (a tribune), threatens to ignite civil war and exemplifies Vertot's claim that the republic is an inherently unstable form of government.

Vertot's eighty-three-year-old tract acquired new resonance in post-Revolutionary Vienna. Since 1790, Francis II (then Archduke) had supported counter-revolutionary efforts in Austria, including the restoration of censorship, the expansion of police powers, and the monitoring of clubs and assemblies. When, shortly after his accession, a Jacobin plot to assassinate the emperor and overthrow the monarchy came to light in summer 1794, he increased police surveillance and the use of secret agents, and put new pressure on the Freemasons, many of whom were arrested as a result of the conspiracy.[37] In this context, Vertot's history offered a potent historical illustration of the dangers of revolution and, by implication, the advantages of the monarchic state (a point that a reviewer for the *Annalen der Österreichischen Literatur* in 1802 made explicit).[38] Nor would this fact have been lost on the edition's German translator, Anton

36. "Coriolan war weise, genügsam, uneigennützig, bieder und in der Handhabung der Gesetze unerschütterlich . . . für einen Republikaner zu stolz." Vertot, *Revolutions-Geschichte*, 79.

37. I draw here on Jean Bérenger, *A History of the Habsburg Empire: 1700–1918*, trans. C. A. Simpson (London and New York: Routledge, 2014; originally published 1990), 128.

38. Wrote a reviewer of the 1802 edition, "The idea to translate a Vertot, who in the beginning of the 18th century wrote about revolutions, at the end of the revolutions of this century, is very appropriate to the needs of our time and our fatherland. The author shows by clear example of the Roman republic, says Herr Meusel in his *Bibliotheca Historica*, that the advantages derived from the condition of monarchies are manifold and more remarkable than those commonly granted to republics." ("Die Idee, einen Vertot, der im Anfange des 18ten Jahrhunderts über Revolutionen schrieb, am Ende der Revolutionen dieses Jahrhunderts zu übersetzen, ist den Bedürfnissen unserer Zeit und unseres Vaterlandes sehr angemessen, Commoda, e statu monarchiarum nata, sagt HR. Meusel in seiner Bibliotheca historica . . . multiplicis et majoris monimenti esse, quam ea, quae rebus publicis vulgo tribuantur, auctor exemplo Reip. Rom dilucide commonstrat.") "*Geschichte der römischen Staatsveränderungen von R. A. Vertot*," *Annalen der Österreichischen Literatur* 3 (January 1802): col. 20. My thanks to Faye Peel and Daniel J. DiCenso for their assistance with the Latin translation.

Kreil, a Freemason and professor of philosophy who was forced into retirement by the Emperor in the wake of the Jacobin plot.[39] Coriolanus's death at the hands of the Volscians also provided a cautionary tale for would-be revolutionaries: such a tragic demise, writes Vertot, is "a sad but almost unavoidable fate for all those who have the misfortune to take up arms against their fatherland."[40]

Collin's *Coriolan* likewise turns on the theme of *vaterländische Liebe* as the citizen's highest obligation. At the end of Act One, spurned by the very people he has sworn to protect, Coriolan angrily renounces his ties to Rome. This pivotal reversal is underscored by his destruction of a wreath, a token of his service to the fatherland. His mother (Veturia) and wife (Volumnia) react in horror, and Coriolan's banishment is compounded by his mother's devastation:

Veturia
That I would never have given birth to you! Listen!
If you betray the fatherland, then I
curse you!

Volumnia
Stop! You kill me!

Coriolan
What do you speak
of fatherland?—I have
no fatherland! And you, Veturia
You had a son—the one here—he is
another—curse him!

(Act I, scene 6, pp. 33–4)[41]

In betraying Rome, Coriolan has betrayed himself, and Collin's play focuses largely on the psychological conflict that results from this action. In the end, Coriolan learns his lesson the hard way, when his mother shames him into realizing the implications of his betrayals of both kin and country. Coriolan's dying plea to the Volscian general Attus Tullus reveals that he has grasped the error of

---

39. Alexander Wilfing, "State Censorship of Kant—From Francis II to Count Thun," trans. Katharina Walter, in Violetta L. Waibel, ed., *Detours: Approaches to Immanuel Kant in Vienna, in Austria, and in Eastern Europe* (Vienna: Vienna University Press, 2015), 32–9, 34–5.

40. "ein trauriges aber beynahe unvermeidliches Loos aller derer, die das Unglück haben, gegen ihr Vaterland die Waffen zu ergreifen." Vertot, *Revolutions-Geschichte*, 129–30.

41. Veturia: Daß ich dich nie geboren hätte!—Höre! / Wenn du das Vaterland verräthst,—dann fluch' / Ich dir! Volumnia: Halt ein! Ihr tödtet mich! Coriolan: Was sprichst / Du da vom Vaterland?—Ich habe ja / Kein Vaterland! / Auch du, Veturia, / Du hattest einen Sohn—Der hier—er ist / Ein Andrer—fluch ihm nur!

his ways, albeit too late: "Leave Rome—love your fatherland!" ("*Brich auf von Rom—liebst du dein Vaterland!*").

Coriolanus's fate hence served to model the equation of the citizen's political and personal selves, casting patriotism as an essential human value. But the story's allegorical meanings extended beyond this, and a large part of its historical significance derived not from the actions of Coriolanus himself, but rather from those of his mother. Veturia was seen as both the epitome of the classical female hero and the model of matronly virtue—this despite the fact that her intervention on behalf of Rome precipitates her son's death. She was one of nine "Heroines of History" depicted by the Nuremberg print-maker Virgil Solis (1514–62), along with two other ancient Roman women, three Old Testament heroines, and three female saints.[42] Solis portrays Veturia not with an armament, but with a necklace—a sign of her femininity—and a shield inscribed "SPQR," symbolic of her role as heroic protector of the Roman republic (see Figure 6.2). Veturia's noble heroism was similarly brought to the fore in theatrical works such as *Cajo Marzio Coriolano* (1717), an opera with music by Antonio Caldara and a libretto by Pietro Pariati. Caldara's *Coriolano* was an occasional work, composed and performed in Vienna in celebration of Empress Elisabeth Cristina's twenty-sixth birthday. At first blush, the legend of Coriolanus seems a bizarre topic for a celebratory occasional work. But while the opera preserves the legend in broad outline, it is transformed into something befitting the moment: a C-major trumpet overture proclaims a festive character; emphasis is placed on the relationship between Coriolanus and his wife (Vergilia); and there is a happy ending in which—crucially—Coriolanus's life is spared and his mother is hailed as Rome's savior. By concluding the drama with the construction of a temple dedicated to the female goddess Fortuna, Caldara and Pariati shift the emphasis of the ending away from Coriolanus's fate and toward the celebration of feminine virtue and wisdom. The allegorical implications of Veturia's exemplary actions are spelled out in the closing "Licenza," a fourth-wall-breaking recitative and aria addressed directly to the Empress.[43]

42. The other eight heroines are Lucretia, Virginia, Judith, Esther, Jael, St. Bridget of Sweden, St. Elizabeth of Hungary, and St. Helena.

43. "[Recitative]: Consecrate from Rome to Fortuna that eventful day, which brought her Peace and gave her rest. A more glorious Day, August Elisa, shines for us today. This day of your celebrated birth has splendor and light, and with the double ray, through which it gives greater clarity to your Beauty and your Virtue, it fills us with joy and the world with esteem. This, such a grand Day, we honor and consecrate, adorned with many ornaments, to our Fortune. [Aria]: To her happy days, Fate, which honors you, will add this one too. And filled with good auspices, she will give back to the world, which adores you." ("Si consacri da Roma a la Fortuna quel giorno avventurato, che a lei recò la Pace, e diè il riposo. Un Dì più glorioso, Augusta Elisa, oggi per noi risplende. Egli de' tuoi celebrati natali ha fasto e lume, e con il doppio raggio, onde più chiaro la tua Beltà, la tua Virtude il rende, empie di gaudio, e in un d'ossequio il mondo. Questo da noi si onora e si consacra di

FIGURE 6.2. "Veturia," from *Heroines of History* (1530–62). Engraving by Virgil Solis. © The Trustees of the British Museum. Used by permission.

Coriolanus's relationship with his mother was itself viewed in allegorical terms. In 1790, for instance, the French artist Jean-Jacques Avril engraved the intervention scene—after a 1764 painting by Jean-Jacques François Le Barbier— along with the allegorical title "Coriolan et Véturie, ou le respect filial" (see Figure 6.3). The engraving was issued as part of a series depicting moral subjects drawn from history, which the *Journal de Paris* in 1795 described as "a course of morality in action."[44] The lesson here is, of course, "honor thy mother," but its effect is seemingly undercut by Veturia's inadvertently filicidal approach to parenting. The notion that Coriolanus's relationship with his mother was thought exemplary is all the more striking in light of modern Freudian interpretations of the legend, particularly in Shakespeare's retelling, which have centered on Veturia's (Volumnia's) attempts to "punish," "destroy," or "feminize" her son.[45]

The twin themes of Veturia's noble heroism and Coriolanus's filial devotion (or submission) meet head on in Heinrich Füger's interpretation of the intervention scene, painted in Vienna between 1803 and 1805 (see Figure 6.4). Titled *Veturia fordert Coriolan auf, die Stadt zu verschonen* (Veturia beseeches Coriolanus to spare the city), Füger's painting stands in contrast to well-known renditions of the scene by Eustache Le Sueur (1638–9), Nicolas Poussin (c. 1652), Le Barbier (1764), and Angelika Kauffmann (1765).[46] Rather than depicting Veturia on her knees, Füger presents her standing upright and looming imperiously over her son, whose bowed head and bent right leg signify defeat. Veturia rejects her son's embrace: with her outstretched right hand, she stays his arm, and with her raised left hand, she commands respect. Coriolanus's wife and sons, meanwhile, implore him more tenderly; the younger son, cherubic and seminude, offers up an olive branch, while the older son, fashioned to look

tanti fregi adorno, a la nostra Fortuna un sì gran Giorno. A' giorni suoi felici la Sorte che ti onora quest'anche aggiugnerà. E pien coi lieti auspici al mondo che ti adora essa lo renderà.") Antonio Caldara and Pietro Pariati, *Cajo Marzio Coriolano / Drama / per musica / da rappresentarsi / nell'imperial Favorita, festeg- / -giandosi il felicissimo / giorno natalizio / della / sac. ces. catt. real maesta, l'imperadrice / Elisabetta Cristina / l'anno 1717,* Vienna, Österreichische Nationalbibliothek, Mus.Hs.18232/1-3. I am grateful to Marica Tacconi for her assistance with this translation.

44. "L'amour de la Patrie ou le Combat des Horaces, le respect filial ou Coriolan, Pénélope et Ulysse ou la Pudeur, le Désintéressement de Lycurgue, législateur des Spartiates, ou la Magnanimité font désirer la suite des sujets moraux tirés de l'histoire qu'il [Avril] nous a promis; on peut regarder cette collection comme un cours de morale en action. C'est ainsi que les arts servent à épurer les moeurs, loin de les corrompre. Puissent tous les artistes imiter l'exemple des cit. Avril et Le Barbier." *Journal de Paris* (March 1, 1795), quoted in Ministère de la Culture, de la Communication, des Grands Travaux et du Bicentenaire, *La Révolution française et l'Europe, 1789–1799: XXe exposition du Conseil de l'Europe,* 3 vols. (Paris: Éditions de la Réunion des musées nationaux, 1989), vol. 1, 305.

45. See David George, ed., *Shakespeare: The Critical Tradition: Coriolanus* (Bristol: Thoemmes Continuum, 2004), xvii.

46. The title has been rendered several different ways, one of which refers to the wrong scene ("Coriolan nimmt Abschied von seiner Mutter"). I follow the version given in Robert Keil, *Heinrich Friedrich Füger: 1751–1818: Nur wenigen ist es vergönnt das Licht der Wahrheit zu sehen* (Vienna: Amartis-Verlag, 2009), 110, 366.

CORIOLAN ET VÉTURIE *or* LE RESPECT FILIAL.

FIGURE 6.3. *Coriolan et Véturie, ou le respect filial* (1790). Engraving by Jean-Jacques Avril after a painting by Jean-Jacques François Le Barbier. © The Trustees of the British Museum. Used by permission.

more like his father, pulls at his arm and mantle. On the left, a train of kneeling women recedes into the background where the Roman skyline is depicted; on the right, Volscian soldiers stand in suspense, with Tullus in a threatening pose. Füger's painting is unusual in that it depicts Veturia not in a posture of supplication, but rather in one of conquest over her son. While this choice reflects her authoritative persona, it also—and more importantly—inverts the scene's traditional gender dynamics. Veturia's imperious stance and countenance imbue her with a masculine air, especially in contrast to the other women in the scene. Coriolanus, by contrast, appears to be bowing to his mother; he is, in the words of one contemporary, "reluctantly softened," and by implication feminine.[47]

47. Wrote an attendee of the Leipzig Ostermesse in 1810: "The most imposing sheet that was sold in this fair was undoubtedly Füger's Coriolan, engraved by *Kininger* and published by the Viennese Kunst- und Industriekomtoir. The mother Veturia is emphatically greater than the reluctantly softened Coriolan. But in this masterful engraving, the character of Volumnia and the sons, deliberately made to look older, is also inexpressibly delicate and charming, and the women and Volscians in the background are superbly inspired. What the art of engraving can achieve is accomplished here." (Das

FIGURE 6.4. *Veturia fordert Coriolan auf, die Stadt zu verschonen* (1809). Engraving by Vincenz Georg Kininger after a painting by Heinrich Friedrich Füger. © Österreichische Nationalbibliothek. Used by permission.

(Compare Poussin, where Veturia stays Coriolanus's sword, but the traditional postures and gender roles are retained.)

Ferdinand Laban, who wrote on both Collin and Füger, notes in passing that Füger's painting was inspired by Collin's tragedy.[48] This is certainly plausible, given both the timing and the relationship between the two artists. Collin and Füger knew each other through Dietrichstein's salons and took an interest in each other's work. Like Collin, Füger had achieved a remarkable reputation

imposanteste Blatt, das in dieser Messe verkauft wurde, blieb gewiß Fügers Coriolan von *Kininger* geschabt, im Verlage des Wiener Kunst- und Industriekomtoirs. Die Mutter Veturia ist freilich gröser, als der ungern erweichte Coriolan. Aber unaussprechlich zart und hinreissend ist auch in diesem Meisterstich der Karakter der Volumnia und der absichtlich älter angenommenen Söhne, treflich motiviert jede Umgebung der Frauen und Volsker. Was schwarze Kunst leisten kan, ist hier erreicht. Schade, daß nicht mehr von Schreivogels neuem Kunstverlag auf dem Platz war. Es hätte dafür gewiß nicht an Liebhabern gefehlt.) "Blicke auf die Leipziger Ostermesse 1810 (Fortsetzung)," *Allgemeine Zeitung mit allerhöchsten Priviligien* 306 (November 2, 1810): 1221.

48. Ferdinand Laban, *Heinrich Joseph Collin: Ein Beitrag zur Geschichte der neueren deutschen Literatur in Oesterreich* (Vienna: Carl Gerolds Sohn, 1879), 37.

in Vienna. Born in Heilbronn in 1751, he excelled at an early age as a painter of miniature portraits. After initial studies in drawing and an aborted decision to study law, he moved to Leipzig in 1771, where he studied classical art with Adam Friedrich Oeser. In 1774, he followed the British ambassador Sir Robert Murray Keith to Vienna, where he lived for two years before a seven-year stint in Italy, during which he met Anton Raphael Mengs, Jacques-Louis David, Angelika Kauffmann, and Gavin Hamilton. He returned to Vienna and was appointed vice-director (1783) and later director (1795) of the Akademie der bildenen Künste, becoming the court's most significant portrait painter. In 1806, Füger would leave the academy to become director of the Imperial Gallery in the Belvedere palace. In addition to miniatures, Füger's oeuvre includes portraits, historical paintings, and works on religious topics (most famously, a cycle of illustrations based on Klopstock's *Messias*).[49]

Füger was familiar enough with Collin's *Coriolan* to criticize the poet's omission of the election tribunal scene, in which Coriolan is exiled from Rome. Collin's response provides insight into their different interpretations of the story:

> Füger could not understand that, in the first act of *Coriolan*, I did not depict the general assembly in which Coriolan was exiled. One would then have forgiven his actions even more easily, he believed. That the following acts would have been further weakened through the liveliness of the first, that Coriolan's friends and enemies would therein have to reveal themselves to be very effective, become interesting, and yet subsequently vanish, to that he gave no weight. To him a play is not a painting but a series of paintings.[50]

Collin believed that opening the drama with the tribunal scene would have introduced characters and situations that would ultimately have compromised the unity of the play. Füger, he argues, was less concerned with this overall unity and more interested in crafting a series of powerful tableaux. Collin's response recalls Lessing's belief that "the poet should always paint," but that poetry should restrict itself to the "progressive imitations" of actions in time, while painting should center on individual "moment[s] of action, and must therefore choose [those] which [are] the most pregnant."[51]

---

49. The biographical sketch in this paragraph is indebted to Ingrid Sattel Bernardi, "Füger, Heinrich Friedrich," *Grove Art Online, Oxford Art Online*, Oxford University Press, http://www.oxfordartonline.com/subscriber/article/grove/art/T030108 (accessed August 4, 2017).

50. "Füger konnte nicht begreifen, daß ich im ersten Acte des Coriolan nicht die Volksversammlung darstellte, in der Coriolan verbannt wird. Man würde sogar, meinte er, ihm dann seinen Schritt leichter vergeben. Daß dann die folgenden Acte durch die Lebhaftigkeit des ersten noch mehr geschwächt werden würden, daß die Freunde und Feinde des Coriolan dabey sich sehr wirksam zeigen, interessant werden, und doch in der Folge verschwinden müßten, darauf legte er kein Gewicht. Ihm ist ein Stück eine Folge von Gemählden, nicht ein Gemählde." Collin, *Sämmtliche Werke*, vol. 5, 43–4.

51. Gotthold Ephraim Lessing, *Laocoon*, trans. Sir Robert Phillimore (London: Macmillan, 1874), 161, 150.

Despite Füger's reservations about the first act, he may well have had Collin's play in mind when painting the intervention scene. In Collin, this scene (Act IV, scene 8) begins with Veturia in the same posture in which Füger depicts her—deflecting her son's embrace ("seine Umarmung abwehrend," according to the stage direction, probably adopted from Livy).[52] Torn between motherly love and hatred for her treacherous son, she both receives and resists him, "raging":

> **Veturia**
>
> In my arms, son! Let yourself be pressed
> against this heart! Do you feel how it beats? Still
> I love you!—I should not! You are the enemy
> of the fatherland; I should hate you now.
> But I love you—motherly love prevails!
> Forgive, you gods!—ah, I am too weak!
> I still cannot hate him, no! Still not!
>
> (Act IV, scene 8, p. 105)[53]

As the scene progresses, Veturia's resolve strengthens, and the motherly love that she initially lamented as a weakness proves to be the key to Coriolan's undoing:

> **Veturia**
>
> Volumnia! Now the man's heart prevails!
> I see it! Help me on my knee!—My son!
>
> **Coriolan**
>
> My heart tears apart! Woe!
>
> **Veturia**
>
> I will lie here,
> Pleading at your feet, so long embracing them,
> Until I die from shame.
>
> **Coriolan**
>
> Stand up! Stand up!
> O woe is me! O let me go! Away!

52. Heinrich von Collin, *Coriolan: Ein Trauerspiel in fünf Aufzüge* (Berlin: Johann Friedrich Unger, 1804), 104.

53. Veturia: In meine Arme, Sohn! Laß an dies Herz / Dich drücken! Fühlst du, wie es schlägt? Noch lieb' / Ich dich!—Ich sollte nicht! Du bist der Feind / Des Vaterlands, ich sollte dich nun hassen. /—Doch lieb' ich dich—die Mutterliebe siegt! / Verzeiht, ihr Götter! – ach, ich bin zu schwach! / Noch kann ich ihn nicht hassen, nein! noch nicht!

Veturia

No man, no god will tear me from this spot.

Coriolan

——You have triumphed!

Veturia

Triumphed!!

Volumnia

O thank you, good one!

Veturia

Now cheer, fatherland! I cheer with you!

Coriolan

This is a mad cheer, mother! through
the soul it presses! And if you knew . . . ? Now,
It ends, as it should. Yet, dear mother,
about what do you rejoice? Let Rome rejoice!
For you and us this is a sad victory.

(Act IV, scene 8, pp. 116–17)[54]

If Füger took his cue for Veturia's posture from Collin's opening stage direction, then his depiction of Coriolanus shows him much later in the scene,
after Veturia has "triumphed" (*gesiegt*). At this point in the play, as in virtually
all other sources, Veturia kneels down in a final attempt to sway her son (in
Shakespeare, "Down, ladies; let us shame him with our knees."). Füger, in order
to capture the scene's essence, hence conflates Coriolanus's thwarted embrace
of his mother and his ultimate defeat, depicting a "protracted" moment of the
kind Lessing hails as a trait of the great historical paintings.[55] The painting's
theatricality is further heightened by the composition and use of light. As Wolf
Eiermann has noted, Füger sets the outdoor scene in a tight configuration that

---

54. Veturia: Volumnia! Nun siegt des Mannes Herz! / Ich seh's! Hilf auf die Kniee mir!—Mein
Sohn! Coriolan: So reiß, mein Herz! Weh! Veturia: Liegen will ich hier, / Die Füße flehend dir so
lang' umfassen, / Bis ich vor Scham vergeh'. Coriolan: Steh' auf! Steh' auf!! / O wehe mir! O laßt
mich los! Hinweg! Veturia: Mich reißt kein Mensch, kein Gott von dieser Stelle. Coriolan:——Ihr
habt gesiegt! Veturia: Gesiegt!! Volumnia: O Dank dir, Guter! Veturia: Nun jauchze, Vaterland! ich
jauchze mit! Coriolan: Das ist ein wildes Jauchzen, Mutter! durch / Die Seele dringt's! Und wenn
du wüßtest . . . ? Nun, / Es endet, wie es soll. Doch, liebe Mutter, / Worüber freust du dich? Laß
Rom sich freuen! / Für dich und uns ist traurig dieser Sieg!

55. Lessing, *Laocoon*, 172.

focuses the view on the characters rather than the cityscape or landscape, suggesting actors on a stage set. The central group of figures is illuminated, as if by footlights, in contrast to the figures on the periphery, who appear darkened. The Roman skyline, meanwhile, suggests the arrival of a new dawn.[56] Füger, it should be noted, was an experienced set designer who had painted stage curtains for the Alte Burgtheater in 1794.[57]

With its larger-than-life Veturia and enfeebled Coriolan, Füger's *Coriolan* brings another set of allegorical meanings to the fore. His painting locates Veturia within a culture that increasingly identified the heroic with the feminine, and that elevated such figures as Joan of Arc, Marianne, and their Germanic counterparts. Matthew Head has called attention to the proliferation of this culture during the late German Enlightenment, noting that during the Napoleonic Wars, heroism itself was "frequently subject to female embodiment and involved motifs of transvestitism and androgyny."[58] Most popular, of course, were the stories of female heroism (often involving cross-dressing) that revolved around conjugal fidelity, such as Beethoven's *Leonore*, Cherubini's *Faniska*, and numerous other rescue plots. But women were also equated allegorically with the ideas of patriotism and nation, as for example in Goethe's *Egmont* and Friedrich Dunker's *Leonore Prohaska*, for which plays Beethoven composed incidental music. By the same token, representations of male heroism often valorized "feminine" characteristics such as sensibility, vulnerability, and fragility. Head has argued that the thematic disintegration at the end of Beethoven's *Coriolan* overture itself analogizes the hero's physical body in its most vulnerable state, recalling the "complex gendering of male heroism" in such paintings as Jacques-Louis David's *The Intervention of the Sabine Women* (1795–9) and *The Death of Bara* (1794).[59] Such complex gendering of both female and male heroism is equally central to Füger's *Coriolan*, and it underscores the painter's debt to the French neoclassicists, not least David, whom he knew personally and sought to emulate.

56. I am grateful to Sherry Roush for this observation.

57. Wolf Eiermann, "Füger der Große," in Marc Gundel, ed., *Heinrich Friedrich Füger 1751– 1818: Zwischen Genie und Akademie*, exhibition catalogue, Städtische Museen Heilbronn/ Kunsthalle Vogelmann December 3, 2011–March 11, 2012 (Munich: Hirmer Verlag, 2011), 53–68, 63.

58. Matthew Head, *Sovereign Feminine: Music and Gender in Eighteenth-Century Germany* (Berkeley: University of California Press, 2013), 191. Head's chapter 6 is a revised version of his earlier article, "Beethoven Heroine: A Female Allegory of Music and Authorship in Egmont," *19th-Century Music* 30, no. 2 (Fall 2006): 97–132. I quote from the more recent version here.

59. Head, *Sovereign Feminine*, 196.

"ALL ARTS ARE INTERCONNECTED": BEETHOVEN'S *Coriolan* AND THE STATUS OF THE PROGRAM

By the time Beethoven completed his overture in early 1807, then, Viennese concertgoers already had multiple ways to familiarize themselves with the Coriolanus story. The overture's direct Viennese antecedents were Collin's play (1802) and Füger's painting (1805), but these were only the most recent entries in a tradition that included modern translations of the classics and popular histories of Rome, all widely available to consumers. To whatever extent the overture was a response to Collin's play, it was also a response to this wider context. Whether Beethoven was influenced by Füger's painting specifically, however, is difficult to determine. Beethoven may have visited Füger's studio in 1801, when he acquired a copy of his painting *Antiochus und Stratonice* (c. 1790) for his friend Franz Wegeler, who was back in Bonn.[60] Beethoven and Füger also overlapped at the salons of Dietrichstein, in which both, along with Collin, were frequent participants. His interest would doubtless have been piqued by Füger's *Coriolan*, though there is no evidence that he knew it. Nonetheless, by 1809, Collin's play, Beethoven's overture, and Füger's painting—engraved by Vincenz Georg Kininger—were all available for purchase, inviting consumers to compare treatments of the Coriolanus story by three Viennese masters (four, counting Kininger), all working in different media.[61]

This confluence of responses to the Coriolanus story is made all the more significant by the fact that Collin, Füger, and Beethoven were equally invested at this time in probing the boundaries of the arts and their relationship to each other. While Füger composed his paintings to look like theatrical scenes, Collin looked to the plastic arts and music for inspiration. In his 1806 memo to the theater management, he recommended the multitalented Joseph Lange as a director not just because of his acting abilities but also because "as a painter, he understands positions and groupings better than anyone."[62] (Lange's

---

60. *Briefwechsel*, vol. 1, no. 65, pp. 78–83, 80; Anderson, vol. 1, no. 51, pp. 57–62, 61.

61. Kininger's engraving, published by the Viennese Bureau des Arts et d'Industrie, was announced as early as December 1807, coincidentally in the same advertisement that publicized the "six new large works by *Beethoven*" that the firm would issue in 1808 (opuses 58 through 62, including 61a). Ironically, the advertisement describes in detail all but the sixth Beethoven work—the *Coriolan* Overture—and hence misses an opportunity for cross-promotion. "Korrespondenz- und Notizen-Blatt," *Zeitung für die elegante Welt* 197 (December 10, 1807): cols. 1573–4. Kininger later designed the frontispieces (engraved by Friedrich John) for the first five volumes of Collin's complete works, based on scenes from Collin's plays: vol. 1—*Regulus*, vol. 2—*Bianca della Porta*, vol. 3—*Die Horatier und Curiatier*, vol. 4—*Kaiser Albrechts Hund*, vol. 5—*Rudolph und Lobkowitz*. The sixth and final volume includes Lange's portrait of Collin, also engraved by John.

62. "Lange kann als Senior darauf Anspruch machen, und für sich anführen, daß er das, was nun allmählich von dem Theater verschwindet, Anstand, Würde, Majestät, guten Ton, Welt, Feinheit und Delicatesse vorzüglich besitze, und als Mahler Stellungen und Gruppirungen besser als jeder versehe." Collin, *Sämmtliche Werke*, vol. 5, 333.

performance in *Coriolan*'s title role was itself hailed as being "like a progressive painting.")[63] Elsewhere, Collin described the importance of painting and music on his conception of drama:

> All arts are interconnected. Yet it is dangerous for the artist if he exclusively studies a second art outside of his own. He should learn from all of them. From Füger I want to study the expression, composition, and unity of paintings; from Mozart, by contrast, the rising of passion to an unimagined level, as from Haydn the order out of confusion, the rest after the struggle.[64]

Collin also expressed his desire for a closer relationship between poetry and music in an open letter on opera, published in the *Morgenblatt für gebildete Stände* on May 21, 1807. Inspired by a new production of Gluck's *Iphigenia in Tauris* at the Kärntnerthortheater on January 1, 1807, the letter, based in part on his 1806 memo to the theater management, is Collin's Gluckian manifesto. While poetry "in its highest perfection becomes music," music, its "twin sister," strives not for novel harmonies or melodies but for "expression." In language that looks back to Gluck while also prefiguring Wagner, he writes that the goal of opera should be the reunion of the arts such that, one day, "drama and opera will merge into one, and Greek theater in its full Olympian splendor will appear before us."[65]

While Collin formulated these ideas, Beethoven was at work on the *Coriolan* overture, and it is worthwhile to consider the status of the overture's "program" in light of their and other contemporaries' thinking about the relationships among poetry, painting, and music. Lessing, who never completed the parts of *Laocoon* that were to deal with music, likened painting and poetry to "two equitable friendly neighboring states" which "do not indeed permit one to take unbecoming liberties in the interior of the empire of the other, but freely allow a mutual indulgence to prevail on their extreme frontiers."[66] In his view, painting and poetry could never truly interpenetrate because painting was bound to the imitation of bodies in space, whereas poetry was bound to the imitation of actions in time. But the notion that the arts were subject to amalgamation on

---

63. "Ueber das Spiel des k. k. Hoffschauspielers Herrn Lange auf dem Grätzer-Theater im Monath July 1805," *Wiener Hof-Theater Taschenbuch auf das Jahr 1806* (Vienna, 1806): 112–37, 129. Lange painted the best-known portrait of Collin, reproduced on Füger's funeral monument and in the complete edition of Collin's works edited by Matthäus von Collin. His painting of his brother-in-law Mozart was described by Mozart's sister as the best likeness of the composer.

64. "Alle Künste stehen mit einander in Verbindung. Doch ist es für den Künstler gefährlich, wenn er, außer seiner Kunst, auschließend eine zweyte studiert. Von allen soll er lernen. Von Füger will ich Ausdruck, Anordnung, Einheit der Gemählde studiren, von Mozart hingegen das Steigen der Leidenschaft zur ungeahndeten Höhe, wie von Haydn die Ordnung aus der Verwirrung, die Ruhe nach dem Kampfe." Collin, *Sämmtliche Werke*, vol. 5, 43.

65. Heinrich Joseph von Collin, "Brief über das gesungene Drama," *Morgenblatt für gebildete Stände* 121 (May 21, 1807): 481–2, 481.

66. Lessing, *Laocoon*, 171–2.

their "extreme frontiers" was provocative, and how this notion applied to music was a topic taken up by many authors, including Johann Georg Sulzer (1771–4), Johann Jakob Engel (1780), and Heinrich Christoph Koch (1802). Beethoven had himself struggled with these issues in composing an overture to *Leonore*. *Leonore No. 2* (1804–5), and to a greater extent, its successor *Leonore No. 3* (1805–6), allude to numerous moments in the opera. As a result, there are so many tempo changes and new musical ideas (especially in *No. 3*) that the overture's program threatens to outweigh the musical demands of the form. Beethoven, perhaps aware of this problem, wrote a more condensed version of the overture in 1807 (*Leonore No. 1*, for a planned performance in Prague), a version that still referred to the key moments in the dungeon scene and the duet between Florestan and Leonore, but in a way that gave more precedence to the overture's sonata-form design. In the end, of course, he chose to eliminate the references to the opera altogether (*Fidelio*, 1814), something that implies that his views on the overture's function changed as time went on.

As Beethoven's experience with the *Leonore* overtures suggests, the dramatic overture posed a unique problem for composers in that it forced one to take a position on the issue of musical representation. As Gluck had put it in the preface to his *Alceste*, "the overture ought to apprise the spectators of the nature of the action that is to be represented and to form, so to speak, the argument."[67] There were a number of ways in which composers could attempt to articulate a drama's argument, whether through references to "exotic" musical styles (the "Chinese" overture to Gluck's *Le Cinesi* [1754] or the "Turkish" overture to his *La rencontre imprévue* [1764]), direct quotations of musical ideas that would appear later in the drama (the overture to Mozart's *Don Giovanni* [1787], with its foreshadowing of the Don's encounter with the Stone Guest; the *Leonore* overtures; or the overture to Beethoven's *Egmont* [1810], with its preview of the "Victory Symphony" that ends the play), or, more unusually, explicit tone painting (the overture to Rameau's *Pygmalion* [1748], which depicts the sculptor chiseling the creation with which he is to fall in love). One commentator in 1807 arguably heard elements of tone painting in the *Coriolan* overture, writing that it "represented in the most masterly way Coriolan's infuriated temper and the sudden, terrible change in his destiny, and produced sublime emotion."[68] It is telling, however, that this commentator refers to the Coriolanus story only in the broadest possible terms and without reference to any specific source.

67. Christoph Willibald Gluck, "Dedication for *Alceste*," in Oliver Strunk, ed., *Source Readings in Music History*, rev. ed., ed. Leo Treitler (New York: Norton Press, 1998), 932–4, 933.

68. "Wenn gediegene Kraft und die Fülle tiefer Empfindung den Deutschen charakterisiren, so darf man Beethoven vorzugsweise einen *deutschen* Künstler nennen. In diesem seinem neusten Werke bewundert man die ausdrucksvolle Tiefe seiner Kunst, die, ohne auf jene mit Recht gerügten Abwege neuerer Musik sich zu verirren, das wild bewegte Gemüth Coriolans und den plötzlich schrecklichen Wechsel seines Schicksals auf das herrlichste darstellte, und die erhabene Rührung hervorbrachte." "Korrespondenz-Nachrichten. Wien." *Morgenblatt für gebildete Stände* 84 (April 8, 1807): 336.

While Beethoven doubtless intended his overture to be read in the context of the Coriolanus legend, attempting to understand it from a purely programmatic standpoint (as some commentators have done) hence involves a substantial amount of assumption and guesswork. It also seems to contradict Beethoven's most definitive statement about the issue of musical representation during this period, the subtitle to his *Pastoral* Symphony, as printed in the first edition of the parts (Breitkopf & Härtel, 1809): "more the expression of feeling than tone painting" (*mehr Ausdruck der Empfindung als Mahlerey*). This elegant phrase was itself the result of considerable revision; interspersed among the sketches for the symphony are a number of Beethoven's attempts to formulate the title:

"The listeners should be allowed to discover the situations."
"Sinfonia caracteristica, or remembrance of country life."
"A remembrance of country life."
"All painting in instrumental music, if pushed too far, is a failure."
"Sinfonia pastorella. Anyone who has an idea of country life can make out for himself the intentions of the author without many titles."
"People will not require titles to recognize the general intention to be more a matter of feeling than of painting in sounds."
"Pastoral Symphony: no painting, but something in which the emotions are expressed which are aroused in men by the pleasure of the country (or), in which some feelings of country life are set forth."[69]

These comments reveal an attitude toward the illustrative potential of both the *Pastoral* and instrumental music in general that is more complex than the final version of the title might be thought to suggest. Beethoven is wary of tone painting, it is true, as we may judge from his remark that "the general intention [is] more a matter of feeling than painting in sounds," but his use of the designations "caracteristica" and "pastorella" situate his symphony within a tradition of illustrative music that had existed since the baroque period. Although he consistently places emphasis on abstract notions such as "feeling," "emotion," and "remembrance," when he suggests that "the listeners should be allowed to discover the situations," he implies that there are indeed situations to be discovered. Similarly, when he claims, "All painting in instrumental music, if pushed too far, is a failure," he implies that painting, when used in moderation, could produce a desirable effect. As these comments indicate, whatever Beethoven's ambivalence about musical representation—and despite his pupil

---

69. The translations are slightly emended from George Grove, *Beethoven and His Nine Symphonies*, reprint of the 1898 edition (Mineola, NY: Dover Publications, 1962), 191. For the German originals, see Gustav Nottebohm, *Zweite Beethoveniana* (New York and London: Johnson Reprint Company, 1970), 375, 504. See also the discussion in David Wyn Jones, *Beethoven: Pastoral Symphony*, Cambridge Music Handbooks (Cambridge: Cambridge University Press, 1995), 30ff.

Ries's assertion that he "often laughed at and inveighed against descriptive music"—Beethoven was aware not only of music's illustrative potential, but also of the attendant aesthetic and philosophical problems that potential implies.[70] Put differently, Beethoven—to borrow Lessing's formulation—was eager to traverse the frontiers between music and its sister arts, but skeptical about venturing too deep into foreign territory.

All of this suggests that to understand the *Coriolan* overture as a kind of tone poem *avant la lettre* is to go too far. At the same time, one need not reject the overture's extramusical associations as somehow extrinsic to the work—on the contrary. Indeed, both of these views are less a product of Beethoven's own time than of the later nineteenth century, when the ideals of absolute and program music crystallized and began to be viewed as mutually exclusive. Contemporaries who experienced Collin's play or Füger's painting inevitably compared these modern interpretations of the Coriolanus story to earlier ones, including Shakespeare.[71] As artists like Collin, Füger, and Beethoven probed the boundaries of their arts, philosophers and everyday listeners weighed the relative merits of the arts and looked to elucidate them through comparison. The rich visual, literary, and political associations of the Coriolanus story as it was known in Vienna, far from being incidental to Beethoven's overture, are, in this sense, indispensable to understanding it. These associations mediated the work's composition, performance, and reception in ways that illuminate its many possible meanings for Beethoven and his contemporaries. One need not take the idea that Beethoven composed his overture "for" Collin, then, as a restriction on interpretation. Rather, by reading the overture in terms of Beethoven's relationship with Collin, one opens up a wide array of interpretations. While this necessarily complicates how one approaches the overture from an analytical standpoint, it also acknowledges the historical contingency of analysis itself, inviting one instead to engage with the complexity, richness, and messiness, of Beethoven's moment.

70. Franz Wegeler and Ferdinand Ries, *Remembering Beethoven: The Biographical Notes of Franz Wegeler and Ferdinand Ries*, ed. Eva Badura-Skoda (London: André Deutsch, 1988), 67.

71. For a contemporary comparison of Shakespeare's *Coriolanus* and Collin's *Coriolan*, see C. Stück, "Schöne Künste," *Neue Leipziger Literaturzeitung* 100 (August 2, 1805): cols. 1585–600.

CONCLUSION

"Everyday" Beethoven

In this book I have tried to make unfamiliar the familiar, to reassess how we think about one of music's most revered figures. To be sure, it is neither the first nor will it be the last study to contribute to the demystification of Beethoven, an individual whose Romantic legacy has acquired not just the force but also the durability of myth. Everyone likes a good story, and one sometimes has the impression that studies of history or context will never be enough to transform the popularized account of Beethoven's life as a journey of struggle and transcendence marked by a handful of profound crises and turning points. Still, it remains important to agitate for a more complex picture of this complex individual, not only for the sake of setting the record straight but also because appreciating the contours of Beethoven's life promises to enhance our appreciation of his music.

One goal of this book has been to offer a more nuanced view of Beethoven's so-called middle period. As I have argued, there are compelling musical affinities among the instrumental works of 1806–7, suggesting a stylistic turn from the "heroic phase" of 1803–5. This turn seems to have been partly a response to criticisms of works like *Leonore* and the *Eroica*, and partly a reaction to the changing political situation in the wake of the Peace of Pressburg. At the same time, it is much less of an aesthetic about-face than it has seemed to many critics. While, in the Fourth Piano Concerto, Fourth Symphony, and Violin Concerto, Beethoven avoids certain elements that scholars have associated with his heroic style (learned counterpoint, expanded orchestration, and extramusical references, to name just three), in other respects—such as the moments of suspended time that Adorno heard as evidence of the music's "subjectivity"— these works suggest an intensification of the heroic impulse. Meanwhile, in the *Coriolan* Overture and Thirty-Two Variations on an Original Theme, both in C minor, Beethoven continues to probe the realm of pathos and tragedy that is central to the heroic ethos but does not attempt to bring about the resultant sense of affirmation and triumph that is typically seen as this style's sine qua non. The "Razumovsky" Quartets offer a more complex case, with multiple styles coexisting in close proximity. In the final analysis, no stylistic label can adequately account for the entire expressive range of Beethoven's instrumental music. And although well-worn dichotomies such as the "heroic" versus the "lyrical," the "sublime" versus the "beautiful," or the "innovative" versus the "traditional" have provided convenient hermeneutic windows, they ultimately serve as a critical shorthand that too often masks the unique aspects of individual artworks.

While it is difficult to imagine a world free of phases, styles, periods, and the like, I have aimed to suggest a different way to conceptualize the music of 1806 and early 1807. By approaching each work individually and through the lens of Beethoven's relationships, I have attempted to show how these works were the products and catalysts of numerous mediations. Crucial to this thesis is the notion that Beethoven's social world provided much more than the context in which his artworks were composed; it rather informed the design of these artworks in significant ways. In Beethoven studies, where the aesthetic and the social have often been viewed as distinctly separate realms, the idea of mediation—particularly in combination with microhistory—offers a path forward, a bridge between text and context.

One of the most interesting questions about the genre of microhistory is whether or to what extent it differs from the case study. In a roundtable discussion at Duke University published in the *Journal of Medieval and Early Modern Studies*, the historian Thomas V. Cohen offered the following reflection:

> Let's pick up the case study for a moment. One who takes up a case study says "I have a phenomenon," and, to explore it, I will pick an example. With a case study, the phenomenon itself, not the case, guides the research and the exposition. So the very mentality of case study in the mind of the researcher starts with the problem to be solved—to solve that problem I'm going to look at something. But the microhistorian, I imagine, is really led into the problem by fascination with the particular, which leads the inquiry to "how do I ever work out these puzzles?" The writer is led by puzzlement.[1]

I gladly confess to having been "led by puzzlement" in my approach to this study. Indeed, for me the year 1806 has been an intriguing subject precisely because it is marked neither by one of Beethoven's unequivocal watershed compositions nor by any of the truly canonical "moments" in Napoleonic political history against which Beethoven's musical output has typically been measured. The absence of a ready-made backdrop in this sense forces one to

---

1. Thomas Robisheaux, ed., "Microhistory Today: A Roundtable Discussion," in *Journal of Medieval and Early Modern Studies* 47, no. 1 (January 2017): 7–52, 11.

think about context in a more intricate way, and in this respect mediation offers an indispensable tool.

Focusing on Beethoven's relationships and the ways in which they mediated his music not only helps us to better understand the complexity of his creative process but also restores a sense of Beethoven as a historical actor, something that is often missing in macrohistorical accounts. For as dramatic as Beethoven's life was, it is easy for even the conscientious critic to fall back on the familiar plot points of the biography and let those govern the discussion of the music, rather than considering the crucial question of what precisely these works did for Beethoven in the moment they were created—and for his audience in the moment in which they were first heard. No history is free of what Hayden White called "emplotment," the tendency to impose a narrative form on historical data, but microhistories can add nuance to the macrohistorical account, and in aggregate, perhaps even transform it.[2]

In many respects, Beethoven in 1806 was an "everyday" composer—he even seems to have wanted to present himself this way. Consider Neugass's 1806 portrait of Beethoven, reproduced in chapter 4, in contrast to Mähler's more famous portrait from just a few years earlier, reproduced in the Introduction. The Mähler portrait is rich in symbolism: Beethoven assumes a heroic posture, his uplifted hand seemingly mediating between the classical temple of Apollo on his right and the windswept, Romantic landscape on his left. His close-cropped hair reflects Parisian trends, and the lyre-guitar that he holds figures him as a modern-day Orpheus. Neugass's half-length portrait, by contrast, is more naturalistic, even proto-Biedermeier, in style. Unlike Mähler, Neugass presents Beethoven with no attributes. While storm clouds in the background, barely visible, emphasize the presence of nature and the pastoral, the symbolism is more muted—the focus is on capturing Beethoven's likeness more than idealizing him. Neugass's Beethoven portrait also contrasts significantly with the painter's 1806 celebrity portrait of Haydn (discussed in chapter 4), which shows Haydn in the act of composing while a statue of Apollo and a bust of J. S. Bach look on. Indeed, the only truly unusual element in Neugass's Beethoven is a mundane one: the lorgnette ribbon on Beethoven's neck, a detail that corroborates contemporary descriptions of the other disability from which Beethoven suffered, near-sightedness.

Scholars of Beethoven's image have called Neugass a "weak" painter, describing his portrait of Beethoven as both "inept" and "insignificant in so far as documenting Beethoven's physiognomy."[3] It certainly remains among

---

2. See Hayden White, *Metahistory: The Historical Imagination in Nineteenth-Century Europe* (Baltimore: Johns Hopkins University Press, 1975), esp. 7ff.

3. Alessandra Comini, *The Changing Image of Beethoven: A Study in Mythmaking*, rev. ed. (Santa Fe: Sunstone Press, 2008), 421, note 55.

the least known and least often reproduced of Beethoven portraits. But one senses that its low esteem has less to do with the perceived inaccuracies of the portrayal than with the absence of the iconographical features that have come to be thought of as quintessentially Beethovenian—whether these be the heroic stance and determined glare of the Mähler or the tousled hair and infamous scowl of Joseph Karl Stieler's 1820 portrait. However inaccurate the likeness, Neugass's Beethoven is noteworthy for its portrayal of a different side of Beethoven, a more modest, more ordinary one. Beethoven was an idealist, to be sure, but he was also an opportunist, someone who sought to build an international reputation, cultivate connections, and earn a living through his art. Embracing the "everyday" Beethoven allows us to better appreciate the full measure of his creative life. It also—and more importantly—opens up a new aesthetics of his music, one that focuses less on a priori schemes and more on the ways in which his music responded to and helped to shape the world in which he lived.

WORKS CITED

Abraham, Gerald. *Beethoven's Second-Period Quartets*. The Musical Pilgrim. London: Oxford University Press, 1942.

———, ed. *The Age of Beethoven 1790–1830*. Vol. 8 of *The New Oxford History of Music*. 1982. Reprint, Oxford and New York: Oxford University Press, 2007.

Adelson, Robert, Alain Roudier, Jenny Nex, Laure Barthel, and Michel Foussard, eds. *The History of the Erard Piano and Harp in Letters and Documents, 1785–1959*. 2 vols. Cambridge: Cambridge University Press, 2015.

Adorno, Theodor W. *Beethoven: The Philosophy of Music*. Edited by Rolf Tiedemann. Translated by Edmund Jephcott. Stanford: Stanford University Press, 1998.

———. *Essays on Music*. Edited by Richard Leppert. Translated by Susan H. Gillespie. Berkeley: University of California Press, 2002.

Albrecht, Theodore, trans. and ed. *Letters to Beethoven and Other Correspondence*. 3 vols. Lincoln: University of Nebraska Press, 1996.

———. "The Musicians in Balthasar Wigand's Depiction of the Performance of Haydn's *Die Schöpfung*, Vienna, 27 March 1808." *Music in Art* 29, no. 1–2 (2004): 123–33.

"Allgemeine Weltgeschichte und alte Geschichte." *Neue Allgemeine Deutsche Bibliothek* 85, part 2, no. 7 (1803), 420.

Alper, Clifford D. "Beethoven's *Coriolan* Overture, Opus 62, Three Points of View." *The Beethoven Newsletter* 6, no. 2 (Summer 1991): 43–9.

Anderson, Emily, ed. *The Letters of Mozart and His Family*. 3 vols. London: Macmillan, 1938.

Antolini, Bianca Maria, and Costantino Mastroprimiano, eds. *Muzio Clementi: Compositore, (Forte)pianista, Editore*. Strumenti della ricerca musicale 9. Lucca, LIM: 2006.

Auslander, Philip. "Musical Personae." *The Drama Review* 50, no. 1 (Spring 2006): 100–19.

Bach, Carl Philipp Emanuel. *Essay on the True Art of Playing Keyboard Instruments*. Translated and edited by William J. Mitchell. New York and London: W.W. Norton & Company, 1949.

Beethoven, Ludwig van. *Briefwechsel: Gesamtausgabe*. 7 vols. Edited by Sieghard Brandenburg. Munich: G. Henle, 1996–2001.

———. *The Letters of Beethoven*. 3 vols. Translated and edited by Emily Anderson. New York: St. Martin's Press, 1961.

———. *Trente deux variations pour le pianoforte composées par Louis van Beethoven*. Vienna: Bureau des Arts et d'Industrie, 1807.

————. *Trois quatuors pour deux violons, alto, et violoncello. Composés par Louis van Beethoven. Oeuvre 59ᵐᵉ.* Vienna: Bureau des Arts et d'Industrie, 1808.

Bekker, Paul. *Beethoven.* Translated by M. M. Bozman. London and New York, 1925. Reprint, New York: AMS, 1971.

Bennett, Joseph. "Second Concert: Thursday, March 24, 1904." *Analytical and Historical Programme.* London: Philharmonic Society, 1904.

Benton, Rita. "Pleyel's *Bibliothèque musicale.*" *The Music Review* 36, no. 1 (February 1975): 1–4.

Bérenger, Jean. *A History of the Habsburg Empire: 1700–1918.* Translated by C. A. Simpson. London and New York: Routledge, 2014. Originally published 1990.

Berger, Karol. *Bach's Cycle, Mozart's Arrow: An Essay on the Origins of Musical Modernity.* Berkeley and Los Angeles: University of California Press, 2007.

Bernardi, Ingrid Sattel. "Füger, Heinrich Friedrich." *Grove Art Online. Oxford Art Online.* Oxford University Press, accessed August 4, 2017, http://www.oxfordartonline.com/subscriber/article/grove/art/T030108.

Biamonte, Nicole. "Modality in Beethoven's Folk-song Settings." *Beethoven Forum* 13, no. 1 (Spring 2006): 28–63.

Biba, Otto, ed. *"Eben komme ich von Haydn . . . ": Georg August Griesingers Korrespondenz mit Joseph Haydns Verleger Breitkopf & Härtel 1799–1819.* Zurich: Atlantis Musikbuch-Verlag, 1987.

Blanning, Tim. *The Pursuit of Glory: The Five Revolutions That Made Modern Europe: 1648–1815.* New York: Penguin Books, 2007.

"Blicke auf die Leipziger Ostermesse 1810 (Fortsetzung)." *Allgemeine Zeitung mit allerhöchsten Priviligien* 306 (November 2, 1810): 1221.

Bonds, Mark Evan. "Haydn, Laurence Sterne, and the Origins of Musical Irony." *Journal of the American Musicological Society* 44, no. 1 (Spring 1991): 57–91.

————. *Music as Thought: Listening to the Symphony in the Age of Beethoven.* Princeton: Princeton University Press, 2006.

Born, Georgina. "For a Relational Musicology: Music and Interdisciplinarity, beyond the Practice Turn." *Journal of the Royal Musical Association* 135, no. 2 (2010): 205–43.

Botticelli, Andrea. "'Creating Tone': The Relationship between Beethoven's Piano Sonority and Evolving Instrument Designs, 1800–1810." DMA thesis, University of Toronto, 2014.

Bourdieu, Pierre. "The Forms of Capital." In *Handbook of Theory and Research for the Sociology of Education,* edited by J. Richardson, 241–58. Westport, CT: Greenwood Press, 1986.

Bouyer, Pierre, and Sophie Liger. *Beethoven et le pianoforte Érard: Variation & pièces diverses à 2 et 4 mains, 1803–1806.* Diligence, DIL6, 2007, compact disc.

Bowles, Edmund A. *The Timpani: A History in Pictures and Documents.* Hillsdale, NY: Pendragon Press, 2002.

Breaugh, Martin. *The Plebeian Experience: A Discontinuous History of Political Freedom.* Translated by Lazer Lederhendler. New York: Columbia University Press, 2013. Originally published 2007.

Breitman, David. "The Damper Pedal and the Beethoven Piano Sonatas: A Historical Perspective." DMA thesis, Cornell University, 1993.

"Briefe über den jetzigen Zustand der Musik in Russland." Pts. 1–3. *Allgemeine musikalische Zeitung* 4, no. 21 (February 17, 1802): cols. 346–50; no. 22 (February 24, 1802): cols. 353–65; and no. 23 (March 3, 1802): cols. 369–80.

Brown, A. Peter. "*The Creation* and *The Seasons*: Some Allusions, Quotations, and Models from Handel to Mendelssohn." *Current Musicology* 51 (1991): 26–58.

———. *The Symphonic Repertoire.* Vol. 2, *The First Golden Age of the Viennese Symphony: Haydn, Mozart, Beethoven, and Schubert.* Bloomington: Indiana University Press, 2002.

Brown, Clive. *Classical and Romantic Performing Practice 1750–1900.* Oxford: Oxford University Press, 2004. Originally published 1999.

Brown, Malcolm Hamrick, ed. *A Collection of Russian Folk Songs by Nikolai Lvov and Ivan Prach.* Facsimile of the 1806 edition. Ann Arbor: UMI Research Press, 1987.

Broyles, Michael. *Beethoven in America.* Bloomington: Indiana University Press, 2011.

———. *Beethoven: The Emergence and Evolution of Beethoven's Heroic Style.* New York: Excelsior Music Publishing, 1987.

Burke, Edmund. *A Philosophical Enquiry into the Origin of Our Ideas of the Sublime and Beautiful.* Edited by Adam Phillips. Oxford and New York: Oxford University Press, 1999. Originally published in 1757.

Burke, Peter. *New Perspectives on Historical Writing.* 2nd ed. University Park: Pennsylvania State University Press, 2001.

Burnham, Scott. *Beethoven Hero.* Princeton: Princeton University Press, 1995.

Burnham, Scott, and Michael Steinberg, eds. *Beethoven and His World.* Princeton: Princeton University Press, 2000.

Burstein, L. Poundie. "The Off-Tonic Return in Beethoven's Piano Concerto No. 4 in G Major, Op. 58, and Other Works." *Music Analysis* 24, no. 3 (October 2005): 305–47.

Caplin, William. *Classical Form: A Theory of Formal Functions for the Instrumental Music of Haydn, Mozart, and Beethoven.* Oxford: Oxford University Press, 1998.

Cappi, Johann, ed. *Musikalisches Wochenblat das ist: Eine Sammlung der besten Arien, Duetten, Terzetten, Maersche, Rondo's und Ouverturen aus den vorzüglichsten Opern, und Balleten, für Gesang und Forte-Piano.* Vol. 1. Vienna: Johann Cappi, 1807.

Charlton, David, ed., and Martyn Clarke, trans. *E. T. A. Hoffmann's Musical Writings.* Cambridge: Cambridge University Press, 1989.

Chop, Max. *Erläuterungen zu Ludwig van Beethovens Symphonien: Geschichtlich und musikalisch analysiert mit zahlreichen Notenbeispielen.* 2 vols. Leipzig: Reclam, 1910.

Churgin, Bathia. "Beethoven and Mozart's Requiem: A New Connection." *Journal of Musicology* 5, no. 4 (Autumn 1987): 457–77.

———, ed. *Beethoven Werke: Symphonien II.* Munich: G. Henle, 2013.

Clarke, Christopher. "Erard and Broadwood in the Classical Era: Two Schools of Piano Making." *Musique–Images–Instruments* 11 (2009): 98–125.

Clayton, Martin, Trevor Herbert, and Richard Middleton, eds. *The Cultural Study of Music: A Critical Introduction*. London: Routledge, 2003.

Clive, Peter. *Beethoven and His World: A Biographical Dictionary*. Oxford and New York: Oxford University Press, 2001.

Coldicott, Anne-Louise. "Performance Practice in Beethoven's Day." In *The Beethoven Compendium: A Guide to Beethoven's Life and Music*, edited by Barry Cooper, 280–9. London: Thames & Hudson, 1991.

Collin, Heinrich Joseph von. "Brief über das gesungene Drama." *Morgenblatt für gebildete Stände* 121 (May 21, 1807): 481–2.

———. *Coriolan: Ein Trauerspiel in fünf Aufzüge*. Berlin: Johann Friedrich Unger, 1804.

———. *Sämmtliche Werke*. Edited by Matthäus von Collin. 6 vols. Vienna: Strauß, 1812–14.

Comini, Alessandra. *The Changing Image of Beethoven: A Study in Mythmaking*. Rev. ed. Santa Fe: Sunstone Press, 2008.

"Concerning Beethoven's Symphonies: A Talk with Sir Henry Wood." *Musical Times* 68, no. 1009 (March 1927): 216–19.

Cone, Edward T. "Beethoven's Orpheus—or Jander's?" *19th-Century Music* 8, no. 3 (Spring 1985): 283–6.

Cook, Nicholas. *Beyond the Score: Music as Performance*. Oxford and New York: Oxford University Press, 2013.

———. "The Other Beethoven: Heroism, the Canon, and the Works of 1813–14. *19th-Century Music* 27, no. 1 (Summer 2003): 3–24.

Cook, Nicolas, and Richard Pettengill, eds. *Taking It to the Bridge: Music as Performance*. Ann Arbor: University of Michigan Press, 2013.

Cooper, Barry. "Beethoven's Fourth Piano Concerto Revisited: A Response to Hans-Werner Küthen." *Beethoven Journal* 13, no. 2 (Winter 1998): 70–2.

———. "Beethoven's Revisions to His Fourth Piano Concerto." In *Performing Beethoven*, edited by Robin Stowell, 23–48. Cambridge: Cambridge University Press, 1994.

———, ed. *The Beethoven Compendium: A Guide to Beethoven's Life and Music*. Ann Arbor: Borders Press, 1991.

———. "The Clementi-Beethoven Contract of 1807, a Reinvestigation." In *Muzio Clementi: Studies and Prospects*, edited by Roberto Illiano, Luca Sala, and Massimiliano Sala, 337–53. Bologna: Ut Orpheus, 2002.

———. "The Evolution of the First Movement of Beethoven's 'Waldstein' Sonata." *Music and Letters* 58, no. 2 (April 1977): 170–91.

Costa, Neal Peres da. *Off the Record: Performing Practices in Romantic Piano Playing*. Oxford and New York: Oxford University Press, 2012.

Cramer, J[ohann] B[aptist]. *Étude pour le piano forte en quarante deux exercises dans les differents tons*. Paris: Erard, 1804.

Curry, Robert, David Gable, and Robert L. Marshall, eds. *Variations on the Canon: Essays on Music from Bach to Boulez in Honor of Charles Rosen on His Eightieth Birthday*. Rochester: University of Rochester Press, 2008.

Cvejić, Žarko. *The Virtuoso as Subject: The Reception of Instrumental Virtuosity, c. 1815–c. 1850*. Newcastle upon Tyne: Cambridge Scholars Publishing, 2016.

Czartoryski, Adam. *Memoirs of Prince Adam Czartoryski and His Correspondence with Alexander I: With Documents Relative to the Prince's Negotiations with Pitt, Fox, and Brougham, and an Account of His Conversations with Lord Palmerston and Other English Statesmen in London in 1832*. Edited by Adam Gielgud. 2 vols. London: Remington & Co., 1888. Reprint, New York: Arno Press, 1971.

Czerny, Carl. *On the Proper Performance of All Beethoven's Works for the Piano: Czerny's Reminiscences of Beethoven and Chapters II and III from Volume IV of the Complete Theoretical and Practical Piano Forte School, Op. 500*. Edited by Paul Badura-Skoda. Vienna: Universal Edition, 1970.

———. *Vollständige theoretisch-practische Pianoforte-Schule*, Op. 500. 4 vols. Vienna: Anton Diabelli, 1839.

Dahlhaus, Carl, et al., eds. *Bericht über den internationalen musikwissenschaftlichen Kongress Bonn, 1970*. Kassel: Bärenreiter, 1971.

———. *Nineteenth-Century Music*. California Studies in 19th-Century Music 5. Berkeley: University of California Press, 1989.

Dahlstrom, Daniel O., ed. and trans. *Moses Mendelssohn: Philosophical Writings*. Cambridge: Cambridge University Press, 1997.

"Darstellung des gegenwärtigen Zustandes der Musik in Russland, vornämlich in St. Petersburg." *Allgemeine musikalische Zeitung* 8, no. 5 (October 30, 1805): cols. 65–72.

Dean, Winton. "German Opera." In *The Age of Beethoven: 1790–1830*, edited by Gerald Abraham, 452–522. Vol. 8 of *The New Oxford History of Music*. 1982. Reprint, Oxford and New York: Oxford University Press, 2007.

Del Mar, Jonathan. *Beethoven, Concerto in D Major for Violin and Orchestra, op. 61: Urtext*. Kassel: Bärenreiter, 2012.

———. *Beethoven, Concerto No. 4 in G Major for Pianoforte and Orchestra, op. 58: Critical Commentary*. Kassel: Bärenreiter, 2015.

———. *Beethoven, Concerto No. 4 in G Major for Pianoforte and Orchestra, op. 58: Urtext*. Kassel: Bärenreiter, 2014.

———. *Beethoven, Symphony No. 4 in B-flat Major, op. 60: Critical Commentary*. Kassel: Bärenreiter, 1999.

———. *Beethoven, Symphony No. 4 in B-flat Major, op. 60: Urtext*. Kassel: Bärenreiter, 2001.

DeNora, Tia. *Beethoven and the Construction of Genius: Musical Politics in Vienna, 1792–1803*. Berkeley: University of California Press, 1995.

DeNora, Tia, and Charles Rosen. "Beethoven's Genius: An Exchange." *New York Review of Books* 44, no. 6 (April 10, 1997). Accessed October 17, 2015. http://www.nybooks.com/articles/archives/1997/apr/10/beethovens-genius-an-exchange/.

Derrida, Jacques. *Positions*. Translated by Alan Bass. Chicago: University of Chicago Press, 1981.

Dietrichstein, Moritz von. *Ueber das Denkmahl des k. k. Hofrathes und Ritters des Leopold-Ordens, Heinrich Joseph Edlen von Collin.* Vienna: Anton Strauß, 1813.

Dorfmüller, Kurt, and Georg Kinsky, eds. *Beiträge zur Beethoven-Bibliographie: Studien und Materialien zum Werkverzeichnis von Kinsky-Halm.* Munich: G. Henle, 1978.

Dorfmüller, Kurt, Norbert Gertsch, and Julia Ronge, eds. *Ludwig van Beethoven: Thematisch-bibliographisches Werkverzeichnis.* 2 vols. Revised and expanded edition of the thematic catalogue by Georg Kinsky and Hans Halm. Munich: G. Henle, 2014.

Eiermann, Wolf. "Füger der Große." In *Heinrich Friedrich Füger 1751–1818: Zwischen Genie und Akademie,* edited by Marc Gundel, 53–68. Munich: Hirmer Verlag, 2011.

Eisen, Cliff. "The Rise (and Fall) of the Concerto Virtuoso." In *The Cambridge Companion to the Concerto,* edited by Simon P. Keefe, 177–91. Cambridge: Cambridge University Press, 2005.

Elias, Norbert. *The Civilizing Process.* Vol. 1, *The History of Manners.* Translated by Edmund Jephcott. New York: Urizen Books, 1978.

Ellison, Paul. *The Key to Beethoven: Connecting Tonality and Meaning in His Music.* Hillsdale, NY: Pendragon Press, 2012.

Engel, Johann Jakob. *Über die musikalische Malerey.* Berlin: C. F. Voss und Sohn, 1780.

Erasmus, Desiderius. *Liber aureus Erasmi Roterodami de civitate morum puerilium; das ist: Ein guldenes Buchlein.* Translated by J. W. Pause. Revised by [James] Jacob Bruce. Hamburg, 1678.

Everist, Mark. *Music Drama at the Paris Odéon, 1824–1828.* Berkeley and Los Angeles: University of California Press, 2002.

Fallows, David. "Andante." In *Grove Music Online. Oxford Music Online.* Oxford University Press, accessed October 3, 2011. http://www.oxfordmusiconline.com/subscriber/article/grove/music/00854.

Felski, Rita. "Context Stinks!" *New Literary History* 42, no. 4 (Autumn 2011): 573–91.

Ferraguto, Mark. "Beethoven *à la moujik*: Russianness and Learned Style in the 'Razumovsky' String Quartets." *Journal of the American Musicological Society* 67, no. 1 (Spring 2014): 77–123.

———. "Beethoven's Fourth Symphony: Reception, Aesthetics, Performance History." PhD diss., Cornell University, 2012.

———. "Representing Russia: Luxury and Diplomacy at the Razumovsky Palace in Vienna, 1803–1815." *Music and Letters* 97, no. 3 (August 2016): 383–408.

Figes, Orlando. *Natasha's Dance: A Cultural History of Russia.* New York: Metropolitan Books, 2002.

Finscher, Ludwig, and Christoph-Hellmut Mahling, eds. *Festschrift für Walter Wiora zum 30. Dezember 1966.* Kassel: Bärenreiter, 1967.

Forkel, Johann Nikolaus. *Allgemeine Litteratur der Musik.* Leipzig: Schwickert, 1792.

Förster, Emanuel Aloys. *Anleitung zum General-Bass.* 2 vols. Vienna: J. Träg & Sohn, 1805.

Frimmel, Theodor von. *Beethoven-Handbuch.* 2 vols. Leipzig: Breitkopf & Härtel, 1926.

Fulcher, Jane F., ed. *The Oxford Handbook of the New Cultural History of Music.* Oxford and New York: Oxford University Press, 2011.

Gallagher, Sean, and Thomas Forrest Kelly, eds. *The Century of Bach and Mozart: Perspectives on Historiography, Composition, Theory, and Performance*. Isham Library Papers 7. Harvard Publications in Music 22. Cambridge, MA: Harvard University Press, 2008.

Gardiner, John Eliot, director. *Beethoven: The Piano Concertos / Choral Fantasy*. Orchestre Révolutionnaire et Romantique with Robert Levin, fortepiano. Archiv Produktion, 1999, 4 compact discs.

Gebauer, Johannes. "Zur Entstehung eines Klassikers: Die Aufführungen von Beethovens Violinkonzert op. 61 von der Uraufführung bis 1844." *Bonner Beethoven-Studien* 12 (2016): 9–26.

Geiringer, Karl. *Instruments in the History of Western Music*. 3rd ed. New York: Oxford University Press, 1978.

Gelbart, Matthew. *The Invention of "Folk Music" and "Art Music": Emerging Categories from Ossian to Wagner*. New Perspectives in Music History and Criticism. Cambridge: Cambridge University Press, 2007.

Gentz, Friedrich von. *Tagebücher: Mit einem Vor- und Nachwort von K. A. Varnhagen von Ense*. Leipzig: F. A. Brockhaus, 1861.

George, David, ed. *Shakespeare: The Critical Tradition: Coriolanus*. Bristol: Thoemmes Continuum, 2004.

"*Geschichte der römischen Staatsveränderungen von R. A. Vertot.*" *Annalen der Österreichischen Literatur* 3 (January 1802): col. 20.

Gibbs, Christopher H., and Dana Gooley, eds. *Franz Liszt and His World*. Princeton: Princeton University Press, 2006.

Gluck, Christoph Willibald. "Dedication for *Alceste*." In *Source Readings in Music History*, edited by Oliver Strunk, 932–4. Rev. ed. edited by Leo Treitler. New York: Norton Press, 1998.

Golianek, Ryszard Daniel. "Towards a New Aesthetics of the Viennese Singspiel in the Early Nineteenth Century: Beethoven's *Fidelio* and Cherubini's *Faniska*." Translated by John Comber. In *Beethoven 6: Studien und Interpretationen*, edited by Mieczyław Tomaszewski and Magdalena Chrenkoff, 403–11. Muzyczna: Kraków Akad., 2015.

Gooley, Dana. "The Battle against Instrumental Virtuosity in the Early Nineteenth Century." In *Franz Liszt and His World*, edited by Christopher H. Gibbs and Dana Gooley, 75–111. Princeton: Princeton University Press, 2006.

Gramit, David. *Cultivating Music: The Aspirations, Interests, and Limits of German Musical Culture, 1770–1848*. Berkeley: University of California Press, 2002.

Greene, David B. *Temporal Processes in Beethoven's Music*. New York: Gordon & Breach, 1982.

Green, Emily H. "A Patron among Peers: Dedications to Haydn and the Economy of Celebrity." *Eighteenth-Century Music* 8, no. 2 (September 2011): 215–37.

Grimsted, Patricia Kennedy. *The Foreign Ministers of Alexander I: Political Attitudes and the Conduct of Russian Diplomacy, 1801–1825*. Russian and East European Studies. Berkeley: University of California Press, 1969.

Grove, George. "Analytical Review of L. van Beethoven, Op. 60, Symphony in B Flat, No. 4." In *Analytical Reviews of Classical and Modern Compositions, for the Use of Amateurs at Musical Entertainments*, vol. 5, 1–8. New York: C. F. Tretbar, c. 1877–8.

Gundel, Marc, ed. *Heinrich Friedrich Füger 1751–1818: Zwischen Genie und Akademie.* Exhibition catalogue, Städtische Museen Heilbronn/Kunsthalle Vogelmann 3 December 2011–11 March 2012. Munich: Hirmer Verlag, 2011.

Haas, Robert. "The Viennese Violinist, Franz Clement." *The Musical Quarterly* 34, no. 1 (January 1948): 15–27.

Hanslick, Eduard. *On the Musically Beautiful: A Contribution towards the Revision of the Aesthetics of Music.* Translated by Geoffrey Payzant. Indianapolis: Hackett Publishing Company, 1986.

Hatch, Christopher. "Internal and External References in Beethoven's Fourth Symphony." *College Music Symposium* 24, no. 1 (Spring 1984): 107–17.

Haydn, Joseph. *Joseph Haydn Werke.* Series I, vol. 15, *Londoner Sinfonien: 1. Folge.* Edited by Gernod Gruber and Robert v. Zahn. Munich: G. Henle, 2005.

———. *Oeuvres de Haydn en Partitions.* Vols. 1–4 (Symphonies Nos. 103, 104, 102, 99). In *Bibliothèque musicale*, edited by Ignaz Pleyel. Paris: Richault, n.d. [1802–3].

Head, Matthew. "Beethoven Heroine: A Female Allegory of Music and Authorship in *Egmont.*" *19th-Century Music* 30, no. 2 (Fall 2006): 97–132.

———. *Sovereign Feminine: Music and Gender in Eighteenth-Century Germany.* Berkeley: University of California Press, 2013.

Hegel, G. W. F. *Phenomenology of Mind.* Translated by J. B. Baillie. Reprint of the 1910 edition. Mineola, NY: Dover Publications, 2003.

Hennion, Antoine. "Music and Mediation: Towards a new Sociology of Music." In *The Cultural Study of Music: A Critical Introduction*, edited by Martin Clayton, Trevor Herbert, and Richard Middleton, 80–91. London: Routledge, 2003.

Hepokoski, James, and Warren Darcy. *Elements of Sonata Theory: Norms, Types, and Deformations in the Late-Eighteenth-Century Sonata.* New York: Oxford University Press, 2006.

Heusinger, J[ohann] H[einrich] G[eorg]. *Handbuch der Aesthetik.* Gotha: Justus Perthes, 1797.

Hiller, Johann Adam, ed. *Musikalische Nachrichten und Anmerkungen.* Vol. 4. Leipzig, 1770.

Hoffmann, E. T. A. "Review of Beethoven's Overture to *Coriolan.*" In *E. T. A. Hoffmann's Musical Writings*, edited by David Charlton and translated by Martyn Clarke, 286–93. Cambridge: Cambridge University Press, 1989. Originally published in the *Allgemeine musikalische Zeitung* 14, no. 5 (August 1812): cols. 519–26.

Huber, Alfons. "Beethovens 'Erard'-Flügel: Überlegungen zu seiner Restaurierung." *Restauro* 3 (1990): 181–8.

Hübsch, Lini. *Ludwig van Beethoven: Die Rasumowsky-Quartette: Op. 59 Nr. 1 F-dur, Nr. 2 e-moll, Nr. 3 C-dur.* Meisterwerke der Musik 40. Munich: Wilhelm Fink, 1983.

Hughes, Lindsey. "'The Crown of Maidenly Honour and Virtue': Redefining Femininity in Peter I's Russia." In *Women and Gender in 18th-Century Russia*, edited by Wendy Rosslyn, 35–50. Aldershot, UK, and Burlington, VT: Ashgate, 2003.

Hunter, Mary. "'To Play as if from the Soul of the Composer': The Idea of the Performer in Early Romantic Aesthetics." *Journal of the American Musicological Society* 58, no. 2 (Summer 2005): 357–98.

Hunter, Mary, and Richard Will, eds. *Engaging Haydn: Culture, Context, and Criticism.* Cambridge: Cambridge University Press, 2012.

Husarik, Stephen. "Musical Direction and the Wedge in Beethoven's High Comedy, *Grosse Fuge* Op. 133." *Musical Times* 153, no. 1920 (Autumn 2012): 53–66.

Illiano, Roberto, Luca Sala, and Massimiliano Sala, eds. *Muzio Clementi: Studies and Prospects.* Bologna: Ut Orpheus, 2002.

Irving, John. "The Invention of Tradition." In *The Cambridge History of Nineteenth-Century Music*, edited by Jim Samson, 178–212. Cambridge Histories of Music. Cambridge: Cambridge University Press, 2001.

Jahn, Michael. "Aspekte der Rezeption von Cherubinis Opern im Wien des 19. Jahrhunderts." *Studien zur Musikwissenschaft* 49 (2002): 213–44.

James, Burnett. *Beethoven and Human Destiny.* London: Phoenix House, 1960.

Jander, Owen. *Beethoven's "Orpheus" Concerto: The Fourth Piano Concerto in Its Cultural Context.* Hillsdale, NY: Pendragon Press, 2009.

———. "Beethoven's 'Orpheus in Hades': The *Andante con moto* of the Fourth Piano Concerto." *19th-Century Music* 8, no. 3 (Spring 1985): 195–212.

———. "Orpheus Revisited: A Ten-Year Retrospect on the Andante con moto of Beethoven's Fourth Piano Concerto." *19th-Century Music* 19, no. 1 (Summer 1995): 31–49.

———. "Romantic Form and Content in the Slow Movement of Beethoven's Violin Concerto." *The Musical Quarterly* 69, no. 2 (Spring 1983): 159–79.

Johnson, Douglas. "1794–1795: Decisive Years in Beethoven's Early Development." In *Beethoven Studies 3*, edited by Alan Tyson, 1–28. Cambridge: Cambridge University Press, 1982.

Johnson, Douglas, Alan Tyson, and Robert Winter. *The Beethoven Sketchbooks: History, Reconstruction, Inventory.* Edited by Douglas Johnson. California Studies in 19th-Century Music 4. Berkeley: University of California Press, 1985.

Jones, David Wyn. *Beethoven: Pastoral Symphony.* Cambridge Music Handbooks. Cambridge: Cambridge University Press, 1995.

———. *Music in Vienna: 1700, 1800, 1900.* Woodbridge: The Boydell Press, 2016.

———. "Some Aspects of Clementi's Career as a Publisher." In *Muzio Clementi: Compositore, (Forte)pianista, Editore,* edited by Bianca Maria Antolini and Costantino Mastroprimiano, 3–20. Strumenti della ricerca musicale 9. Lucca: LIM, 2006.

Jost, Christa. "*32 Variationen c-Moll für Klavier WoO 80.*" In *Beethoven: Interpretationen seiner Werke,* 2 vols., edited by Albrecht Riethmüller, Carl Dahlhaus, and Alexander L. Ringer, 2: 481–5. Laaber: Laaber-Verlag, 1996.

Kawabata, Maiko. "Virtuoso Codes of Violin Performance: Power, Military Heroism, and Gender (1789–1830)." *19th-Century Music* 28, no. 2 (Fall 2004): 89–107.

Keefe, Simon P., ed. *The Cambridge Companion to the Concerto.* Cambridge: Cambridge University Press, 2005.

———, ed. *The Cambridge History of Eighteenth-Century Music.* Cambridge: Cambridge University Press, 2009.

Keil, Robert. *Heinrich Friedrich Füger: 1751–1818: Nur wenigen ist es vergönnt das Licht der Wahrheit zu sehen.* Vienna: Amartis-Verlag, 2009.

Kelly, Catriona. *Refining Russia: Advice Literature, Polite Culture, and Gender from Catherine to Yeltsin.* Oxford: Oxford University Press, 2001.

Kerman, Joseph. *The Beethoven Quartets.* New York: Norton, 1979. Originally published 1966.

———. "Beethoven's Minority." In *Write All These Down: Essays on Music,* 217–37. Berkeley: University of California Press, 1994.

———. "Representing a Relationship: Notes on a Beethoven Concerto." *Representations* 39 (Summer 1992): 80–101.

———. *Write All These Down: Essays on Music.* Berkeley: University of California Press, 1994.

Kerman, Joseph, et al. "Beethoven, Ludwig van." In *Grove Music Online. Oxford Music Online.* Oxford University Press. http://www.oxfordmusiconline.com/subscriber/article/grove/music/40026.

Kerst, Friedrich. *Die Erinnerungen an Beethoven.* 2 vols. Stuttgart: Julius Hoffmann, 1913.

Kinderman, William. *Beethoven.* 2nd ed. Oxford and New York: Oxford University Press, 2009. Originally published 1995 by University of California Press.

———, ed. *The String Quartets of Beethoven.* Urbana: University of Illinois Press, 2006.

King, David. *Vienna 1814: How the Conquerors of Napoleon Made Love, War, and Peace at the Congress of Vienna.* New York: Harmony Books, 2008.

Kinsky, Georg, and Hans Halm. *Das Werk Beethovens: Thematisch-bibliographisches Verzeichnis seiner sämtlichen vollendeten Kompositionen.* Munich: G. Henle, 1955.

Kirkendale, Warren. *Fugue and Fugato in Rococo and Classical Chamber Music.* Translated by Warren Kirkendale and Margaret Bent. Durham, NC: Duke University Press, 1979.

Knittel, K. M. "The Construction of Beethoven." In *The Cambridge History of Nineteenth-Century Music,* edited by Jim Samson, 118–50. Cambridge: Cambridge University Press, 2001.

Koch, Heinrich Christoph. *Musikalisches Lexikon.* Frankfurt am Main: August Hermann dem Jüngern, 1802.

"Korrespondenz-Nachrichten. Wien." *Morgenblatt für gebildete Stände* 84 (April 8, 1807): 336.

"Korrespondenz- und Notizen-Blatt." *Zeitung für die elegante Welt* 197 (December 10, 1807): cols. 1573–4.

Kramer, Lawrence. "The Strange Case of Beethoven's *Coriolan*: Romantic Aesthetics, Modern Subjectivity, and the Cult of Shakespeare." *The Musical Quarterly* 79, no. 2 (Summer 1995): 256–80.

Kregor, Jonathan. *Program Music*. Cambridge Introductions to Music. Cambridge: Cambridge University Press, 2015.

Kropfinger, Klaus. *Wagner and Beethoven: Richard Wagner's Reception of Beethoven.* Translated by Peter Palmer. Cambridge: Cambridge University Press, 1991. Originally published as *Wagner und Beethoven* (Regensburg: Gustav Bosse Verlag, 1974).

Kuhnau, Johann. *The Musical Charlatan.* Translated by John B. Russell with an introduction by James Hardin. Columbia, SC: Camden House, 1997.

Küthen, Hans-Werner. "Die authentische Kammerfassung von Beethovens Viertem Klavierkonzert für Klavier und Streichquintett (1807)." *Bonner Beethoven-Studien* 1 (1999): 49–90.

———. "The Newly Discovered Authorized 1807 Arrangement of Beethoven's Fourth Fortepiano Concerto for Fortepiano and String Quintet: An Adventurous Variant in the Style of the Late Cadenzas." *Beethoven Journal* 13, no. 1 (Summer 1998): 2–11.

Laban, Ferdinand. *Heinrich Joseph Collin: Ein Beitrag zur Geschichte der neueren deutschen Literatur in Oesterreich.* Vienna: Carl Gerolds Sohn, 1879.

Landon, H. C. Robbins. *Haydn: Chronicle and Works.* 5 vols. London: Thames & Hudson, 1977.

LaRue, Jan. "Harmonic Rhythm in the Beethoven Symphonies." *Journal of Musicology* 18, no. 2 (Spring 2001): 221–48.

Latour, Bruno. *Reassembling the Social: An Introduction to Actor-Network Theory.* Oxford and New York: Oxford University Press, 2005.

League of American Orchestras. "2007–2008 Season Orchestra Repertoire Report." Accessed July 24, 2017. http://www.americanorchestras.org/interest_areas/librarians.html.

Lessing, Gotthold Ephraim. *Laocoon.* Translated by Sir Robert Phillimore. London: Macmillan, 1874.

Lenz, Wilhelm von. *Beethoven: Eine Kunststudie.* 6 parts in 5 vols. Cassel: Ernst Balde, and Hamburg: Hoffmann & Campe, 1855–60.

———. *Beethoven et ses trois styles.* Brussels: G. Stapleaux, 1854.

Levi, Giovanni. "On Microhistory." In *New Perspectives on Historical Writing*, 2nd ed., edited by Peter Burke, 97–119. University Park: The Pennsylvania State University Press, 2001.

Levitz, Tamara. *Modernist Mysteries: Perséphone.* Oxford and New York: Oxford University Press, 2012.

L'interprétation de la musique classique de Haydn à Schubert. Colloque International, Evry, 13–15 octobre 1977. Paris: Minkoff, 1980.

Locke, Ralph P. "Program Music." In *The New Harvard Dictionary of Music*, edited by Don Michael Randel, 656–9. Cambridge, MA: Harvard University Press, 1986.

Lockwood, Lewis. "Beethoven, Florestan, and the Varieties of Heroism." In *Beethoven and His World*, edited by Scott Burnham and Michael Steinberg, 27–47. Princeton: Princeton University Press, 2000.

———. *Beethoven: The Music and the Life*. New York: Norton, 2003.

Lockwood, Lewis, and Phyllis Benjamin, eds. *Beethoven Essays: Studies in Honor of Elliot Forbes*. Cambridge, MA: Harvard University Press, 1984.

Lodes, Birgit. "Zur musikalischen Passgenauigkeit von Beethovens Kompositionen mit Widmungen an Adelige: An die ferne Geliebte op. 98 in neuer Deutung." In *Widmungen bei Haydn und Beethoven. Personen—Strategien—Praktiken. Bericht über den Internationalen musikwissenschaftlichen Kongress Bonn, 29. September bis 1. Oktober 2011*, edited by Bernhard R. Appel and Armin Raab (Bonn: Verlag Beethoven-Haus, 2015), 171–202.

Longyear, Rey M. "Beethoven and Romantic Irony." *The Musical Quarterly* 56, no. 4 (October 1970): 647–64.

[Lvov, Nikolai Alexandrovich], and Johann Gottfried ("Ivan") Pratsch [Prach]. *Sobraniye narodnikh russkikh pesen s ikh golosami* [Collection of Russian Folk Songs with Their Tunes]. St. Petersburg, 1790.

Lowe, Melanie. *Pleasure and Meaning in the Classical Symphony*. Bloomington: Indiana University Press, 2007.

Madrid, Alejandro L. "Why Music and Performance Studies? Why Now? An Introduction to the Special Issue." *Trans: Revista Transcultural de Música* 13 (2009). http://www.sibetrans.com/trans/articulo/1/why-music-and-performance-studies-why-now-an-introduction-to-the-special-issue.

Magnússon, Sigurður Gylfi, and István M. Szijártó. *What Is Microhistory? Theory and Practice*. Abingdon, Oxfordshire: Routledge, 2013.

Maniguet, Thierry. "Le piano en forme de clavecin Érard." *Musique–Images–Instruments* 11 (2009): 82–98.

Mann, Alfred, ed. *The Study of Fugue*. New York: Dover, 1987.

Marliave, Joseph de. *Beethoven's Quartets*. Translated by Hilda Andrews. Reprint of the 1928 edition. Mineola, NY: Dover, 2004.

Marpurg, Friedrich Wilhelm. "Selections from *Abhandlung von der Fuge*." Translated by Alfred Mann. In *The Study of Fugue*, edited by Alfred Mann, 142–212. New York: Dover, 1987.

Marshall, Robert L. "Sonority and Structure: Observations on Beethoven's Early and Middle-Period Piano Compositions." In *Variations on the Canon: Essays on Music from Bach to Boulez in Honor of Charles Rosen on His Eightieth Birthday*, edited by Robert Curry, David Gable, and Robert L. Marshall, 100–29. Rochester: University of Rochester Press, 2008.

Martin, Robert. "The Quartets in Performance: A Player's Perspective." In *The Beethoven Quartet Companion*, edited by Robert Winter and Robert Martin, 111–41. Berkeley: University of California Press, 1994.

Marx, Adolf Bernhard. *Ludwig van Beethoven: Leben und Schaffen.* 2 vols. Leipzig: A. Schumann, 1902. Originally published 1859 by O. Janke.

Mason, Daniel Gregory. *The Quartets of Beethoven.* New York: Oxford University Press, 1947.

Mathew, Nicholas. "Beethoven and His Others: Criticism, Difference, and the Composer's Many Voices." *Beethoven Forum* 13, no. 2 (Fall 2006): 148–87.

———. "Beethoven's Political Music and the Idea of the Heroic Style." PhD diss., Cornell University, 2006.

———. *Political Beethoven.* New Perspectives in Music History and Criticism. Cambridge: Cambridge University Press, 2013.

McErlean, J. M. P. "Razumovskii, Andrei Kirillovich." In *The Modern Encyclopedia of Russian and Soviet History*, 60 vols., edited by Joseph L. Wieczynski, 30: 210–14. Gulf Breeze, FL: Academic International Press, 1982.

McVeigh, Simon. "Concerto of the Individual." In *The Cambridge History of Eighteenth-Century Music*, edited by Simon P. Keefe, 583–612. Cambridge: Cambridge University Press, 2009.

"Merkwürdige Novität." *Allgemeine musikalische Zeitung* 8, no. 39 (June 25, 1806): cols. 616–22.

Metzner, Paul. *Crescendo of the Virtuoso: Spectacle, Skill, and Self-Promotion in Paris during the Age of Revolution.* Berkeley: University of California Press, 1998.

Meyer, Stephen. "Terror and Transcendence in the Operatic Prison, 1790–1815." *Journal of the American Musicological Society* 55, no. 3 (Winter 2002): 477–523.

Mies, Paul, ed. *Beethoven: Streichquartette II.* Munich: G. Henle, 1968.

———. "Die Bedeutung der Pauke in den Werken Ludwig van Beethovens." *Beethoven-Jahrbuch* 8 (1975): 49–71.

———. "Zur Coriolan-Ouvertüre op. 62." *Beethoven-Jahrbuch* 6 (1969): 260–8. Originally published 1938 in *Zeitschrift für Musik.*

Miller, Malcolm. "Peak Experience: High Register and Structure in the 'Razumovsky' Quartets, Op. 59." In *The String Quartets of Beethoven*, edited by William Kinderman, 60–88. Urbana: University of Illinois Press, 2006.

Ministère de la Culture, de la Communication, des Grands Travaux et du Bicentenaire. *La Révolution française et l'Europe, 1789–1799: XXe exposition du Conseil de l'Europe.* 3 vols. Paris: Éditions de la Réunion des musées nationaux, 1989.

Mirka, Danuta, ed. *The Oxford Handbook of Topic Theory.* New York: Oxford University Press, 2014.

Misch, Ludwig. *Die Faktoren der Einheit in der Mehrsätzigkeit der Werke Beethovens.* Munich and Duisberg: G. Henle, 1958.

———. "Ein unbemerkter thematischer Zusammenhang in Beethovens IV. Symphonie." In *Neue Beethoven-Studien und andere Themen*, 56–8. Bonn: Beethoven-Haus, 1967.

Montagu, Jeremy. *Timpani and Percussion.* The Yale Musical Instrument Series. New Haven and London: Yale University Press, 2002.

Mohr, Wilhelm. "Beethovens Klavierfassung seines Violinkonzerts op. 61." In *Bericht über den internationalen musikwissenschaftlichen Kongress Bonn, 1970*, edited by Carl Dalhaus, 509–11. Kassel: Bärenreiter, 1971.

———. "Die Klavierfassung von Beethovens Violinkonzert." *Österreichische Musikzeitschrift* 27, no. 2 (February 1972): 71–5.

Mosel, Ignaz von. "Uebersicht des gegenwärtigen Zustandes der Tonkunst in Wien." *Vaterländische Blätter für den Österreichischen Kaiserstaat* 1, no. 6 (May 27, 1808): 39–44; and no. 7 (May 31, 1808): 49–54.

Mozart, Leopold. *Treatise on the Fundamental Principles of Violin Playing*. Translated by Editha Knocker. London: Oxford University Press, 1951.

"Music: Philharmonic Society." *London Literary Gazette and Journal of Belles Lettres, Arts, Sciences, etc. for the Year 1831*. London: James Moyes, 1831.

"Nachrichten." *Allgemeine musikalische Zeitung* 7, no. 31 (May 1, 1805): cols. 500–4.

"Nachrichten." *Allgemeine musikalische Zeitung* 8, no. 24 (March 12, 1806): cols. 376–7.

Nef, Karl. "Haydn-Reminiszenzen bei Beethoven." *Sammelbände der Internationalen Musikgesellschaft* 13, no. 2 (January–March 1912): 336–48.

Newman, William S. *Beethoven on Beethoven: Playing His Piano Music His Way*. New York and London: W. W. Norton & Company, 1988.

———. "Yet Another Major Beethoven Forgery by Schindler?" *Journal of Musicology* 3, no. 4 (Autumn 1984): 397–422.

Nietzsche, Friedrich. *The Gay Science*. Translated by Josefine Nauckhoff. Cambridge: Cambridge University Press, 2001.

Nisbet, H. B., ed. *Winckelmann, Lessing, Hamann, Herder, Schiller and Goethe*. Vol. 3 of *German Aesthetic and Literary Criticism*. Cambridge: Cambridge University Press, 1985.

Nottebohm, Gustav. *Zweite Beethoveniana: Nachgelassene Aufsäze*. Leipzig: Peters, 1887. Reprint, New York: Johnson Reprint Corporation, 1970.

November, Nancy. *Beethoven's Theatrical Quartets: Opp. 59, 74, and 95*. Cambridge: Cambridge University Press, 2013.

Oulibicheff [Ulybyshev], Alexandre. *Beethoven, ses critiques, et ses glossateurs*. Leipzig and Paris: F. A. Brockhaus & Jules Gavelot, 1857.

Oster, Ernst. "The Dramatic Character of the *Egmont* Overture." In *Aspects of Schenkerian Theory*, edited by David W. Beach, 209–22. New Haven: Yale University Press, 1983. Originally published in *Musicology* 2, no. 3 (1949): 269–85.

Plantinga, Leon. "Beethoven, Napoleon, and Political Romanticism." In *The Oxford Handbook of the New Cultural History of Music*, edited by Jane F. Fulcher, 484–500. Oxford and New York: Oxford University Press, 2011.

———. *Beethoven's Concertos: History, Style, Performance*. New York and London: W. W. Norton & Co., 1999.

Plutarch. "The Life of Martius Coriolanus." Translated by Sir Thomas North. In *Shakespeare's Plutarch*, edited by T. J. B. Spencer, 296–362. Baltimore: Penguin Books, 1964.

Raab, Armin, and Bernhard Appel, eds. *Widmungen bei Haydn und Beethoven: Personen—Strategien—Praktiken*. Bonn: Beethoven-Haus, 2015.

Radano, Ronald, and Philip V. Bohlman, eds. *Music and the Racial Imagination*. Chicago: University of Chicago Press, 2000.

Radcliffe, Philip. *Beethoven's String Quartets*. London: Hutchinson, 1965.

Randel, Don Michael, ed. *The Harvard Dictionary of Music*. 4th ed. Cambridge, MA: Harvard University Press, 2003.

Rasch, Rudolf. "Muzio Clementi, the Last Composer-Publisher." In *Muzio Clementi: Studies and Prospects*, edited by Roberto Illiano, Luca Sala, and Massimiliano Sala, 355–66. Bologna: Ut Orpheus, 2002.

Razumovsky, Maria. *Die Rasumovskys: Eine Familie am Zarenhof*. Cologne: Böhlau, 1998.

"Recension." *Allgemeine musikalische Zeitung* 4, no. 44 (July 28, 1802): cols. 705–18.

Reimer, Erich. "Der Begriff des wahren Virtuosen in der Musikästhetik des späten 18. und frühen 19. Jahrhunderts." *Basler Jahrbuch für historische Musikpraxis: Eine Veröffentlichung der Schola Cantorum Basiliensis an der Musik-Akademie der Stadt Basel* 20 (1996): 61–72.

Reeve, Henry. *Journal of a Residence at Vienna and Berlin in the Eventful Winter 1805–6*. London: Longmans, Green, & Co., 1877.

Reichardt, Johann Friedrich. *Vertraute Briefe geschrieben auf einer Reise nach Wien und den Oesterreichischen Staaten zu Ende des Jahres 1808 und zu Anfang 1809*. Edited by Gustav Gugitz. 2 vols. Munich: G. Müller, 1915. Originally published 1810 by Kunst- und Industrie-Comptoir.

Rellstab, Ludwig. "Reiseberichte von Rellstab. No. 4, Wien." *Berliner allgemeine musikalische Zeitung* 3 (May 18 and 25, 1825): 161–3, 169.

Rice, John A. *Empress Marie Therese and Music at the Viennese Court, 1792–1807*. Reprint. Cambridge: Cambridge University Press, 2007. Originally published 2003.

Riethmüller, Albrecht, ed. *Das Beethoven-Handbuch*. 2nd ed. 6 vols. Laaber: Laaber-Verlag, 2008–16.

Riethmüller, Albrecht, Carl Dahlhaus, and Alexander L. Ringer, eds. *Beethoven: Interpretationen seiner Werke*. 2 vols. Laaber: Laaber-Verlag, 1994–6.

Riezler, Walter. *Beethoven*. Translated by G. D. H. Pidcock. London: M. C. Forrester, 1938.

Riley, Matthew. *Musical Listening in the German Enlightenment: Attention, Wonder, and Astonishment*. London and New York: Routledge, 2016. Originally published 2004.

Ringer, Alexander L. "Beethoven and the London Pianoforte School." *The Musical Quarterly* 56, no. 4 (October 1970): 742–58.

Ristow, Nicole, Wolfgang Sandberger, and Dorothea Schröder, eds. *"Critica musica": Studien zum 17. und 18. Jahrhundert: Festschrift Hans Joachim Marx zum 65. Geburtstag*. Stuttgart: J. B. Metzler, 2001.

Ritzarev, Marina. *Eighteenth-Century Russian Music*. Aldershot, UK: Ashgate, 2006.

Robisheaux Thomas, ed. "Microhistory Today: A Roundtable Discussion." *Journal of Medieval and Early Modern Studies* 47, no. 1 (January 2017): 7–52.

Rosen, Charles. "Did Beethoven Have All the Luck?" *New York Review of Books* 43, no. 18 (November 14, 1996). Accessed October 17, 2015. http://www.nybooks.com/articles/archives/1996/nov/14/did-beethoven-have-all-the-luck/.

———. *The Classical Style: Haydn, Mozart, Beethoven*. Rev. ed. New York: Norton, 1997.

———. *The Romantic Generation*. Cambridge, MA: Harvard University Press, 1998.

———. *Sonata Forms*. New York: Norton, 1988.

Rose van Epenhuysen, Maria. "Beethoven and His 'French Piano': Proof of Purchase." *Musique–Images–Instruments* 7 (2005): 110–22.

Rosslyn, Wendy, ed. *Women and Gender in 18th-Century Russia*. Aldershot, UK, and Burlington, VT: Ashgate, 2003.

Rowland, David. "Beethoven's Pianoforte Pedaling." In *Performing Beethoven*, edited by Robin Stowell, 46–9. Cambridge: Cambridge University Press, 1994.

Rumph, Stephen. *Beethoven after Napoleon: Political Romanticism in the Late Works*. California Studies in 19th-Century Music 14. Berkeley: University of California Press, 2004.

———. "What Beethoven Learned from K. 464." *Eighteenth-Century Music* 11, no. 1 (March 2014): 55–77.

Salmen, Walter. "Zur Gestaltung der 'Thèmes russes' in Beethovens Opus 59." In *Festschrift für Walter Wiora zum 30. Dezember 1966*, edited by Ludwig Finscher and Christoph-Hellmut Mahling, 397–404. Kassel: Bärenreiter, 1967.

Samson, Jim, ed. *The Cambridge History of Nineteenth-Century Music*. Cambridge Histories of Music. Cambridge: Cambridge University Press, 2001.

Schauffler, Robert Haven. *Beethoven: The Man Who Freed Music*. 2 vols. Garden City, NY: Doubleday, Doran, & Co., 1929.

Schiller, Friedrich. "On Naive and Sentimental Poetry." Translated by Julius A. Elias. In *German Aesthetic and Literary Criticism*, vol. 3, *Winckelmann, Lessing, Hamann, Herder, Schiller and Goethe*, edited by H. B. Nisbet, 177–232. Cambridge: Cambridge University Press, 1985.

———. *Schillers sämmtliche Schriften*. Edited by Karl Goedecke. Stuttgart: Cotta, 1871.

Schindler, Anton Felix. "Aus Frankfurt am Main." *Niederrheinische Musik-Zeitung* 8, no. 43 (October 20, 1860): 337–40.

———. *Beethoven as I Knew Him*. Translated by Constance S. Jolly and edited by Donald W. MacArdle. Mineola, NY: Dover, 1996. Originally published 1966.

Schirach, Gottlob Benedict von, ed. and trans. *Biographien des Plutarchs. Mit Anmerkungen von Gottlob Benedict von Schirach*. 8 vols. Vienna and Prague: Franz Haas, 1796.

Schmalfeldt, Janet. *In the Process of Becoming: Analytic and Philosophical Perspectives on Form in Early Nineteenth-Century Music*. Oxford and New York: Oxford University Press, 2011.

Schmelz, Peter J. "'Shostakovich' Fights the Cold War: Reflections from Great to Small." *Journal of Musicological Research* 34, no. 2 (2015): 91–140.

Schreiber, C[hristian]. "Etwas über Volkslieder." *Allgemeine musikalische Zeitung* 6, no. 43 (July 25, 1804): cols. 713–18.

Schroeder, David. *Haydn and the Enlightenment: The Late Symphonies and Their Audience.* Oxford: Clarendon Press, 1990.

Schubart, Christian Friedrich Daniel. *Ideen zu einer Ästhetik der Tonkunst.* Vienna: J. V. Degen, 1806.

Schukoff, Nadeschda. *Russland in Wien.* Television documentary. Directed by Alexander Schukoff. Vienna: Österreichischer Rundfunk, 2006.

Schulz, Johann Abraham Peter. "Vortrag." In *Allgemeine Theorie der schönen Künste,* edited by Johann Georg Sulzer, vol. 2, 1247–58. Leipzig: Weidemann, 1771–4.

Scott, Marion M. *Beethoven.* Revised by Sir Jack Westrup. London: Dent & Sons, 1974.

Senner, Wayne M., and William Meredith, eds., and Robin Wallace, trans. and ed. *The Critical Reception of Beethoven's Compositions by His German Contemporaries.* Lincoln and London: University of Nebraska Press, 2001.

Sipe, Thomas. *Beethoven, Eroica Symphony.* Cambridge Music Handbooks. Cambridge: Cambridge University Press, 1998.

Sisman, Elaine R. "After the Heroic Style: Fantasia and the 'Characteristic' Sonatas of 1809." *Beethoven Forum* 6 (1998): 67–96.

———, ed. *Haydn and His World.* Princeton: Princeton University Press, 1997.

———. "Haydn's Career and the Idea of the Multiple Audience." In *The Cambridge Companion to Haydn,* edited by Caryl Clark, 3–16. Cambridge: Cambridge University Press, 2005.

———. *Mozart: The "Jupiter" Symphony, No. 41 in C Major, K. 551.* Cambridge Music Handbooks. Cambridge: Cambridge University Press, 1993.

———. "'The Spirit of Mozart from Haydn's Hands': Beethoven's Musical Inheritance." In *The Cambridge Companion to Beethoven,* edited by Glenn Stanley, 45–63. Cambridge: Cambridge University Press, 2000.

Skowroneck, Tilman. "Beethoven's Erard Piano: Its Influence on His Compositions and on Viennese Fortepiano Building." *Early Music* 30, no. 4 (November 2002): 522–38.

———. *Beethoven the Pianist.* Musical Performance and Reception. Cambridge: Cambridge University Press, 2010.

Skowroneck, Tilman, and Andrew Pinnock. "Grand and Grander: Economic Sidelights on Piano Design and Piano Salesmanship in Early Nineteenth-Century Vienna." In *Interpreting Historical Keyboard Music: Sources, Contexts and Performance,* edited by Andrew Woolley and John Kitchen, 221–32. Farnham, UK, and Burlington, VT: Ashgate, 2013.

Small, Christopher. *Musicking: The Meanings of Performing and Listening.* Middletown, CT: Wesleyan University Press, 1998.

Solomon, Maynard. *Beethoven.* 1977. Rev. ed. New York: Schirmer, 1998.

———. "The End of a Beginning: The 'Diabelli' Variations." In *Late Beethoven: Music, Thought, Imagination,* 11–26. Berkeley: University of California Press, 2003.

———. "Some Images of Creation in Music of the Viennese Classical School." *The Musical Quarterly* 89, no. 1 (Spring 2006): 121–35.

Sonneck, O. G., ed. *Beethoven: Impressions by His Contemporaries*. New York: Dover Publications, 1967.

Staehelin, Martin. "'auf eine wirklich ganz *alte* Manier'? Händel-Anlehnung und Eigenständigkeit in Beethovens Klavier-Variationen c-Moll WoO 80." In "*Critica musica*": *Studien zum 17. und 18. Jahrhundert: Festschrift Hans Joachim Marx zum 65. Geburtstag*, edited by Nicole Ristow, Wolfgang Sandberger, and Dorothea Schröder, 281–97. Stuttgart: J. B. Metzler, 2001.

Stählin, Jacob von. "Nachrichten von der Musik in Rußland." Pts. 1–13. In *Musikalische Nachrichten und Anmerkungen*, edited by Johann Adam Hiller (Leipzig, 1770), vol. 4, no. 18 (April 30): 135–9; no. 19 (May 7): 143–7; no. 20 (May 14): 151–5; no. 21 (May 21): 159–65; no. 22 (May 28): 167–73; no. 23 (June 4): 175–9; no. 24 (June 11): 183–90; no. 25 (June 18): 191–8; no. 26 (June 25): 199–204; no. 27 (July 2): 205–12; no. 28 (July 9): 213–17; no. 29 (July 16): 221–6; no. 30 (July 23): 229–32.

Stanley, Glenn, ed. *The Cambridge Companion to Beethoven*. Cambridge: Cambridge University Press, 2000.

Steblin, Rita. *A History of Key Characteristics in the Eighteenth and Early Nineteenth Centuries*. 1983. Rev. ed. Rochester, NY: University of Rochester Press, 2002.

Steibelt, Daniel. *Étude pour le pianoforte contenant 50 exercices de différents genres, partagé en deux Livraisons*. Leipzig: Breitkopf & Härtel, [1805].

———. *Méthode de Piano ou l'art d'enseigner cet Instrument/Pianoforte-Schule*. Leipzig: Breitkopf & Härtel, [1809].

Steinberg, Michael. *The Concerto: A Listener's Guide*. New York: Oxford University Press, 1998.

———. "The Middle Quartets." In *The Beethoven Quartet Companion*, edited by Robert Winter and Robert Martin, 175–213. Berkeley: University of California Press, 1994.

Stowell, Robin. *Beethoven: Violin Concerto*. Cambridge Music Handbooks. Cambridge: Cambridge University Press, 1998.

———, ed. *Performing Beethoven*. Cambridge: Cambridge University Press, 1994.

Strunk, Oliver, ed. *Source Readings in Music History*. Rev. ed. edited by Leo Treitler. New York: Norton Press, 1998.

Stück, C. "Schöne Künste," *Neue Leipziger Literaturzeitung* 100 (August 2, 1805): cols. 1585–600.

Sullivan, J. W. N. *Beethoven: His Spiritual Development*. London: Unwin Books, 1964. Originally published 1927 by J. Cape.

Sulzer, Johann Georg. *Allgemeine Theorie der schönen Künste*. 2 vols. Leipzig: Weidemann, 1771–4.

Suurpää, Lauri. *Music and Drama in Six Beethoven Overtures: Interaction between Programmatic Tensions and Tonal Structure*. Studia musica. Helsinki: Hakapaino Oy for the Sibelius Academy, 1997.

Swafford, Jan. *Beethoven: Anguish and Triumph*. Boston and New York: Houghton Mifflin Harcourt, 2014.

Szondi, Peter. "Das Naïve ist das Sentimentalische: Zur Begriffsdialektik in Schillers Abhandlung." *Euphorion* 66 (1972): 174–206.

Tame, David. *Beethoven and the Spiritual Path.* Wheaton, IL: Quest Books, 1994.

Taruskin, Richard. *Musorgsky: Eight Essays and an Epilogue.* Princeton: Princeton University Press, 1993.

———. *On Russian Music.* Berkeley: University of California Press, 2009.

Thayer, Alexander Wheelock. *Ludwig van Beethovens Leben von Alexander Wheelock Thayer nach dem Original-Manuskript.* Edited by Hermann Deiters and Hugo Riemann. 3rd ed. 3 vols. Leipzig: Breitkopf & Härtel, 1917–23.

———. *Thayer's Life of Beethoven.* Revised and edited by Elliot Forbes. 2 vols. Reprint. Princeton: Princeton University Press, 1991. Originally published 1967.

"Theatre und Musik in Wien in den letzten Wintermonaten 1806. Wien den 16. April 1806." *Journal des Luxus und der Moden* (May 1806): 284–91.

Thoré, T[héophile]. "Salon de 1838: Dernier Article." *Revue de Paris,* n.s., 53 (1838): 50–9.

Thormählen, Wiebke. "Franz Clement, Violin Concerto in D Major (1805), ed. Clive Brown." *Eighteenth-Century Music* 5, no. 2 (2008): 255–7.

Tolley, Thomas. *Painting the Cannon's Roar: Music, the Visual Arts, and the Rise of an Attentive Public in the Age of Haydn, c. 1750 to c. 1810.* Aldershot, UK: Ashgate Press, 2001.

Tomaszewski, Mieczyław, and Magdalena Chrenkoff, eds. *Beethoven 6: Studien und Interpretationen.* Muzyczna: Kraków Akad., 2015.

Tovey, Donald Francis. *Beethoven.* London and New York: Oxford University Press, 1945.

———. *Essays in Musical Analysis.* 6 vols. London: Oxford University Press, 1935–9. Reprint, 2 vols. London: Oxford University Press, 1981.

"Trente deux variations p. le pianoforte comp. par Louis v. Beethoven." *Allgemeine musikalische Zeitung* 10, no. 6 (November 4, 1807): cols. 94–6.

Triest, Johann Karl Friedrich. "Abhandlung: Ueber reisende Virtuosen." *Allgemeine musikalische Zeitung* 4, no. 46 (August 11, 1802): cols. 737–49, no. 47 (August 18, 1802): cols. 753–60, and no. 48 (August 23, 1802): cols. 769–75.

———. "Remarks on the Development of the Art of Music in Germany." Translated by Susan Gillespie. In *Haydn and His World,* edited by Elaine R. Sisman, 321–94. Princeton: Princeton University Press, 1997.

Tusa, Michael. "Beethoven's 'C-Minor Mood': Some Thoughts on the Structural Implications of Key Choice." In *Beethoven Forum 2,* edited by Lewis Lockwood and James Webster, 1–27. Lincoln: University of Nebraska Press, 1993.

Tyson, Alan. *The Authentic English Editions of Beethoven.* London: Faber and Faber, 1963.

———. "Beethoven's Heroic Phase." *Musical Times* 110, no. 1512 (February 1969): 139–41.

———, ed. *Beethoven Studies 3.* Cambridge: Cambridge University Press, 1982.

———. "The 'Razumovsky' Quartets: Some Aspects of the Sources." In *Beethoven Studies 3,* edited by Alan Tyson, 107–40. Cambridge: Cambridge University Press, 1982.

———. Review of "Beethoven, Ludwig van: Klavierkonzert nach dem Violinkonzert, op. 61." *Musical Times* 111, no. 1530 (August 1970): 827.

"Ueber das Spiel des k. k. Hoffschauspielers Herrn Lange auf dem Grätzer-Theater im Monath July 1805." *Wiener Hof-Theater Taschenbuch auf das Jahr 1806*.Vienna, 1806.

van der Meer, J. H. "Beethoven et le pianoforte." In *L'interprétation de la musique classique de Haydn à Schubert. Colloque International, Evry, 13–15 octobre 1977*, 67–85. Paris: Minkoff, 1980.

Vann, James Allen. "Habsburg Policy and the Austrian War of 1809." *Central European History* 7, no. 4 (December 1974): 291–310.

van Oort, Bart. "The English Classical Piano Style and Its Influence on Haydn and Beethoven." DMA thesis, Cornell University, 1993.

———. "Haydn and the English Classical Piano Style." *Early Music* 28, no. 1 (February 2000): 73–89.

Vertot, René-Aubert. *Revolutions-Geschichte des alten Roms*.Translated by Anton Kreil. 2 vols.Vienna: J.V. Degen, 1802. Originally published as *Histoire des révolutions arrivées dans le gouvernement de la République romaine*, 3 vols. Paris: F. Barois, 1719.

Volek, Tomislav, and Jaroslav Macek. "Beethoven's Rehearsals at the Lobkowitz's." *Musical Times* 127, no. 1716 (February 1986): 75–80.

———. "Beethoven und Fürst Lobkowitz." In *Beethoven und Böhmen: Beiträge zu Biographie und Wirkungsgeschichte Beethovens*, edited by Sieghard Brandenburg and Martella Gutiérrez-Denhoff, 203–17. Bonn: Beethoven-Haus, 1988.

Wagner, Richard. *Richard Wagner's Prose Works*.Translated by William Ashton Ellis. 8 vols. London: Kegan Paul, Trench, Trübner and Co., 1892–9.

Waibel, Violetta L., ed. *Detours: Approaches to Immanuel Kant in Vienna, in Austria, and in Eastern Europe*. Göttingen: Vienna University Press, 2015.

Waldoff, Jessica. "Does Haydn Have a C-minor Mood?" In *Engaging Haydn: Culture, Context, and Criticism*, edited by Mary Hunter and Richard Will, 158–86. Cambridge: Cambridge University Press, 2012.

W[alker], E[rnest]. "*Beethoven's Second-Period Quartets* by Gerald Abraham." *Music and Letters* 24, no. 2 (April 1943): 112–13.

Wallace, Robin. *Beethoven's Critics: Aesthetic Dilemmas and Resolutions during the Composer's Lifetime*. Cambridge: Cambridge University Press, 1986.

Warner, Elizabeth A., and Evgenii S. Kustovskii. *Russian Traditional Folk Song*. Hull, UK: Hull University Press, 1990.

Wassiltchikow, Alexandre. *Les Razoumowski*. Translated by Alexandre Brückner. 3 vols. Halle: Tausch & Grosse, 1893–4.

Webster, James. "The Century of Handel and Haydn." In *The Century of Bach and Mozart: Perspectives on Historiography, Composition, Theory, and Performance*, edited by Sean Gallagher and Thomas Forrest Kelly, 297–315. Cambridge, MA: Harvard University Press, 2008.

———. "*The Creation*, Haydn's Late Vocal Music, and the Musical Sublime." In *Haydn and His World*, edited by Elaine R. Sisman, 57–102. Princeton: Princeton University Press, 1997.

————. "The Falling-Out between Haydn and Beethoven: The Evidence of the Sources." In *Beethoven Essays: Studies in Honor of Elliot Forbes*, edited by Lewis Lockwood and Phyllis Benjamin, 3–45. Cambridge, MA: Harvard University Press, 1984.

————. *Haydn's "Farewell" Symphony and the Idea of Classical Style*. Cambridge Studies in Music Theory and Analysis. Cambridge: Cambridge University Press, 1991.

————. "Traditional Elements in Beethoven's Middle-Period String Quartets." In *Beethoven, Performers, and Critics: The International Beethoven Congress, Detroit, 1977*, edited by Robert Winter and Bruce Carr, 94–133. Detroit: Wayne State University Press, 1980.

Wegeler, Franz Gerhard, and Ferdinand Ries. *Biographische Notizen über Ludwig van Beethoven*. Coblenz: K. Bädeker, 1838.

————. *Remembering Beethoven: The Biographical Notes of Franz Wegeler and Ferdinand Ries*. Translated by Frederick Noonan with an introduction by Eva Badura-Skoda. London: André Deutsch, 1988.

Weldmann, Franz Carl. *Moritz, Graf von Dietrichstein: Sein Leben und Wirken*. Vienna: Wilhelm Braumüller, 1867.

White, Hayden. *Metahistory: The Historical Imagination in Nineteenth-Century Europe*. Baltimore: Johns Hopkins University Press, 1973. Reprint, 1975.

Whiting, Steven M. "Beethovens *Coriolan*-Ouvertüre (nach Collin)." In Oliver Korte and Albrecht Riethmüller, eds., *Das Beethoven-Handbuch*, 6 vols., vol. 1: *Beethovens Orchestermusik und Konzerte*, 449–61. Laaber: Laaber-Verlag, 2013.

Wieczynski, Joseph L., ed. *The Modern Encyclopedia of Russian and Soviet History*. 60 vols. Gulf Breeze, FL: Academic International Press, 1982.

Wilfing, Alexander. "State Censorship of Kant—From Francis II to Count Thun." Translated by Katharina Walter. In *Detours: Approaches to Immanuel Kant in Vienna, in Austria, and in Eastern Europe*, edited by Violetta L. Waibel, 32–9. Göttingen: Vienna University Press, 2015.

Will, Richard. *The Characteristic Symphony in the Age of Haydn and Beethoven*. Cambridge: Cambridge University Press, 2002.

Wilson, John David. "Of Hunting, Horns, and Heroes: A Brief History of E♭ Major before the *Eroica*." *Journal of Musicological Research* 32, nos. 2–3 (2013): 163–82.

Winter, Robert, and Bruce Carr, eds. *Beethoven, Performers, and Critics: The International Beethoven Congress, Detroit, 1977*. Detroit: Wayne State University Press, 1980.

Winter, Robert, and Robert Martin, eds. *The Beethoven Quartet Companion*. Berkeley: University of California Press, 1994.

Wood, Michael. "A World without Literature?" *Dædalus* 138, no. 1 (Winter 2009): 58–67.

Woolley, Andrew, and John Kitchen, eds. *Interpreting Historical Keyboard Music: Sources, Contexts and Performance*. Farnham, UK, and Burlington, VT: Ashgate, 2013.

INDEX

Note: Tables and figures are indicated by *t* and *f* following the page number

For the benefit of digital users, indexed terms that span two pages (e.g., 52–53) may, on occasion, appear on only one of those pages.